ASHE Higher Education Report: Volume 31, Number 6
Kelly Ward, Lisa E. Wolf-Wendel, Series Editors

Rethinking the "L" Word in Higher Education

The Revolution in Research on Leadership

Adrianna J. Kezar, Rozana Carducci,
Melissa Contreras-McGavin

Rethinking the "L" Word in Higher Education: The Revolution in Research on Leadership
Adrianna J. Kezar, Rozana Carducci, Melissa Contreras-McGavin
ASHE Higher Education Report: Volume 31, Number 6
Kelly Ward, Lisa Wolf-Wendel, Series Editors

ISSN 1551-6970   electronic ISSN 1554-6306   ISBN 0-7879-8677-1

The ASHE Higher Education Report is part of the Jossey-Bass Higher and Adult Education Series and is published six times a year by Wiley Subscription Services, Inc., A Wiley Company, at Jossey-Bass, 989 Market Street, San Francisco, California 94103-1741.

For subscription information, see the Back Issue/Subscription Order Form in the back of this volume.

CALL FOR PROPOSALS: Prospective authors are strongly encouraged to contact Kelly Ward (kaward@wsu.edu) or Lisa Wolf-Wendel (lwolf@ku.edu). See "About the ASHE Higher Education Report Series" in the back of this volume.

Visit the Jossey-Bass Web site at www.josseybass.com.

Advisory Board

The ASHE Higher Education Report Series is sponsored by the Association for the Study of Higher Education (ASHE), which provides an editorial advisory board of ASHE members.

Contents

Executive Summary

In these times of change and challenge in higher education, pleas for leadership have become frequent and repeated. But the type of leadership required in this new context of globalization, demographic changes, technological advancement, and questioning of social authority may require different skills and thus reeducation of campus stakeholders if they want to be successful leaders. In the past twenty years, a revolution has occurred in the way leadership is conceptualized across most fields and disciplines. Leadership has moved from being leader centered, individualistic, hierarchical, focused on universal characteristics, and emphasizing power over followers to a new vision in which leadership is process centered, collective, context bound, nonhierarchical, and focused on mutual power and influence. This book summarizes research and literature related to new concepts of leadership to inform practice.

This change in conceptualizing leadership has occurred as new paradigms and theories have been applied to the study of leadership. In particular, social constructivism, critical, and postmodern paradigms have made the context and process much more important to the study of leadership, meaning making, and power. In addition, new theories highlight new aspects that expand our view such as transformational leadership, chaos and complexity theories, social and cultural theories, contingency theories, and relational or team theories of leadership. As a result, leadership researchers and practitioners are now beginning to understand the incredible complexity of organizations and global societies where contemporary leadership takes place, underscoring the need for more adaptive, systems-oriented approaches to leadership that enhance cognitive complexity through learning and team leadership. Researchers have called attention to the significance of leaders' being culturally intelligent and able to understand the perspective of those from different races, cultures, and ethnicity. Leaders need to hone their ability to work in groups and to become more artful at reading organizational and historical contexts.

The application of new paradigms and theories in leadership research has resulted in the emergence of new leadership concepts that are now a major focus of research—ethics or spirituality, collaboration or partnering, empowerment, social change, emotions, globalization, entrepreneurialism, and accountability. Spirituality has long helped to drive leaders and provide a foundation for understanding leadership. Emotions have also long been a part of leadership as one of the key ways to influence and connect with people as leaders. What is new is the emphasis on studying and providing empirical evidence of the importance of ethics and emotions in leadership. Conceptualizing leadership as aligned with social movements also has a long history, even if this history has not been emphasized in recent years, as it does not support the prevailing dominant ideology of the profit-making sector and industrial military complex. Leadership has always been part of the great story of social evolution, however, helping to empower individuals and create social change. Yet the emphasis on empowerment and social change in formal institutions such as organizations, colleges, and universities is a newer affiliation. Although people disagree as to whether globalization is a wholly new concept, today's world does seem to represent some new challenges for leaders who may find themselves interacting with people from many different cultures in a world where power is distributed differently among countries. And although leaders throughout history have been entrepreneurial, taking risks, and working toward transformation, what is new is that leaders more generally are being called on to be entrepreneurial as well as accountable to a broader set of stakeholders.

Most of the theories that have emerged in the general leadership literature have been applied to the context of higher education, with the exception of chaos theory. Cognitive theories represent a rich area with a significant body of data to guide practitioners, whereas the higher education community needs significant research related to chaos theory, transformational leadership, and the link between learning and leadership. In general, higher education research and practice have indeed experienced a revolution in the way leadership is conceptualized. No longer is the college president considered the sole leader on campus or the campus hierarchy the place to look for change agents. Instead, both practitioners and researchers realize that leadership is a collective process found among many different individuals and groups on campus, usually involving the work of teams and collaboration. Moreover, leaders themselves are conceptualized quite differently. Task orientation is no longer seen as more important than developing relationships and being a strong communicator. Effective leadership is a combination of relational and task skills and involves both transformational and transactional qualities. Successful leaders need to develop cognitive complexity and become skilled in acting as symbolic leaders, become politically savvy, maintain attention to goals and objectives, *and* build strong relationships on campus. They must recognize that leadership takes place in a particular context that has a culture they need to learn and with which they must align their leadership practices. Leaders who foster learning can create change. Our conceptualization of leadership now embraces an understanding of the way culture affects leadership, the importance of leaders' developing cognitive complexity, the impact of leaders' and followers' mental models on the leadership process, and the effect of leaders' background and experience on their views and behavior as leaders.

Few of the new concepts have been examined, however, and reflect important areas for future research and examination by practitioners. Higher education would benefit as a field if more studies would use critical and postmodern paradigms to uncover new ways to conceptualize leadership; explore explicit examinations of power dynamics embedded in leadership processes; focus on failed examples of leadership; study the implications of globalization for leadership; focus on entrepreneurialism, accountability, and cross-cultural leadership; explore empirical studies of specific cultural phenomena that affect leadership in higher education such as symbols or story telling; develop empirical research from the perspective of social movement; study the interaction of various levels (micro, meso, macro) and aspects (different units) of the higher education context; focus on negotiating conflicts that are inevitable with collective forms of leadership; use interdisciplinary research to understand ethics, global leadership, and empowerment; and study leadership over time, as relationships take time to develop.

Foreword

In 1989, Bensimon, Neumann, and Birnbaum published an ASHE-ERIC monograph titled *Making Sense of Administrative Leadership: The "L" Word in Higher Education*. At that time the editor of the monograph series, Jonathan Fife, predicted that the monograph would "have a major impact in the understanding of higher education leadership for many years to come." His prediction came true: the original work served the field well and has become one of the most widely cited references on higher education leadership. As time has passed, however, the research and our understanding about what makes an effective leader in higher education have changed. New paradigms and perspectives on leadership were not conceptualized when the original work was published. The present monograph builds on the 1989 edition by thoughtfully and carefully leading the reader through the new theories about leadership that have been proposed in light of the changing context of higher education.

A lot has been written about leadership, some of it reading like a self-help guide to becoming a "great leader." Other works on leadership are so theoretical and abstract that their practical application is questionable. This situation creates a challenge for those seeking to understand higher education leadership: How can one sort through the array of sources and perspectives and make meaning of them? This monograph engages theoretical perspectives in a practical way, meeting that rather difficult goal of being both conceptually strong and practical. Like its predecessor, this monograph serves as a guide to those wishing to understand leadership in the context of contemporary higher education. One of the most important components of this monograph is that it views leadership not as an end but as a means to achieving the goals of higher education. It is not a book about the habits of effective presidents; rather, it is a thoughtful review of how leadership can help higher education respond to the many challenges it faces.

This work explores the new leadership perspectives brought about through the uses of postmodern, critical, and social constructivist lenses and illuminates the growing complexity of higher education leadership. It does an exceptional job of synthesizing the literature and offering insight into the application of the theories and research. One of its strengths is that it introduces readers to these new paradigms and concepts in a straightforward way, cutting through the jargon to reveal the essence of the ideas. The authors do not shy away from talking about the relationship between leadership and such topics as ethics, spirituality, and emotion and exploring more mainstream leadership concepts such as collaboration, globalization, entrepreneurialism, and accountability. The monograph stresses the collective process of leadership and the context in which leadership occurs. It presents several case studies to illustrate leadership in action and provides analytical questions attached to each case. These additions to the monograph will serve as excellent teaching cases for graduate programs but will also prove helpful for administrators and campus leaders to consider and discuss. This monograph is not just an academic review of the leadership literature: it also offers a means to understand the complex terrain of leadership research and theory and provides practical advice for leaders to consider as they seek to improve their institutions.

Lisa E. Wolf-Wendel
Series Editor

Preface

As editor of the ASHE Higher Education Report Series, I frequently received inquiries regarding the update or revision of classic texts. In recent years many individuals contacted me, hoping that the leadership book published in 1989 by Bensimon, Neumann, and Birnbaum would be updated. I tried to find interested authors, and when no one emerged, I thought it seemed like something I should tackle. Given that I have conducted research and written on leadership, I took on the task. I had no idea what I was in for! The amount of literature written in recent years is staggering. The number of books published on leadership doubled between the 1980s and the 1990s. The result is many new ideas and concepts to absorb about leadership. Immediately, I realized the value and importance of creating this new volume, and I was lucky enough to recruit two coauthors to help make sense of this new literature base.

—Adrianna J. Kezar

Acknowledgments

Adrianna Kezar dedicates this book to future leaders like Constance Kezar, Keaton Kezar, Maxwell Kezar, and Tait Viskovich. She also thanks her father for being such a strong role model of leadership.

Rozana Carducci thanks Seth Taper, Andra Evans, Bernie Carducci, and Theda Evans for their love, laughter, support, and patience. She is a lucky woman.

Melissa Contreras-McGavin dedicates this book to her father, Omega Contreras, who provided her inspiration, spirit, and great love.

 Published online in Wiley InterScience
(www.interscience.wiley.com) • DOI: 10.1002/aehe.3106

The Revolution in Leadership

BENSIMON, NEUMANN, AND BIRNBAUM'S ORIGINAL volume (1989) had the ambitious task of noting the importance of leadership, describing how leadership is defined, and reviewing six main theories of leadership across the interdisciplinary research base. It examined leadership within the context of organizational theory and reviewed how leadership had been explored in higher education research through the lens of the six theories: trait, behavioral, power and influence, contingency, cognitive, and cultural/symbolic.

The Continued Need for Leadership in a Changed Context

In 1989, Bensimon, Neumann, and Birnbaum noted that some policymakers and several blue ribbon commissions were calling for better, stronger, and bolder leadership. The need for leadership in higher education has only become more urgent as the fat days with regular increases from state governments are long over, and the days of accountability and assessment, globalization, and competition are here to stay, providing new pressures for colleges and universities. Policymakers regularly implore campuses to integrate technology, respond to community needs, and provide a higher quality education for less money. In these times of change and challenge, pleas for leadership have become frequent and repeated. The type of leadership required in this new context, however, may call for different skills and the reeducation of campus stakeholders if they want to be successful leaders. As

Lakomski (2005) suggests, it is the end of leadership as we have known it in the past. For some the change is so dramatic they may no longer see this phenomenon as leadership.

In the past twenty years, a revolution has occurred in the way leadership is conceptualized across most fields and disciplines. Many ask what we mean by revolution. Leadership has been studied and written about for more than 2000 years (perhaps longer), and much of its history is hierarchical in nature and emphasizes social control. In the last twenty years, however, nonhierarchical and increasingly democratic forms of leadership have been conceptualized. We believe that both leadership research and the practice of leadership have changed and that these two processes are often linked (that is, leadership research changes as leadership practices change; and leadership practice changes as research conceptualizations change). This revolution in leadership research is visually represented in Figure 1. Moving away from static, highly structured, and value-neutral leadership frameworks, contemporary scholars have embraced dynamic, globalized, and processed-oriented perspectives of leadership that emphasize cross-cultural understanding, collaboration, and social responsibility for others.

The heroic leaders were often the focus, but now teams and collectives are emphasized and studied. In addition, scientific views of leadership that have

FIGURE 1
The Revolution in Leadership Research

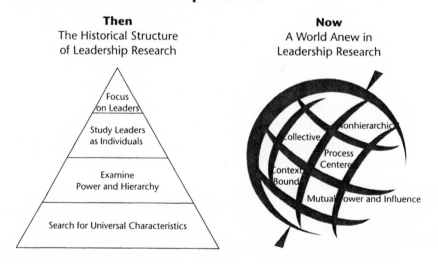

Then	Now
The Historical Structure of Leadership Research	A World Anew in Leadership Research

Focus on Leaders

Study Leaders as Individuals

Examine Power and Hierarchy

Search for Universal Characteristics

Nonhierarchical

Collective

Process Centered

Context Bound

Mutual Power and Influence

held sway for most of the last century have been challenged and tempered by other views of leadership as an art, craft, or spiritual practice. Further, the positivist approach to studying leadership has given way to studies from social constructivist, postmodern, and critical paradigms. Revolution also refers to the way that some long-forgotten topics have become important again within leadership. In other words concepts such as spirituality are "revolving" back into fashion. Throughout this manuscript, we refer to the ways that leadership has changed in ways that we consider revolutionary from its past as well as the way that older concepts are revolving back into importance.

Many hypothesized reasons for the change in leadership scholarship are described more thoroughly in the volume but are briefly mentioned in this introduction. The two major reasons suggested are that the context in which leadership takes place has changed and that new perspectives and ideas about leadership have been introduced from scholars and practitioners. These two forces are interdependent and are hard to separate. The radical social and political changes of the 1960s and 1970s opened the door for people to think about leadership in new ways from the past. Feminism and Marxism provided the foundation for different views of leadership. Many of the democratic, collaborative, and nonhierarchical trends in leadership are associated with the challenges to authority that took place during this time. Many of the trends reviewed in this book—collaboration, empowerment, multiculturalism, and leadership as a collective process—are related to these historical changes. In the 1980s and 1990s, the world economy shifted, creating a more interdependent system that has been called a global economy. The emphasis on interdependence reinforces the importance of collaboration and working in teams for enacting leadership. As people throughout the world connect and work together in greater frequency, cultural and social differences have become recognized and have been studied in relation to leadership. Various forms of technology have sped up decision time, connected people across the globe, and made more local forms of leadership possible (Lipman-Blumen, 1996, 2000), leading to the democratization of leadership as well as to a more complex and diffuse process. Interdependence is a central concept of the leadership revolution and will be found throughout the book as we review paradigms, theories, and concepts.

The revolution in leadership, however, has not gone unchallenged. Two main countermovements—academic capitalism and managerialism—adopt hierarchical leadership with centralized forms of power. These movements will be described throughout the text but are mentioned here to demonstrate that it is not entirely a linear progression from hierarchical, individualistic forms of leadership to more collaborative, collective, and nonhierarchical forms. New views are emerging from traditional, functionalist circles of leadership, competing as countertendencies that draw individuals back to top-down, command, and control leadership.

Organization of the Book

Given the major changes that have occurred, it is important to examine the state of leadership research in higher education. This volume updates the 1989 Bensimon, Neumann, and Birnbaum volume. Rather than rewrite a book that nicely summarized research on leadership until the late 1980s, this book focuses on reviewing advances in paradigms, theories, concepts, and research concerns and agendas. The next chapter, "A World Apart," reviews the new paradigms—social constructivism, postmodernism, and critical theory—that have been applied to the study of leadership and revolutionized how we think about leadership. Love and Estanek (2004) define a paradigm "as a system of assumptions about the nature of reality that is integrated, pervasive, holistic, and internally consistent. . . . It is from within a paradigm that human beings understand what is real, what is false, what is possible, and to what they should pay attention" (p. 1). This book examines how the underlying assumptions, beliefs, and values of the social constructivist, postmodern, and critical theory paradigms have shaped the way leadership research is conducted. We choose these three paradigms, as they are the most cited new paradigms to be applied to leadership. The following chapter, "A World Anew," updates several schools of thought presented in the original volume of this book—contingency theory, cultural theories, and cognitive theories—and describes new theories that have emerged such as complexity theory, organizational learning, processual theories, and team approach. Theories are complex explanations of social phenomena. When a variety of related theories emerge and are followed up by many different researchers, they form a school of thought. Because schools of thought represent what scholars believe are promising areas of study, they are emphasized and reviewed in the text. Theories and paradigms differ in important ways. Theories offer complex explanations for why and how a phenomenon (for example, leadership) occurs and are supported by empirical evidence, whereas paradigms are underlying assumptions that generally have no empirical grounding. Paradigms focus on macrolevel assumptions examining issues such as ontology (the nature of reality) or epistemology (the nature of knowledge).

The next chapter, "Revolutionary Concepts of Leadership," reviews some of the main concepts that have emerged in the leadership research and literature such as ethics, empowerment, collaboration, and networks. Concepts are important ideas that are combined to develop theories but on their own represent important areas for people to consider as they examine the phenomenon. "Higher Education Leadership in the New World" presents the research specifically in higher education that has been conducted since 1989, focusing on developments that advance our thinking such as cognitive and cultural theories of leadership. "Revolutionary Leadership Concepts in Higher Education" reviews the degree to which the new concepts that have emerged in that general leadership literature have been pursued by higher education researchers. In the last two chapters, the implications of this vast body of new research are reviewed and directions for future research provided. Throughout the text, vignettes and summaries are presented to help bring the main concepts presented in this book to life and made more concrete. An appendix includes case studies designed to provide readers with opportunities to apply the theories and concepts reviewed in the book. We want to introduce one major assumption here that will be reinforced throughout the text: we do not believe there is any best way to lead. Instead, we believe that by understanding a variety of paradigms, theories, and concepts leaders can learn tools to approach various leadership situations that fit in particular contexts. In addition, leaders have varied strengths and weaknesses, and they can use these tools to complement and build on their personal styles.

Key Terms and Theories

Because this volume builds on the earlier ASHE-ERIC volume, *Making Sense of Administrative Leadership: The "L" Word in Higher Education* (Bensimon, Neumann, and Birnbaum, 1989), it is important to briefly note and define the theories that were central to the earlier volume—trait, behavioral, power and influence, contingency, cognitive, and cultural/symbolic. Although we direct readers to the original volume for lengthy discussions of these various theories, the following definitions will help when these concepts are brought up in this volume. In addition, Table 1 summarizes the major assumptions, key findings, and criticisms of each of these six theories, facilitating comparisons across conceptual approaches. Moreover, a distinction is made in these various schools of thought related to *leader* and *leadership*. In trait and behavioral theories, leadership is synonymous with leader. Later theories of culture and power and influence examine leadership as a process, and leader is no longer synonymous with leadership.

Trait theories identify specific personal characteristics that contribute to a person's ability to assume and successfully function in positions of leadership (Bensimon, Neumann, and Birnbaum, 1989). An example of a study from a trait perspective is a survey of leaders that examines the top five traits they feel make them effective. The traits reviewed might include integrity, competence, intelligence, or experience. Researchers using this theory tend to identify identical traits for all leaders, transcending all contexts, and thus focus their efforts on developing a definitive list of leadership traits. Further, trait theorists assume the existence of objective trait definitions and thus assert that people perceive traits similarly.

Behavioral theories study leadership by examining the roles, categories of behavior, and tasks associated with leadership (Bensimon, Neumann, and Birnbaum, 1989). Behavioral studies identify tasks such as planning, fundraising, or mentoring as key to understanding leadership. These studies also examine leader orientation to tasks versus relationships, attempting to identify whether one or the other orientation is more effective. Behaviors tend to be generic ones, applicable to all types of leaders and organizations. Similar to trait theories, behavioral theories rely solely on leaders for understanding leadership.

TABLE 1
Six Leadership Theories Reviewed in *Making Sense of Administrative Leadership*

	Trait	Behavioral	Power and Influence	Contingency	Cognitive	Cultural/Symbolic
Definition and Emergence	Seeks to identify a definitive list of individual traits associated with successful leaders Prominent in early twentieth century but continues to be researched today	Examines the behaviors of effective leaders Gained prominence in midtwentieth century	Sees leadership as a social exchange process characterized by the acquisition and demonstration of power Prominent throughout the twentieth century	Leaders and leadership behaviors influenced by situational variables (task, followers' characteristics) Focus of research during the last half of the twentieth century	Examines the influence of cognitive processes (attribution, error judgment) on leadership Emerged in late twentieth century	Explores the symbolic and cultural functions of leadership (how a leader's use of rituals can inspire change) Gained prominence at the end of the twentieth century
Major Assumptions and Contributions	Leader-centered theory Leaders possess specific traits that distinguish them from followers Universal (objective) definitions of traits exist	Leader-centered theory Leaders use a combination of task and relational behaviors to guide interactions with subordinates	Leaders use power to influence followers More recent research considers the reciprocal relationship between leaders and followers	Different leaders and leadership behaviors called for in different situations Situational factors influence who emerges as a leader	Cognitive processes influence perceptions of leaders and leadership behaviors Introduced the possibility of leadership as a socially	Leadership seen as a social construct that differs across cultural contexts Individuals foster shared meaning and cultural norms through interactions

(Continued)

TABLE 1 (*Continued*)
Six Leadership Theories Reviewed in *Making Sense of Administrative Leadership*

Trait	Behavioral	Power and Influence	Contingency	Cognitive	Cultural/Symbolic
Theory intuitively appealing, given the perceived difference between leaders and followers	and achieve leadership goals Views leadership as something that can be learned Provides specific skills for leaders to be trained in	Introduces a process-oriented view of leadership that emphasizes the needs and values of followers as well as leaders	Provides predictive models of leadership effectiveness by assessing the match between the leader's style and the situation Expands views of leadership to include context, not just individuals, as an important source of influence on leadership	constructed rather than objective phenomenon Examined the cognitive processes of followers as well as leaders	Symbolic processes (rituals, stories) make leadership meaningful Values and beliefs important to understand leadership Helped highlight perceptions, context, interaction, and symbolism

Key Insights	Abundance of empirical research documents the importance of key leadership traits (self-confidence, integrity, sociability, determination, and intelligence)	Leadership process comprises task and relational behaviors Leadership effectiveness is product of the leader's ability to balance task and relational behaviors Research attempts to determine which behaviors are most appropriate for particular situations	Leaders draw on multiple sources of power (reward, expert, coercive) to influence followers Leaders' authority and influence constrained by followers' expectations Transformational leaders draw on charisma, visionary leadership, and authentic concern for others to influence and motivate followers	Leadership effectiveness a product of matching the leader's style with the needs of the situation	Cognitive biases influence leadership attributions and judgments of both leaders and followers	Effective leaders use cultural symbols, language, rituals, and so on to influence followers

(Continued)

TABLE 1 (Continued)
Six Leadership Theories Reviewed in Making Sense of Administrative Leadership

	Trait	Behavioral	Power and Influence	Contingency	Cognitive	Cultural/Symbolic
Criticisms and Limitations	Has not resulted in a definitive list of leadership traits Traits difficult to measure Does not consider leadership context	Inadequate relationship established between leaders' behaviors and outcomes Has not generated a universal style of leadership Does not adequately address the influence of leadership contexts	Lacks conceptual clarity and as a result is difficult to measure empirically Perpetuates directive and hierarchical views of leadership	Ambiguous concepts make empirical research challenging Difficult to translate into practice, given the numerous variables that must be assessed before determining a leader's effectiveness	Limited practical use, given the difficulty associated with assessing and changing the cognitive processes of others	Lacks empirical research connecting cultural leadership practices to organizational outcomes

Power and influence theories consider leadership in terms of the source and amount of power available to leaders and the manner in which the leaders exercise that power. Reciprocal approaches to studying leadership focus on the process as relational and emphasize followership as critical to success (Komives, Lucas, and McMahon, 1998). A researcher using power and influence theories might study the ability of leaders to use persuasion to achieve desired organizational outcomes.

Contingency theories emphasize the way situational factors such as the groups (for example, followers) involved or the external environment affect leadership (Bensimon, Neumann, and Birnbaum, 1989). The followers, however, are seen mostly as having limited human agency and as reactive to the leader. Contingency theorists in higher education explore different organizational subsystems, including the bureaucratic, collegial, political, and symbolic subsystems. Leadership becomes more closely related to perspective or vantage point through contingency theory.

Cognitive theories focus on the influence of cognitive processes (such as perception) to develop an understanding of leadership. These theories frequently inform the development of leadership research that is centered on understanding how followers make leadership attributions. For example, attribution studies have examined the degree to which followers attribute change to leaders, compared with the actual work leaders do to enact change.

Finally, cultural theories explore the importance of context for understanding leadership, emphasize interaction, and explore the symbolic functions of leadership. A study of leadership through a cultural lens might examine a leader's use of rituals and traditions to inspire people toward change.

Challenges and Missed Opportunities in the Study of Leadership in Higher Education

Many of the struggles and tensions described in the earlier volume still hold true and will be reinforced in this volume. The difficulty in precisely defining leadership continues to remain a challenge. Various theories provide additional lenses, but there continues to be no agreed-upon definition of leadership. The application of new theories and concepts from the general leadership literature to the higher education literature also remains incomplete. For example, the importance of the leadership process in producing learning so that people can be more successful in creating change, providing organizational direction, and supporting organizational effectiveness is not emphasized in the higher education literature and is critical in the leadership literature or business. The lack of these important ideas represents missed opportunities to more fully understand leadership in the higher education setting. For example, the importance of examining leadership in the organizational context remains important today. Many studies have reinforced that leadership is affected by the organizational context and that leadership is perceived in an institutional context (Birnbaum, 1992). As Birnbaum has quipped in various articles, good leadership depends on the perspectives of the individuals in an organization whose opinions are shaped by the institutional history and culture. We would add that not only the organizational context affects perceptions but also the societal influences and previous experiences of individuals. Context needs to be thought of much more broadly than the organization, but many studies examine leadership without grounding it in any context. In addition, practitioners' embracing a more complex representation of leadership continues to be of importance. The continued popularity of and interest in books that promise leaders that they will have a recipe for success by following ten simple steps demonstrate that complex and holistic views are still not favored.

New Directions in Higher Education Leadership

Even though higher education researchers have missed some important opportunities for exploring leadership, the literature has changed markedly in the last fifteen years. For example, the earlier volume focused primarily on research about college presidents, but the leadership literature has broadened and now examines deans, department chairs, and professional staff across the university, students, and nonpositional change agents. Leadership is studied as a phenomenon that can be found throughout the institution. Another major change is that the controversy about whether leaders must exert direct authority and control to be considered leaders has been resolved. No longer is the literature concerned with the perception that presidents and other leaders are weak if they do not mandate change or exert power. Instead, models of servant leaders and collective leadership have replaced the command-and-control leader reflective of much of the writings on leadership in the 1970s and 1980s. This change will be demonstrated through a variety of leadership theories, including team leadership, organizational learning, and cultural and symbolic use of leadership. In addition, the main concepts described in leadership also reflect this change from command and control to power sharing such as the emphasis on collaboration and leadership as a social movement. During this period of change, Birnbaum (1992) noted that people questioned whether leadership mattered. It was a timely question when authoritative forms of leadership were falling out of favor. People found themselves confused about whether leadership existed or was important outside the authoritative, directive forms of leadership described throughout the 1970s and 1980s. This skepticism and concern about leadership, however, have passed away as new forms of leadership have emerged and become institutionalized, embracing a more collective and empowering view of leadership. Birnbaum (1992) describes some of these fallacies of leadership that were generally embraced in the 1970s and 1980s. For example, for many years it was assumed that the vision of the institution must be developed by the president. That view has been replaced by a belief that a shared vision developed by constituents is a more effective form of leadership. Many other myths have been challenged in the leadership literature over the past fifteen years such as the importance of charisma to successful leadership, the myth that leaders should be distant from followers, or that some definable traits or styles that make leaders effective can be used in all situations (see Woodard, Love, and Komives, 2000, for more details of myths). It is hard to know whether they were myths or whether views of effective leadership have merely changed. Regardless, the picture of leadership today is vastly different from fifteen years ago. In fact one might say that we have had a revolution in our views of leadership. It is this revolution that is the underlying theme of this volume.

Contributions of This Book

This volume complements and is different from other recent leadership texts. Most textbooks such as Northouse's *Leadership: Theory and Practice* (2004) review the classic theories and empirical research on leadership and provide readers with little if any information about the new trends and approaches for studying leadership. Northouse's work examines trait, style, exchanges between leaders and members, and situational and transformational leadership theories, for example. Other texts tend to focus on one of the new theories of leadership such as complexity (Heifetz's *Leadership Without Easy Answers*, 1994), learning (Senge's *The Fifth Discipline*, 1990a), or relational (Lipman-Blumen's *The Connective Edge*, 1996). This volume is one of the first to summarize and review the newer theories and concepts of leadership. It can be used in leadership courses to complement classic texts or to introduce the revolution and leadership literature.

This volume is also novel in that it presents a thorough discussion of the influential role paradigms play in framing contemporary studies of leadership. Few books mention research paradigms and how they affect the study of leadership. Some journal articles reference paradigms but usually focus on one particular paradigm in which the author's study was conducted. Comparing and contrasting paradigms and examining each one's strengths and weaknesses relative to the study of leadership are important contributions of this book.

Because it is one of the few to synthesize the literature on higher education research and compare it with the general leadership literature, this work provides an opportunity to establish a research agenda for the field of higher education for the coming years. It will be particularly helpful for graduate students and new scholars attempting to familiarize themselves with this vast literature base. And the book provides an introduction to a set of concepts, theories, and paradigms that can inform leadership practitioners' thinking about leadership in complex and multifaceted ways, bringing together various works that they have read.

A World Apart: New Paradigms of Leadership

IN 1989, BENSIMON, NEUMANN, AND BIRNBAUM NOTED that most research on leadership had been conducted using traditional, empirical scientific methods and assumptions (positivist or functionalist paradigms). The word *paradigm* refers to a worldview and in the context of this book relates to the main assumptions brought to the study of leadership. The rise of cultural theories of leadership in the 1980s provided the foundation and opened the door to the use of other paradigms in examining leadership because it focused on meaning-making processes, symbolic elements, and the role of values. For example, the examination of values identified varying perspectives of leadership based on interpretation (Schein, 1992).

A major change in the leadership literature in the past decade is the rise in use of alternative paradigms to examine leadership. Social constructivism, postmodernism, and critical theory are now applied in studies of leadership, providing new insights (see Table 2). Although we describe these three approaches separately, they share many similar assumptions. In addition, we review the major tenets of each paradigm. Given that any given paradigm includes multiple strands of researchers (for example, critical race theory and critical cultural studies are both encompassed under the paradigm of critical theory), a static description of core assumptions is unable to capture the complexity inherent in the study of paradigms. These descriptions are meant only to provide an introduction for further reading (Alston, 2002; Anderson, 1999; Barker, 2002; Blackmore, 1999; Grint, 1997; Hunt, 1991; Kezar, 2000; Palestini, 1999; Pettigrew, 1997; Rost, 1991).

TABLE 2
Leadership Paradigms

Paradigms	Functionalist	Social Constructivism	Critical	Postmodern
Major Assumptions	Leadership is a social reality that can be described, has an essence, and has generalizable qualities and predictable outcomes.	Leadership is a social construction; subjective experience important to how leadership emerges; culture and context have a significant effect on leadership, an ever-evolving concept that has changed over time.	Leadership has a history of oppression and is therefore viewed with suspicion; it is typically used by those in power as a means of maintaining authority and control; it is possible for leadership to serve a broader goal of social change if power dynamics are watched carefully and new language is used that empowers individuals and groups historically marginalized.	Leadership has been an expression of the will to power but is more complicated than that generalization; it is a contingent, human construction affected by local conditions, history, and the ambiguity and complexity of the human experience; it is a reflection of human identity shaped by history.
Purpose of Research	To predict leader outcomes based on behavior; to develop generalizable principles to help direct the action and behavior of leaders	To interpret and understand what people perceive or attribute as leadership; to help leaders in understanding their frameworks and how their perspectives as leaders affect a leadership process	To develop representations and strategies of leadership that are empowering and create social change	To question the concept of leadership itself; to examine whether it is merely the will to power; to explore whether certain complex conditions can result in leadership

Approach to Research	Survey of leader traits, behaviors, and influence strategies	Interviews of leaders in a particular setting; surveys of perceptions of followers; study interaction of leaders and followers	Case study and ethnography of leadership contexts focused on power dynamics and interactions	Case study and ethnography of leadership contexts focused on power dynamics and interactions
Role of Values	Functionalist theories took neutral stance on values	Values seen as shifting based on perspectives and situations	Values believed central for creating leadership that empowers and creates social change	Values questioned as inherently serving some power interest
Criticisms or Limitations	Fails to acknowledge the influence of context, culture, and individual differences on leadership; limited ability to create universal or general principles of leadership	Provides few specific directives for action; does not examine the role of power	Does not emphasize effectiveness or outcomes important for societal and organizational survival	Provides few specific directives for action; some people question whether the global economy and postmodern condition truly exist

Positivist Paradigm

It might help to understand the positivist research assumptions that affected the early studies of leadership (Crotty, 1998). Positivism maintains a realist ontological view—a researcher can come to know a singular, objective, shared reality. Knowledge is grounded in facts that are conceptualized as objective statements of truth. Universal truths can be discovered, and knowledge is generalizable. Researchers strive to identify generalizable principles to guide leaders and to predict how they will affect outcomes. Researchers acknowledge that we can only probabilistically and imperfectly apprehend the singular reality. When thinking about the extant leadership research, for example, we can see that positivist assumptions underlie trait theories, behavioral theories, power and influence theories, and contingency theories. Traits and behaviors are seen as transcending all contexts, and it is assumed that all people perceive traits and behaviors similarly. The emphasis in these theories has been universal traits or power and influence processes as well as universal perceptions of these traits or power and influence processes. Even contingency theory, which appears to examine context and emphasizes situational and organizational variables, still sees these contexts as perceived identically by individuals within the context and representing a singular reality. Another important assumption in positivism is that a phenomenon can be separated from its context and isolated for study. Therefore, leadership could be studied in a laboratory and involve scenarios rather than real leadership situations. Positivists believe that they must (and can) design research that guards against the impact of their beliefs and normative values on the conceptualization of leadership research. Therefore, a male or female researcher would perceive leadership in a context in similar ways, for example. The goal of research is to develop predictions about behavior so that human situations can be controlled. This perspective on studying leadership resulted in universal, context-free, value-free representations and theories of leadership. These positivist assumptions began to be challenged in the 1980s through cognitive and cultural theories that focused on interpretation and context, but their full impact was not realized until the 1990s as the new paradigms of social constructivism, critical theory, and postmodernism were applied to the study of leadership.

Social Constructivism Paradigm

Social constructivism is the belief that reality is developed through one's interpretation of the world and a denial of essences or universal qualities. Reality is a social and cultural construction. By examining multiple interpretations, we can detect a shared sense of reality, yet our understanding of reality is always partial and imperfect. Because perception and interpretation are so significant, these scholars reshape the approach to understanding leadership. In applying social constructivism to leadership, these scholars focus on ways that leadership itself is a social construct developed through interaction and that the way people define leadership differs based on their experience and background (Grint, 1997; Kezar, 2002b; Parry, 1998; Rhoads and Tierney, 1992; Tierney, 1988; Weick, 1995). The way people interpret leaders' behaviors is also important to understand (Birnbaum, 1992). There is no single reality of how followers or others interpret leadership, and these perceptions affect notions of effectiveness and quality (Birnbaum, 1992; Grint, 1997). In addition, when and if a situation requires leadership is determined through analysis of individual perspectives. Because social interaction is so important in the constructivist framework, research focuses on the interactions between leaders and followers and on the social environment and culture itself. Thus, understanding leadership requires studying the various perceptions and interpretations of people throughout the leadership setting. Grint (1997) notes that rhetoric may be a key skill for leadership as it focuses on persuasion, networking, and negotiation—three behaviors that are critical to an understanding of leadership as a socially constructed phenomenon.

In addition to the importance of individual perception and interaction, context is particularly important for interpreting and understanding the perceptions and subjective experiences of people in relationship to leadership. Thus, leadership must be studied in a particular context, looking at the interaction between how the context shapes perspective as well and how perspectives shape the leadership context. An example of this process is how leadership differs between secondary schools and higher education based on the varying structures and cultures of these environments and experiences of individuals in these environments.

Some social constructivist scholars view leadership itself as an attempt by certain individuals to frame and define reality, which can become a form of social control (Chemers, 1997). These researchers examine how leaders, through their positions of authority, create social reality by managing and interpreting meaning (Bolman and Deal, 2003). For example, a leader may be told by his or her board of directors that layoffs are necessary to improve profits. The leader realizes that this action could affect the morale of people in the organization and lower productivity, so instead of presenting the layoffs as necessary to improve profits (which only focuses on shareholders' interests, not workers'), the leader describes layoffs as necessary for the survival of the company and says that a few must be sacrificed to save the many.

Scholars operating from the social constructivist paradigm focus attention on understanding various interpretations of leadership situations to paint more complex pictures than we have had in the past—for example, how may normative beliefs of a culture or organization shape the expected qualities of the leader and create an environment in which only certain individuals are considered leaders? From this perspective, agency lies in the group or its dominant members, and social norms establish the conditions in which a leader can operate. Here the focus is not so much on an individual's subjective experience but on examining how individual perspectives work together to shape norms.

Several strands of research such as attribution theory suggest that leadership itself is not real in an empirical sense but that individuals attribute certain processes and actions to leaders. Studies have found that more outcomes are attributed to leaders than they are actually responsible for and that people are biased to exaggerate the importance of leadership as a cause of organizational performance (Yukl, 1998). In this line of research, leaders are largely illusory except insofar as leadership positions provide a place for people to attribute organizational actions and processes. In a confusing and ambiguous world where people are trying to construct meaning, leaders serve as a visible place for understanding why things happen as well as a scapegoat for problems.

Common among researchers in the social constructivist paradigm is an emphasis on interpretation, multiple realities, meaning making, perception, and subjective experience as they are important to understanding leadership (Grint, 1997). To understand leadership, language and discourse become primary sites for examining perceptions and views. Earlier research from a behavioral or trait perspective often focused on observation for understanding leadership. Researchers from a social constructivist perspective shift their methodological emphasis to the words of leaders and followers as well as observe the interaction between individuals in leadership contexts.

Critical Paradigm

Critical theory evolved from scholarship by Karl Marx and focuses on how economics, capital, and the market drive social progress and processes. This paradigm critiques and questions the class-based society that currently exists. Many different schools of thought have evolved from Marx, including the Frankfurt school. Feminism and other radical traditions such as critical race theory that challenge traditional societal norms are also often considered part of critical theory, as they also question the ways social processes privilege certain groups in society. Although many different traditions exist, certain characteristics underlie each strand: (1) an examination of power dynamics; (2) the importance of acknowledging that research is not neutral or value free; (3) the need to develop new constructs; and (4) seeing research as political and a form of activism.

Critical theorists who study leadership question the value-free representation of leadership and focus primarily on power dynamics that are hidden in the phenomenon of leadership, particularly oppression and abuses of power (Ashcroft, Griffiths, and Tiffin, 1995; Blackmore, 1999; Calas and Smircich, 1992; Chliwniak, 1997; Grint, 1997; Kezar, 2000, 2002b, 2002c; Kezar and Moriarty, 2000; Palestini, 1999; Popper, 2001; Rhode, 2003; Skrla, 2000; Tierney, 1993a; Young and Skrla, 2003). These scholars work to unearth and deconstruct hidden assumptions involved in the process of leadership. For example, are hierarchical arrangements between leader and follower merely socially constructed and not natural or inherent? And are they used to disempower and privilege certain groups? Is the language of followership and leadership used to subordinate certain groups? How do leaders use power or persuasion to keep certain groups or individuals marginalized? Why are the traits and behaviors associated with leadership such as masculinity and dominance gendered? How does representation of leadership ignore race? Popper (2001), in *Hypnotic Leadership: Leaders, Followers, and the Loss of Self,* describes the dangers of the distinction between leader and follower prevalent in most leadership literature as a problematic power relationship that ends up erasing followers in the leadership process. Jean Lipman-Blumen (2004) describes how people are often attracted to toxic leaders.

In addition to questioning traditional notions of leadership for reinforcing oppressive power conditions and distinctions among people, critical scholars also work to develop a new approach to leadership. Critical theorists suggest the work of leaders is to liberate people to do what is required of them in the most humane way. Feminist researchers have been one of the major strands of critical research focusing on new concepts such as empowerment, a more collaborative approach to leadership, teams and partnerships, equity, and rethinking the ends or outcomes of leadership to be social change or social critique (Young and Skrla, 2003). In feminist research the leadership process, outcomes, and associated characteristics and qualities are markedly different from earlier visions of leadership that emerged mainly out of the military, business, and politics. Leadership involves empowerment and an ethic of care, and it focuses on being reflective, constantly having the leaders evaluate their motives to avoid the oppression and marginalization prevalent in many earlier definitions and theories of leadership. Early feminist studies of leadership focused on why women were absent from leadership positions, the glass ceiling for women, and the way gender inequities were structured into institutions (Blackmore, 1999; Young and Skrla, 2003). The majority of these studies concluded that male characteristics had been normalized as defining leadership and that women's experiences and values were therefore ignored. The most recent research examines the overlap of race, gender, social class, and a variety of differences, avoiding the problem of making certain differences essential to overly broad social categories, realizing that social and cultural categories are changing (Kezar, 2002b).

In addition, leadership has been viewed as a social movement. Deborah Meyerson's book, *Tempered Radicals* (2003), provides an in-depth look at individuals in several different organizations who played a leadership role by resisting the dominant discourse and eventually creating changes in the cultures of the organizations where they were situated. Critical researchers study resistance as a form of leadership; resistance also demonstrates the role of human agency, not just victimization or marginalization, which some people commonly associate with strands of critical theory. These researchers also see their own studies as a form of activism helping to change the practice of leadership, which can help in changing power dynamics and relationships in society.

Postmodern Paradigm

Postmodernism is a complicated word that has emerged as an area of academic study only since the mid-1980s. It is hard to define because it is a concept that appears in a wide variety of disciplines and areas of study, including art, music, literature, sociology, communications, and technology. In its simplest terms, it is a rejection of modernist views of the world—including a belief in an objective, continuous, linear view of reality with an autonomous individual who controls his or her destiny. Instead, postmodernism emphasizes subjective and local experiences, history and context, fluidity and change. Postmodern thought favors reflexivity and self-consciousness, fragmentation, complexity, ambiguity, and simultaneity. Some of the main underlying concepts in postmodernism are local conditions, subjective experience, ambiguity, and power (described in greater detail below). Although it might not sound as though it has implications for leadership studies, it does. Scholars who have conducted studies using postmodern theory to understand leadership have developed novel insights (Anderson, 1999; Grint, 1997; Popper, 2001; Schier, 2000).

Postmodernists deconstruct modernist, positivist approaches to science in which universal truths and essences about leadership are sought because there is no objective vantage point and our perceptions are the only thing we can come to know. Like social constructivists, they question whether universal essences or truths even exist beyond our perceptions and thus focus on social and cultural norms that shape perspectives. One such norm is the qualities that have been associated with leadership. Postmodernist scholars question the characteristics identified in earlier trait, behavioral, and power or influence theories as highlighting the qualities of white, male elites and labeling them as leadership. Postmodernists want to bring norms and values to light so that they can be examined. Social constructivists also examine perceptions, but postmodernists examine these perspectives critically. The critical stance in post-modernism differs from critical theorists in that postmodernists focus more on human agency and the ability of people to shape their existence rather than studying followers as victims of leaders and those in power.

Leadership is seen as contingent on local conditions and contexts. Post-modernists question whether any form of universal leadership such as transformational leadership makes sense, as leadership varies by local context and culture. Social constructivists also see context affecting perspective, but postmodernists define context in a slightly different way. They focus more on the dynamics of local context but at the same time connect the local context to larger, global trends.

They also make apparent the complexities and ambiguities inherent in leadership—whether leadership is always good for a community, the difficulty of determining when it might be used for good, and the difficulty entailed in making good leadership decisions because information is incomplete and human processes are imperfect (Kezar, 2004). Critical theorists do not focus on ambiguities, and social constructivist see ambiguity but not as problematic as the way postmodernists conceive ambiguity.

Similar to critical theorists, postmodernists focus on power dynamics and their effect on how leadership is defined and understood. For example, does transformational leadership merely keep certain groups marginalized by not empowering them to act while having a heroic figure save communities, organizations, and schools? When examining leadership, postmodernists focus on language and discourse because they are the vehicles through which one expresses ideology and power. They believe most attempts to describe leadership are normative and ideological and serve no other purpose then creating another hegemonic form of reality that serves to oppress "followers."

Many postmodernists focus less on presenting a new conceptualization of leadership, as most researchers think the concept is inherently fraught with problems and deeply entrenched with maintaining the status quo and control for certain groups. Additionally, postmodernists pose questions such as whether leadership and the most appropriate leader should emerge out of community definitions and needs rather than be imposed by researchers' or elites' definitions and constructions (questioning the researcher's role altogether). They also think that researchers are the wrong group to rethink a future direction for leadership and that it needs to be developed and fostered in communities of practice.

Another line of postmodern research argues that organizations have moved into a postmodern era and that they need new operating principles that match this new environment (see Anderson, 1999; Rost, 1991; Wheatley, 1999). In this research, new visions of leadership have emerged such as Wheatley's *Leadership and the New Science* (1999), which is described more fully under chaos and complexity theories of leadership. In short, this line of postmodernism questions linear and directive approaches to decision making and planning as well as individualistic forms of leadership that have modernist and mechanistic orientations that no longer work in a global, interconnected world. Bergquist (1993) describes leaders in a postmodern era through the metaphor of a butterfly in which the leader is constantly changing directions with the wind, analogous to the many external forces that have become more prominent in the postmodern world. To be successful in this environment, however, leaders must be clear about personal and institutional mission and purpose while fluttering in a turbulent environment.

Comparing the Paradigms' Impact

A comparison among paradigms might help illustrate the difference in current lines of research (see Table 2). Previous functionalist or positivist research tried to predict leadership outcomes and come up with verifiable principles for leadership. For example, in trait theory if the leader acts in honest ways, is trustworthy, and relational, then the followers should be content and work toward the goal. In behavioral theories if the leader provides a vision, structures the task appropriately, and builds strong relationships, then the group should work effectively, be satisfied, and create change. In path goal theory if the follower's ability and personality can be determined and the task and formal authority systems matched, then leadership outcomes are obtained as desired. Constructivists suggest that people's subjective experience is too complex to be generalized in these ways. For example, structuring a task is unique to each person; building a strong relationship involves a complex set of dynamics and is fragile and not static. Postmodernists see these previous theories (trait or path goal) as hegemonic approaches being forced on a group of people (that is, people should conform their notions to the one good form of leadership, whether it works or not), and critical theorists question the leader's motives and goals. Even if the theory works, critical theorists wonder whether it is just, fair, or humane (see Table 2 for a comparison of the main assumptions and primary differences among the paradigms).

Although the paradigms are different in several ways, they share some similarities as well. Social constructivists, postmodernists, and critical theorists all question whether *predictable* and *generalizable* leadership processes, traits, behaviors, or outcomes can be determined, as they question the notion that human behavior is predictable and regularized. Instead, they all promote a view of leadership as a human process filled with ambiguity and contradiction and driven by values and ethics. In addition, each focuses on the way that leadership is interpreted and socially constructed in a particular context and affected by culture and history.

Some authors, such as Rost (1991), have characterized the similarities across these three paradigms as a metaparadigm—a postindustrial paradigm. In his book, *Leadership for the Twenty-First Century,* Rost (1991) reviews research from the last one hundred years and identifies an industrial paradigm with several qualities: "dominated by functionalist assumptions . . . , management oriented, personalistic in focusing on only the leader, goal achievement dominated, self interested and individualistic in outlook, male oriented, utilitarian and materialistic in ethical perspective, rationalistic, technocratic, linear, and quantitative" (p. 27). Rost notes an emerging shift and calls for more research and practice in what he terms a postindustrial paradigm that embraces a very different set of assumptions, including chaos, change, dialogue, local and global knowledge and learning, values, connecting partners, integrity, trust, outcomes, and reflection. These characteristics are all represented in the assumptions of social constructivist (learning, dialogue, trust), critical theory (change, values, integrity, outcomes, reflection), and postmodern (chaos, local and global, connecting partners) paradigms. He notes that the world has changed dramatically and that the leadership literature no longer reflects the current realities of globalization, changing demographics, dramatic shifts in power or, as some say, "shared power world," and complexity (Crosby, 1999). Komives, Lucas, and McMahon (1998) suggest the following questions for leaders trying to understand the difference between industrial and postindustrial paradigm thinking. First, how is my life like a machine? (rational, orderly principles). Second, how is my life like a weather system? (unpredictable, uncontrollable, with crises). People often wish their life was like a machine but acknowledge through experience how it can be chaotic. Rost's call for new research in the postindustrial paradigm has been embraced by many researchers in the last fifteen years.

Now that we have introduced the notion of using paradigms to frame and examine leadership, we offer a more concrete example of how paradigms can shape higher education leadership processes and practices. Take, for example, a dean who has been charged with creating a shared vision for the school of engineering. The functionalist paradigm provides a leader with a set of techniques such as describing the vision at every meeting or visiting regularly with department chairs to emphasize the direction the school is moving. After the dean has been working on creating a shared vision for a year or so, she realizes that she has not made as much progress as she had hoped through the techniques promised in functionalist theory. Social constructivism will provide her some tools for examining what prevents people from engaging in a shared vision. As she reads about the way that people make meaning individually, she realizes that more dialogue is necessary between faculty and staff so that they understand the varied perspectives that each has; moreover, increased dialogue provides a way to negotiate these perspectives to move more toward a shared vision. Social constructivism would help the dean to see the need for dialogue, investigate people's beliefs, and make fewer assumptions about the ease of moving to a shared vision. If the dean were to think about her leadership from a critical perspective, she might realize that she has imposed the notion of the shared vision on the school and that her meetings with the department chairs were perceived as forcing her message. At this point, she might reconsider the way she is trying to develop a shared vision and might think of more inclusive ways that involve various people in the school. She decides to have a retreat and work to develop a collective vision first; she then realizes she has more success moving toward a shared vision for the school but that everyone is not yet on board. From a postmodern perspective, she might question whether a shared vision is appropriate for the school. Given the differing cultures of some of the departments and the vastly different backgrounds of people, she might wonder whether it makes sense to allow people to create their own direction in their various departments and units. She might begin to see her role more as facilitating direction among these units than creating a shared vision. This short vignette provides an example of the ways that individuals involved in leadership might use the paradigms to interpret and analyze a situation and develop appropriate approaches to guide their actions.

Finally, the new research paradigms involve new leadership assumptions, including moral, ethical, and value-based components that are being brought back to the study of leadership. Ethics and values remain part of the popular literature on leadership (for example, Robert Greenleaf's *Servant Leadership* [1977]), but these concepts were missing, for the most part, from empirical research conducted throughout most of the last century. In a sense, leadership has come full circle in the last one hundred years. At the turn of the twentieth century, narratives of leaders that emphasized the complexity of leadership, values, and ethics shaped leadership views (Depree, 1989). Then a strong empirical tradition took hold of leadership researchers, and the character of the research changed dramatically, leaving behind many traditional concepts such as the human, complex, and value-laden aspects of leadership. Instead, a reductionist view emerged in which researchers attempted to isolate and study a handful of variables to understand leadership. Although research on leadership is returning to some of these perennial elements and concepts, it is different in many ways as well (Depree, 1989). Some of the significant changes include questioning hierarchy and unequal forms of power, the emphasis on developing as a leader rather than being born as one, and the fact that leadership is shared and not seen as the purview of an elite few.

Summary

The application of these new paradigms has led to the revolution that has altered the face of our understanding of leadership in the last twenty years. If researchers had continued to study leadership from a functionalist or positivist perspective, few of the new theories or concepts would have emerged. For example, no place existed for ethics and spirituality in the functionalist paradigm of leadership. Critical theory, social constructivism, and postmodernism are distinctive lenses on the world that helped reshape and complicate our current views. Although we wish to highlight the important ways that these paradigms have broadened our views of leadership, we also respect the contribution of functionalist theories over the years in helping to understand certain traits, behaviors, and power and influence processes and their role in leadership. Certainly, vision and inspiration are key concepts that will remain important. Some see the increasing complexity and ambiguity brought by these new paradigms as a hindrance to the practice of leadership (Rost, 1991). Only time will tell if this revolution in our thought processes has been enriching or debilitating. Nevertheless, a review of research on leadership demonstrates that our views of leadership have indeed changed for the better.

A World Anew: The Latest Theories of Leadership

THE REVOLUTION IN LEADERSHIP RESEARCH began with the emergence of the new paradigms described in the preceding chapter and has resulted in the application of new theories and approaches to understanding leadership. Accordingly, the new leadership theories reviewed in this chapter complement and build upon the major assumptions and research purposes of the social constructivist, critical, and postmodern paradigms. For example, complexity theory attempts to address postmodernism's questioning of the belief that leadership is or can be a predictable and generalized phenomenon (a conviction held by researchers operating from a functionalist paradigm). The emerging theories of leadership teams and cultural approaches to leadership respond to critical theorists' concerns about the gender and racial biases embedded in earlier leadership research. Social constructivists' views of leadership are reflected in organizational learning approaches in which mental models, interpretation, and cognitive mind-sets are key elements for understanding leadership. In addition, process theories reflect both postmodern and social constructivist calls for approaches to understanding leadership that are grounded in local conditions and take into account the complexity of meaning in social systems.

The new theories also reflect the changing context of leadership in a world where cultural and social differences are more prominent and where multiple, complex forces such as changing demographics, technology, faster decisions, and greater competition make straightforward and insular approaches to leadership problematic at best (Lipman-Blumen, 1996, 2000). As Peter Vaill (1991) noted, we no longer have simple problems with right or wrong answers but are increasingly faced with complex dilemmas. Perhaps the "truth" is that there never were simple solutions but that in working in a functionalist paradigm of authority, one-way power, and the status quo, leadership appeared simpler in earlier times and in traditional schools of thought. As we embrace other perspectives and interpretations, leadership may seem more complex when in reality, past researchers have simply ignored the complexity.

Because the new leadership theories described in this chapter were predominantly developed by researchers using social constructivist and critical paradigms, theory is often not an appropriate term for the research results. As noted in the previous chapter, the aim of functionalist research is building theory that predicts behavior or situations. For example, trait, contingency, and behavior theories seek to predict an outcome (leadership effectiveness) by studying certain traits and actions. In the social constructivist and critical paradigms, however, the goal of research is not to predict behavior; instead, it usually strives to improve understanding and description. As a result, a particular approach to leadership in these paradigms may not have the same type of empirical research support as in the functionalist paradigm. We use the word *theory* because it is most familiar to practitioners, but we acknowledge that much of the new research reviewed in this chapter would not fit that word in its strictest definition.

Given the breadth and density of scholarship on new leadership theories, the following organizational and conceptual roadmaps are offered as a guide for navigating this chapter. For each leadership theory and approach reviewed, we discuss (1) the definition of the theory, its emergence, and key scholars; (2) the theory's major assumptions, contributions, and advantages; (3) key findings and insights from studies, if available; and (4) criticisms, problems, and issues that have emerged with the theory. Disparities in the volume and depth of information presented for each theory reflect differences in the extent to which scholars have adopted a particular theory or approach. Although this volume cannot synthesize all the scholarship in this vast new literature base, we highlight key texts and findings and provide a lengthy list of references so that the reader can continue developing a deeper understanding. In addition, key points are summarized at the end of each discussion of a theory to facilitate comparison across theories. Several vignettes about leadership are also included in this chapter to illustrate how to translate new leadership theories into administrative practice.

Most of the schools of thought reviewed in *Making Sense of Administrative Leadership: The "L" Word in Higher Education* (Bensimon, Neumann, and Birnbaum, 1989) continue to be researched and refined, even those considered less conceptually robust such as trait and behavior theories. These newer studies are not reviewed in this book, however, as there are few new insights to be gleaned (Kouzes and Posner, 2002; Kurke, 2004; Kyle, 1998; Olson, 1991; Rosenbach and Taylor, 2001). Studies do continue to demonstrate the importance of certain traits such as integrity to the leadership process, and studies that reaffirm key leadership insights are reviewed. We do, however, update contingency, cognitive, and cultural theories of leadership given the significance of new findings. One approach in the power and influence school of thought (transformational leadership) reviewed in the earlier book also needs to be updated, as it was just gaining visibility in the 1980s and research on it had just begun. Two new leadership theories reviewed in this chapter could not be placed easily in early schools of thought: complexity and team or relational theories. Complexity theories are very similar to learning theories and might be considered a cognitive approach. Team models emerged from feminist research and might be placed under the social and cultural school of thought. To highlight the distinctive insights and key findings associated with these two new leadership theories, however, we decided not to embed them in our discussion of existing leadership frameworks and instead present them independently.

Figure 2 illustrates the progression and changes that have occurred in the leadership literature before and after the revolution. Over the past twenty years, leadership has moved from being leader centered, individualistic, hierarchical, focused on universal characteristics, and emphasizing power over followers to a new vision in which leadership is processed centered, collective, context bound, nonhierarchical, and focused on mutual power and influence processes (also described by Rost [1991] as the postindustrial paradigm). Although most of the theories reviewed in this chapter reflect the newer vision of leadership depicted on the right side of the diagram, the arrows represent theoretical continuums, not rigid

FIGURE 2
The Revolution in Leadership Research

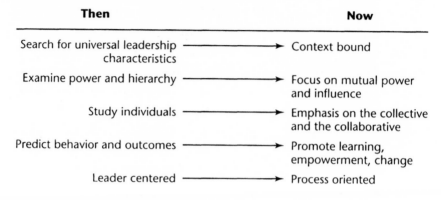

Then	Now
Search for universal leadership characteristics	→ Context bound
Examine power and hierarchy	→ Focus on mutual power and influence
Study individuals	→ Emphasis on the collective and the collaborative
Predict behavior and outcomes	→ Promote learning, empowerment, change
Leader centered	→ Process oriented

endpoints, underscoring the fact that each theory occupies a unique position on each of the five leadership dimensions. For example, transformational leadership theory shares most of the characteristics of older visions of leadership as it is leader centered, individualistic, hierarchical, and focused on universal characteristics. It differs from some of these earlier theories, however, by focusing on mutual power and influence processes. Given the fact that transformational leadership theory is situated on the bridge between traditional and contemporary approaches to understanding leadership, we begin by reviewing the new insights on transformational leadership.

Transformational Leadership

Definition and Emergence

Transformational leadership is typically defined as a power and influence theory in which the leader acts in mutual ways with the followers, appeals to their higher needs, and inspires and motivates followers to move toward a particular purpose (Bensimon, Neumann, and Birnbaum, 1989; Rost, 1991). Transformational leaders attend to the individual needs of followers and offer inspiration and motivation to organizations and their constituents by providing meaning to their work rather than just rewards. Intended to understand how organizations could be led most effectively, this power and influence approach eclipsed traditional notions of transactional leadership. Rather than continue to consider processes in which leaders exchange rewards or administer punishments for following (or not following) their wishes, leaders were relied on to guide followers in organizational processes. Burns (1978) is credited with developing the theory of transformational leadership in his *Leadership*, which many different researchers have elaborated on over the past fifteen years, including Bass (1985), Kouzes and Posner (2002), and Rost (1991). Burns used the word *transforming*, not transformational, but because most scholars use the word *transformational*, we use it throughout the section.

Major Assumptions and Advantages

A central component that defines transformational leadership is the role of ethics and morals (Burns, 1978). In a major contribution to the leadership literature, Burns explains the connection between leaders and moral purpose. In a review of significant leaders throughout history, he defines leadership as a mutual process based on an ethic of care for the follower that is focused on socially desirable ends. To determine socially desirable ends and to act in ways that show caring, leaders need to be guided by ethics and morals. The focus on purpose and the ends of leadership is also a new aspect of this theory. Earlier leadership theories focused on outcomes but almost exclusively on the outcomes of organizational effectiveness and performance. Although effectiveness may be socially desirable, in transformational leadership theory moral ends (such as equity) now take prominence over purely functionalist objectives.

Transformational leadership is still leader focused and hierarchical. As Rost (1991) notes, transformational leadership acts as a bridge between old and new views of leadership. Transformational leadership begins to conceptualize leadership as a process by emphasizing the interaction between leaders and followers. By distinguishing between leaders and followers, however, this approach remains hierarchical in orientation. Most studies of transformational leadership generally focus on the leader and less so on the process and interactions between leader and followers. The focus of research tends to be on the identification of characteristics or qualities of transformational leadership such as inspiration, trust, passion, and commitment.

Many current concepts in the larger leadership literature such as ethics, social change, and empowerment are directly influenced by transformational leadership. A major contribution of transformational leadership research has been its role in bringing new concepts to the study of leadership, many of which are reviewed in the following chapter. Perhaps no other theory in the last twenty years has helped to bring so many new concepts to the practice of leadership and redirected the direction of leadership research as transformational leadership.

Key Findings and Insights

Most current transformational leadership research focuses on providing empirical evidence for the concepts Burns (1978) articulated in his seminal work, *Leadership*. Bass (1985) helped operationalize and test the notion of transformational leadership, developing a survey instrument called the Multifactor Leadership Questionnaire (MLQ), which examines four main factors—charisma, inspiration, individualized consideration, and intellectual stimulation. In his research, Bass asked people to describe individuals they considered to be transformational leaders. He continues to follow up on this work, trying to distinguish between authentic transformational leadership and pseudo-transformational leaders who do not have an ethical underpinning (Bass and Steidlmeier, 1999). Also building on Burns's work, Kouzes and Posner (2002) studied leaders who were considered "great," asking them to write detailed memoirs in an attempt to better understand the qualities of transformational leaders. They identified five types of behavior that is part of transformational leadership: challenging the process (searching for opportunities and experimenting); inspiring a shared vision (motivating people toward a vision); enabling others to act (fostering collaboration and self-development); modeling the way (setting an example); and encouraging the heart (celebrating achievements). After years of conceptualizing and defining transformational leadership with disagreements about the role of morality (Burns versus Bass) and the emphasis on particular behaviors (Bass versus Kouzes and Posner), studies began to be conducted to better describe and understand the effects of transformational leadership. For example, research using the MLQ has consistently shown that transformational leadership behaviors are positively associated with leaders' effectiveness and lead to more satisfaction among followers than transactional leadership behaviors (Avolio and Bass, 1991; Zacharatos, Barling, and Kelloway, 2000). Although disagreement still exists over an exact definition, a consensus is emerging among researchers.

Other important studies of transformational leadership have focused on how leaders develop and cultivate vision, how leaders empower rather than manipulate, the organizational context of transformational leadership, and the importance of transformational leaders' working to construct a functional culture where transformational leadership is possible (Avolio and Bass, 1991; Bass, 1997; Schein, 1992; Zacharatos, Barling, and Kelloway, 2000). Studies have also demonstrated the importance of leaders' articulating a clear and appealing vision that is relevant to the needs and values of followers. Leaders can improve the communication of their vision by using emotional appeals, symbols, metaphors, rituals, and dramatic staged events.

Other researchers have been concerned with the generalizability of transformational leadership attributes across cultures, a topic of growing significance, given the global nature of contemporary society. The Global Leadership and Organizational Effectiveness project (GLOBE) examined transformational leadership behaviors and attributes across sixty-two international cultures (Den Hartog and others, 1999). The goal of this project was to study whether or not certain traits of transformational leadership transcended cultures. Despite traditionally recognized social and cultural differences, the findings of this project support the claim that certain attributes are universally considered to represent transformational leaders. Leaders who were encouraging, positive, motivational, builders of confidence, dynamic, and demonstrated foresight were found to be transformational in most of the cultures studied (Den Hartog and others, 1999). Leadership traits that were considered impediments were also studied, with certain traits such as risk taking found to be valued differently across cultures.

Criticisms, Problems, and Issues

Some concerns about transformational leadership are related to whether the transformational leadership model is a generalizable model in all organizational and societal contexts. Is it a western construction, or, as explored in the GLOBE project, is it relevant in other cultures? (Shamir and Howell, 1999). Concerns also exist about the hierarchical leader–centric nature of this approach. Barker (2001) suggests that the focus on "superior/subordinate" relationships overshadows other important organizational and contextual variables related to leadership.

Bass and Steidlmeier (1999) suggest that many recent studies of transformational leadership lack some of the central components (such as ethics) and as a result are not really studying transformational leadership as defined by Burns (1978). Harkening back to the early notions of transformational leadership in the late 1970s, they assert that for leadership to be considered transformational, it must be guided by moral and ethical considerations. This distinction between what constitutes authentic transformational leadership and other definitions provides one example of how this theory has evolved over the past fifteen years. Scholarly dialogue on the definition and theoretical focus of transformational leadership continues to be relevant, however, given the reemergence of morality and ethics in current leadership literature. As research continues be conducted, transformational leadership remains an important albeit somewhat contested concept for understanding effective leadership.

Summary of Transformational Leadership

Leadership is viewed as a mutual process focused on care for followers and the pursuit of socially desirable ends.

Research, grounded in a power and influence approach to leadership, maintains a focus on hierarchy and positional leaders.

The ethical purposes and moral ends of leadership are prioritized.

Leadership for empowerment and social change are emphasized.

Key transformational leadership research findings include that (1) transformational leadership behaviors such as inspiring vision and celebrating achievement are associated with higher levels of leader effectiveness and follower satisfaction than transactional leadership; (2) the articulation of a clear and compelling vision that matches followers' needs and values is important; and (3) transformational leadership transcends cultural boundaries with certain attributes and behaviors universally recognized as transformational.

Complexity and Chaos Theory

Definition and Emergence

As Rost (1991) noted, scholars became suspicious of the reductionist and simple views of leadership, especially as the context for leadership grew more complex, and they began to search for new ways of understanding leadership more fitting for the times and challenges. One response has been for researchers to study the complexity and chaos of leadership and the organizations where it takes place (Anderson, 1999; Axelrod and Cohen, 1999; Depree, 1992; Handy, 1996; Heifetz and Linsky, 2002; Komives, Lucas, and McMahon, 1998; Marion, 1999; Marion and Uhl-Bien, 2001; Phillips and Hunt, 1992). Chaos theory challenges the simplicity of earlier theories such as contingency approaches where leaders simply match a leadership style to a task or preference of followers. Instead, external challenges and the environment in organizations should be examined and taken into account to understand leadership. For example, as technology alters the ability to communicate and to work together, making access to individuals and information more readily available, it is assumed that it will affect the leadership process. This theory emerged in the hard sciences but has been adapted in recent years to the social sciences and examinations of complexity in human systems. Two major writers addressing this theory are Margaret J. Wheatley (1999) and Ronald A. Heifetz (1994).

Many credit Wheatley's *Leadership and the New Science* (1999) for bridging chaos theory and leadership. Her book describes the implications of chaos theory for organizational life, suggesting we should reexamine our traditional assumptions about how organizations operate and how leadership should be practiced. She also challenges traditional notions of hierarchy and authority in organizations. Decentralization, dedifferentiation of tasks (spanning boundaries and breaking down organizational barriers), collaboration, flexibility and adaptability of structures and processes, participation, and autonomy characterize the postmodern organization. Traditional notions of leadership embedded in centralization, differentiation of task, hierarchy, rigidity and control, exclusiveness, and individuality are poorly suited for organizations needed to respond to the complex environment.

Another work that helps understand leadership as a complex process is Heifetz's *Leadership Without Easy Answers* (1994). The primary assumption of this book is that leadership has often been characterized and studied as routine and technical responses to situations and problems; however, most situations and tasks really require an adaptive and complex response. Routine problems are clearly definable and easily fixed by technical experts. Heifetz believes that routine problems do not require leadership; rather, problems that are difficult to define should be the focus. He notes that adaptive challenges require experiments, new discoveries, and adjustments from numerous places in the organization. Without learning "changing attitudes, values, and behaviors, people cannot make the adaptive leap necessary to thrive in the new environment" (Heifetz and Linksy, 2002, p. 13). Adaptive work is generative, multidimensional, multilevel, chaotic, and anxiety provoking. Leadership takes place in the community by mobilizing expertise and working to develop novel solutions. Routine responses will not help address adaptive challenges that are the work of leadership. Again, leadership is no longer a predictable process that requires the application of a set of characteristics, skills, or behaviors. Instead, it is a process that embraces a complex approach of learning, non-mechanized and innovative solutions, and collective action and reflection. The chaos theory literature continues to expand and helps us rethink leadership as an ambiguous and multifaceted topic.

Major Assumptions and Advantages

As noted, collaboration, breaking down hierarchy, local decision making, and organic processes characterize leadership in chaos theory. In contrast to typical bureaucratic approaches to decision making, systems thinking is emphasized. In chaos theory, the notion of linear, controllable, and universalistic patterns of operation are challenged. Simple, straightforward rules of operation or universalistic principles of leading are shown to be inadequate in a world of complex everchanging conditions (Heifetz and Linsky, 2002; Marion, 1999; Marion and Uhl-Bien, 2001; Phillips and Hunt, 1992; Wheatley, 1999). In chaos theory, local and context-based factors strongly affect institutional operations, but beneath the surface of high levels of autonomy, local conditions, and multiple sources of input are simple organizing principles that undergird all systems. Thus, chaos theory demonstrates that leadership is the practice of combining simple rules that are adaptive to multiple local conditions. A greater order exists that cannot be seen in the chaos of local contexts. The order and the universal laws are found at a holistic or systems level, not in specific organizations. Moreover, the imperfection in our vision (or our inability to identify the order in the chaos) is the reason we have fragmented our work lives into the bureaucratic roles and divisions indicative of modern organizational forms. The essence of a strong organization and good leader is working at a more holistic systems level, focusing on the relationships among roles and tasks rather than seeing them as discrete parts.

This theory also suggests the importance of relationships and connections, as the world is interdependent and connected in a system (Wheatley, 1999). Relationships inside and outside the organization are paramount for cultivating and maintaining leadership activity. Leaders also need to keep connected to the outside world so that they can adjust to environmental changes.

Complexity and chaos theory make several contributions to leadership. First, complexity theory helped leadership researchers to expand their notions of context as they examined the leadership process from broader social and technical system perspectives. Rather than framing context as a static organizational variable, chaos and complexity theorists recognize the dynamic and changing nature of leadership contexts. Second, the notion of the postmodern organization and the way leadership would be unique in this type of organizational context has helped expand leadership research in new directions. For example, many organizations have now transformed the way they operate and are organized. Third, complexity theory introduced new concepts into the leadership vocabulary such as networks and systems thinking as well as reinforced concepts that were emerging such as partnering, collaboration, local decision making, and globalization.

Key Findings and Insights

Research supports the notion that taking complexity into account improves the effectiveness of leaders (Heifetz and Linksy, 2002). Most research on complexity theory, however, suggests it is difficult to study, remains incomplete, and must be more carefully operationalized to study consistently

(Osborn, Hunt, and Jauch, 2002; Satish and Streufert, 1997). Because of the challenges related to measuring elements of complexity and leadership, multiple research approaches (quantitative and qualitative studies) have been used. In essence, few studies have been definitive in terms of understanding the relationship of complexity, chaos, and leadership.

Quantitative studies have primarily been used as a means of prediction and to provide statistical significance associated with complexity. For example, a study by Streufert and Nogami (1989) measured the complexity of managerial behavior and effectiveness using a set of numeric measures. Participants were assessed using structural measurement techniques that ascribed a numerical value to complex traits at various levels: simple activities, breadth, strategy, high-level strategic planning, and the ability to shift network characteristics and environments (Streufert and Nogami, 1989). Performance on these designated tasks correlated meaningfully with leadership complexity. For example, managers who scored highly in addressing nonstable situations scored more highly in leadership complexity than those who performed more efficiently in less chaotic and complex scenarios. These findings indicate the ability to predict how well leaders will perform and adapt to a range of structural and environmental complexities. This study is limited, however, in its predictive capacity and, like many quantitative studies of complexity, by its lack of external validity and practical application (Streufert, 1997).

Because relationships and interactions are so important, complexity studies have focused on examining networks and how they are developed. For example, Regine and Lewin (2000) studied multiple levels of complex dynamics in organizational networks. In an ethnography of a dozen American and British companies that exhibited principles of complexity, they examined the significance of leaders and their practices in creating and enhancing networks. Their findings suggest that in complex systems leaders and agents affect each other in ways that can foster creativity and adaptability. They also found that the creation of networks is one of the most important contributions made by leaders in complex environments (Marion and Uhl-Bien, 2001). These findings are particularly useful in understanding the practices of complex leaders as well as reframing nonlinear and nontraditional organizational practices.

Critiques, Problems, and Issues

On a practical level, we need to understand the trade-offs between the advantages of cognitive complexity and people's capacity to absorb complexity. Perhaps some personality types are better able to adapt to complexity. Myers-Briggs typology, for example, suggests that certain individuals do not respond well to complexity. In a team approach to leadership, group members can work together to confront and engage complexity. We may need to understand the advantages of teams for a leadership process that is tied to complexity. We know teams can be more cognitively complex than individuals (Bensimon and Neumann, 1993); therefore, we need a much deeper understanding that moves from conceptual to practical about how complexity can be best engaged by change agents and groups in day-to-day activities.

From a research perspective, complexity and chaos have proved difficult to study. Some researchers have suggested that to truly understand complexity and chaos in systems all levels need to be examined simultaneously. For leadership, it would mean studying how a particular action of a leader affects individuals, groups, organizational culture and climate, and the external environment or how an action in the external environment affects leaders, groups, and the organizational culture and climate. It is assumed, however, that patterns in the system will be nonlinear and random so that following such patterns is more difficult than in functionalist research. As noted, quantitative studies of complexity often lack external validity and practical application (Streufert, 1997). In describing the importance of appropriate research methods in the study of complexity, Marion and Uhl-Bien (2001) explain the value of qualitative approaches such as ethnography in analyzing complex interactions. They note qualitative methods reach beyond the scope of quantitative studies to capture complicated multidimensional interactions. More studies from a qualitative perspective may help to shed more light on chaos and complexity and their relationship to leadership. If complexity is hard to operationalize in practice and difficult to study, is it a valuable approach?

Summary of Complexity and Chaos Theories

Theoretical framework is grounded in assumptions of postmodern organizational life.

From Conflict to Collaboration: The Benefits of Chaos and Complexity

Upon reviewing the annual reports submitted by department directors in her division, the vice chancellor for student affairs identified several leadership challenges of concern across the division. Specifically, department directors repeatedly articulated frustrations associated with the unrealistic expectations of the university's technology strategic plan, the inflexible nature of the division's assessment model, and rigid personnel policies that hinder the pursuit of balance between personal and professional responsibilities. In addition, constraints on fiscal resources coupled with increased student demand have sparked conflict between department directors competing for discretionary funding from the vice chancellor's office. In an attempt to address these concerns, the vice chancellor pulls Wheatley's *Leadership and the New Science* (1999) and Heifetz's *Leadership Without Easy Answers* (1994) from her bookshelf and begins to sketch out a plan for using chaos and complexity theories of leadership to improve relationships in the division and to enhance organizational performance.

Drawing on the principles of systems thinking, local decision making, organizational adaptability, and collaboration, the vice chancellor begins to work with her staff on revising existing organizational policies and procedures that have historically emphasized control, consistency, and rigid organizational boundaries. Rather than continuing to impose uniform assessment standards and personnel policies on all student affairs departments, the vice chancellor decides to

Traditional notions of hierarchy and bureaucratic decision making are challenged.

Decentralization, dedifferentiation of tasks, collaboration, flexibility, systems thinking, and adaptability of organizational structures are emphasized.

Leaders are called on to operate at the systems level, focusing on the connections between organizational roles and tasks as well as fostering interdependent relationships inside and outside the organization.

Complex leadership challenges require organizational learning, collaboration, reflection, and innovative solutions.

Complexity and chaos theories of leadership are difficult to operationalize for research purposes.

collaborate with staff members on the articulation of a clear organizational vision and guiding set of values that will inform a decentralized decision-making process. In this new model of local leadership and decision making, the directors are provided with the autonomy essential for addressing the specific contextual needs of their departments and encouraged to explore innovative strategies for addressing complex leadership challenges. Rather than continuing to implement the standard program assessment plan that privileges objective measures of program quality (such as attendance, participant satisfaction, and fiscal efficiency), the Office of Multicultural Affairs decides to carry out a qualitative assessment project that seeks to understand the subjective experiences of students involved in multicultural organizations advised by their office. In addition, under this new leadership framework, each student affairs department is encouraged to develop a specific technology plan that reflects the division's commitment to technological advancement yet is grounded in a realistic assessment of the internal and external contextual factors that will shape technology integration in the department. Given that both chaos and complexity theories of leadership place a high value on relationships and collective action, the vice chancellor makes sure that collaboration is included on the list of key organizational values and establishes a discretionary funding framework that promotes boundary-spanning collaborations rather than competition. At the heart of the vice chancellor's new leadership framework is a belief that simple organizing principles, not rigid rules and hierarchical structures, are the most effective means for cultivating organizational environments that demonstrate a focus on learning, reflection, collaboration, and innovation—four dimensions of leadership essential for addressing the complex leadership challenges of the twenty-first century.

Expanding Cognitive Theories: Mental Models and Organizational Learning

Definition and Emergence

An emerging area of research reviewed in the 1989 volume by Bensimon, Neumann, and Birnbaum was cognitive theories of leadership that take into consideration mental processes such as error judgment and attribution. Given that many strands and approaches exist to studying leadership from a cognitive perspective, it is difficult to offer a single definition for cognitive theories of leadership. In general, however, cognitive theories tend to focus on the mental processes of leaders or other individuals involved in leadership processes.

In the last fifteen years, the area of cognition has focused on expanding and testing attribution theories of leadership, examining how people assign causes to interpersonal events and organizational outcomes. These studies help explain the mental processes by which individuals attribute certain actions and outcomes to leaders (Chemers, 1997). Another line of cognitive research using a social constructivist paradigm has studied the dubious value of leadership for explaining organizational outcomes. This research suggests that people want to believe in leadership and therefore mentally construct such a phenomenon to facilitate cognitive processing of organizational events (Chemers, 1997). In addition to these expansions of attribution theories (noted as an emerging area in the 1989 volume), learning and mental models or lenses have been added to the literature in recent years.

Major Assumptions and Advantages

A major assumption of this theoretical perspective is that the meaning and importance of leadership cannot be understood by analyzing traits or behaviors; instead, the thought and interpretation processes of individuals are believed to provide greater insight into all aspects of the leadership process. Intentions, perception, and other mental processes have previously been ignored in the leadership literature. A variety of researchers believe that this omission was a great weakness in our understanding because even if a leader says he or she is exhibiting a particular behavior, it does not mean that followers perceive that behavior the same way the leader intended. In addition, theories such as transformational leadership focus on the emotional side of leadership, ignoring how a leader's thought processes or learning affects his performance.

Some of the advantages of cognitive theories become evident in reviewing these assumptions. First, they recognize an important and unstudied area of leadership—cognitive processes. Second, they open the door for studies from a social constructivist paradigm that also emphasize interpretation and subjective experience. Third, they demystify the importance of the leader and help support emerging leadership theories that focus on leadership as a process. From a practical perspective, leaders find the attention to mental processes helpful, as they perceive such processes to be a dimension of leadership over which they have control and see the potential for skill development.

Key Insights and Research

The notion of mental models or cognitive mind-sets has become a major area of research in the last twenty years. Leadership scholars suggest that the work of leaders is using complex mind-sets to analyze and assess leadership issues. One of the main works that relies on mental models for understanding leadership is Bolman and Deal's *Reframing Organizations* (2003). These authors demonstrate that leaders tend to examine situations through one or more lenses or cognitive orientations (political, symbolic, structural, human resource). Different situations might require different cognitive approaches to leadership; a political orientation might serve a leader in one situation, while a bureaucratic orientation is important in another. Successful leaders move between various lenses or approaches to leadership and use all cognitive lenses rather than focusing on the one or two with which they feel most comfortable. The concept of mental models takes a socially constructed view of leadership in which leaders interpret the situation from multiple perspectives and make assessments to determine an appropriate approach to leadership. In this theoretical framework, leaders are not simply matching a particular leadership style to a fixed organizational reality; rather, they must artfully analyze the specific (and changing) needs of the organization based on data gathered from multiple perspectives. Leaders are encouraged to develop reflection skills, to carefully analyze situations through multiple cognitive lenses, and to realize that leadership contexts are specific to a situation and require individualized responses. (Several specific examples are provided in "Higher Education Leadership in the New World.")

In addition to research on mental models, learning has been a major area of study in cognitive theory. The focus on complexity and ambiguity in the postmodern paradigm led scholars to realize the importance of learning to the leadership process and begin a line of research solely on this concept (Griffin, 2002; Neumann, 1991; Shapiro, 2003; Vaill, 1996). For example, Heifetz (1994) and Wheatley (1999) reviewed the critical role of learning in addressing the adaptive and systems challenges faced by organizations. The concept of learning became particularly important in the 1990s in response to concerns that American firms and their leaders were unable to respond to challenges from the external environment and that bureaucratic structures had created inflexible environments where workers no longer engaged in thoughtful reflection (Senge, 1990a; Vaill, 1991, 1996). The literature on leadership and learning focuses on creating organizations that can be adaptable, flexible, experimental, and innovative. Learning is important to leadership at both the individual and organizational level. Ramsden (1998) and Bennis and Goldsmith (1997) emphasize the importance of leaders' thinking of their own development or learning, providing a blueprint for developing a leadership learning agenda. A renewed focus is apparent on the ways that leaders need to constantly renew their skills and conceptualize leadership as a lifetime journey (Komives, Lucas, and McMahon, 1998; Shapiro, 2003; Tomlinson, 2004; Van Velsor and Drath, 2003).

Another prominent example of the significance of learning for leadership is Lambert and others' *The Constructivist Leader* (2002), which suggests that leadership is about seeking improvement through the open, democratic processes of learning and problem solving. The leader's role is building learning communities committed to improving the lives of her or his stakeholders.[1] The leader's work in building learning communities entails creating trust through social and professional relationships, identifying and reconstructing commonly held assumptions and beliefs, building new shared knowledge, and altering individual and group behaviors to create new ways of working (Shapiro, 2003). Leadership is about leading different types of conversations, including dialogic, inquiring, sustaining, and partnering, which contribute to collaborative sense-making, remembrance and reflection, sharing and building ideas, listening, connectivity, common purpose, and vision (Lambert and others, 2002).

At the organizational level, "leaders are responsible for building organizations where people are continually expanding their capabilities to shape their future—that is, leaders are responsible for learning among others" (Senge, 1990b, p. 9). Additionally, leaders play a critical role in helping institutions surface mental models (basic beliefs and assumptions), detect errors, and create environmental supports for learning (for example, breaking down hierarchical structures). To encourage and overcome threats to learning, Senge (1990a) suggests five disciplines for leaders: systems thinking, mental models, personal mastery, shared vision, and team learning or dialogue. In this framework, the leader plays a very different role in organizations from in the past, when he or she was a charismatic or authoritarian leader. Instead, the leader acts as teacher, designer, and steward. As a teacher, leaders motivate others to develop a learning plan (an approach to personal mastery), linking individual and institutional learning. Essentially the leader's role is to inspire and motivate people to learn, a leadership challenge that can lead the organization in unpredictable and different directions. The predictions and generalizations common in positivist theories of leadership are no longer described in these new cognitive theories of leadership, as the future is largely unknown. The teacher also helps surface mental models that prevent individuals from learning, asking critical questions, and embracing new ideas. As designers, teachers create and develop support for a shared vision that serves to focus people's learning. As stewards, leaders focus on supporting people so that they feel part of a team and the larger purpose of the organization. Systems thinking is key throughout each of the roles described above. For example, it is used in the role of teacher to help people think about their contribution to a complex organization and in the role of designer to develop a structure that supports learning. True to the assumptions of social constructivism, learning theories focus on interpretation and meaning making while also adopting postmodern assumptions about the importance of truly understanding the complexity and ambiguity of organizations through systems thinking.

Critique, Problems, and Issues

Although learning is significant in these models, learning and intellect have historically been downplayed in the leadership literature. Transformational leadership models, for example, do not place any importance on the role of learning or an intellectual role for leaders (although they do note that the leader challenges followers' assumptions, which might be a form of learning, and that one of the common measures of transformational leadership is intellectual stimulation). The importance of learning to leadership varies vastly in the research. For example, limited empirical research to date supports the idea that learning creates more effective leaders, yet a plethora of research suggests that learning is important to other organizational functions such as decision making (Senge, 1990a). More research is needed to determine the importance of learning for leadership and bridge the gap in existing scholarship. Other criticisms have been leveled against cognitive leadership perspectives: some researchers believe learning is a fad focused on creating greater innovation in organizations but is not inherently part of leadership (Birnbaum, 2000), and other scholars assert attribution theories are not helpful and provide no guidance for practice (Rost, 1991).

Summary of Cognitive Theories

Theoretical framework is informed by social constructivist and postmodern paradigms of leadership.

The thought processes and interpretations of individuals involved in the leadership process are the focus of research.

Studies of attribution, learning, and mental models are three prominent strands of cognitive leadership research.

Individuals examine leadership challenges and contexts through one or more cognitive lenses (political, symbolic, structural), with different situations requiring different cognitive orientations.

Individual and organizational learning is critical to the cultivation of adaptable, flexible, and innovative leadership processes.

Limited empirical research exists regarding whether or not learning fosters more effective leaders.

Expanding Cultural and Symbolic Theories: Social and Cultural Theories of Leadership

Definition and Emergence

As noted earlier, cultural and symbolic theories of leadership focus on the importance of values, meaning, interpretation, history and traditions, context, and symbolic elements in leadership processes. Cultural and symbolic theories of leadership are relatively new in this area of scholarship, having emerged in the mid- to late 1980s. In the last ASHE-ERIC volume synthesizing the research on higher education leadership (Bensimon, Neumann, and Birnbaum, 1989), very few studies had been conducted from a cultural and symbolic approach. Many studies now, however, have examined the way leadership is affected by values and symbolic dimensions, the context-based and historical influence on leadership, and the way leadership is interpreted distinctly by followers or how leaders' beliefs shape culture.

The focus in cultural theories is that leadership functions in a complex social system. Earlier trait or behavior theories tended to isolate the leader or examine interactions between leader and followers. Instead, these theories emphasize leadership's taking place in a unit, an organization, and a broader social system. Moreover, cultural theories tend to reflect constructivist assumptions and see leadership as invented or created among people and not as a social reality that is discovered. As this theory emerged, scholars also recognized the important role of leaders in developing and shaping the culture of an organization, institution, or society.

Major Assumptions and Advantages

One advantage and contribution of studying leadership from a cultural perspective is the rising prominence of an important leadership construct that had been overlooked in earlier research—the value dimension of leadership. In many ways, Burns's work (1978) on transformational leadership might be credited with the emergence of cultural theories of leadership, as his book on leadership describes the importance of purpose and values in the leadership process, opening the doors for studies from a cultural perspective. In addition to bringing to light an important area of leadership that had not been studied (values), research from a cultural perspective also emphasizes the importance of context in a new way. In the past context had been studied mostly from an organizational structure perspective (for example, examining whether or not an organization was centralized or decentralized). Context from a cultural perspective examines the history, traditions, rituals, and major assumptions of an institution that shape and frame the way people make meaning. Cultural theories brought a new orientation to the study of context, creating other lines of research such as processual leadership (reviewed in the next section).

The advantages of cultural theory are quite significant. Leadership is seen in a much broader perspective as part of the human condition and a vital part of any culture. In addition to providing many new areas of leadership study such as symbols of meaning, cultural theories of leadership have also provided a temporal perspective to leadership research, recognizing the importance of the history of a society or organization to the leadership process.

Key Insights and Research

Over the last twenty years, numerous studies have examined the relationship between various cultural constructs (history and values, for example) and the leadership process, demonstrating that culture is indeed a very significant and important component of leadership (see details of a variety of studies from the higher education literature in "Higher Education Leadership in the New World"). This chapter highlights the ways that the leadership research from a cultural perspective has evolved in recent years, taking new directions in the study of values, gender, race, and cross-cultural issues (see, for example, Astin and Leland, 1991; Ayman, 1993; Banks, 1995; Bell, 1988; Bensimon, 1989a; Cantor and Bernay, 1992; Helgesen, 1990; Kezar 2000, 2002a, 2002c; Morrison, 1991, 1996; Offermann and Phan, 2002; Rosener, 1990; Statham, 1987; Tierney, 1993b; Valverde, 2003)—cultural phenomena previously ignored by leadership scholars.

As mentioned earlier, the emergence of values as an important leadership construct can be attributed to the rising prominence of research on cultural leadership. Similar to culture, many definitions and interpretations of values exist, and values can be manifested in multiple ways throughout an organization. Not to be mistaken for moral or ethical values (treated elsewhere), values in this section represent what Deal and Peterson (1999) describe as one of a number of central beliefs that construct the "bedrock" of organizational culture. This section focuses narrowly on how leaders' values affect organizations. Although traditionally considered in abstract terms, contemporary research has shown that leaders' values play a significant and precise role in the construction of organizational culture. In *Organizational Culture and Leadership,* Schein (1992) draws on years of research with some of America's most well-known organizations to inform his argument that leaders' values underpin most organizational cultures. He describes culture as being multifaceted and consisting of three key layers. In the first layer, the one closest to the surface, are visible organizational behaviors and practices. Underlying those behaviors in the second layer are espoused values that represent organizational philosophies and understandings. The third and deepest layer of culture consists of values and core beliefs that construct the philosophies represented by organizational actions. It is at this level, the deepest source of organizational ideologies, where leaders' values are most influential. Schein explains that when groups and cultures are first created, they adopt the thoughts, beliefs, and assumptions of certain individuals. Those individuals, who are often later identified as leaders, play a central role in determining the philosophies and subsequent actions of an organization and its constituents. One example from higher education is the founding members of a college or university. The core principles that guide an institutional mission are frequently the direct results of one key individual and his or her beliefs and values. In many instances these values are passed on for centuries without being questioned. A second and more important example involves organizational change. In many instances organizational change cannot take place effectively unless the change is compatible with leaders' values and beliefs (Schein, 1992).

With respect to cultural research on gender and leadership, studies of women leaders have illustrated that women tend to define and understand leadership in ways not reflected in traditional models based on all-male research samples (Astin and Leland, 1991; Bensimon and Neumann, 1993; Kezar, 2000, 2002b, 2002c; Rhode, 2003). For example, women's leadership is associated with a more participatory, relational, and interpersonal style and with different types of power and influence strategies emphasizing reciprocity and collectivity. Moreover, women leaders tend to conceptualize leadership as collective rather than individualistic, emphasize responsibility toward others and the empowerment of others to act in the organization, and deemphasize hierarchical relationships (Amey and Twombley, 1992; Astin and Leland, 1991; Cantor and Bernay, 1992; Ferguson, 1984; Helgesen, 1990; Kezar, 2000, 2002b, 2002c; Rosener, 1990; Statham, 1987).

A few studies of leadership beliefs among people of color in the United States have found distinctions in the way that Native Americans

---

(community oriented, focus on wisdom, spirituality) and African Americans (nonhierarchical, community based, focus on spirituality) define leadership; findings have been mixed for Hispanics (Ayman, 1993; Kezar, 2000, 2002b, 2002c; Kezar and Moriarty, 2000). Some studies also examine the overlap of social and cultural differences (Kezar, 2002b, 2002c). For example, studies of African American women find that they have more direct communication styles than white women and focus more on spirituality (Rhode, 2003). One researcher has developed a pluralistic approach to leadership that demonstrates the importance of leaders' reflecting actively on their backgrounds as well as understanding and engaging the diversity of leadership approaches from people of varying backgrounds (Kezar, 2000, 2002b, 2002c). The cultural and social differences are described as emerging from the specific experiences of being a woman or a minority, not something essential about being a woman or a minority. Therefore, different cultural experiences can result in specific sensitivities or beliefs about leadership.

Cross-cultural studies have exploded in the literature in the last decade (Dickson, Den Hartog, and Mitchelson, 2003; Dorfman, 1996; House, Wright, and Aditya, 1997). Dickson, Den Hartog, and Mitchelson (2003) describe how, since 1996, the quest for universal leadership principles has declined and an awareness of differences risen based on research grounded in Hofstede's cultural dimensions (1980). Cultural leadership research examines a host of issues, including differences between individualist countries (a focus on individual achievement and rights) and collective societies (a focus on collective achievement and rights) as well as the possibility of clustering countries based on similar contexts or histories (Ah Chong and Thomas, 1997; Ensari and Murphy, 2003; Hofstede, 1997; House and others, 2004; Offermann and Phan, 2002). Others have developed complex matrixes representing the differences in the traits, behaviors, and power and influence processes of leaders across a host of countries (Gerstner and Day, 1994). Countries have also been labeled according to cultural norms related to leadership such as performance oriented, team oriented, participative, humane, autonomous, self-protective, and group protective. The studies reveal specific ways that leadership is defined among eastern (collective, holistic, spirituality based) and western (hierarchical, authority based, and individualistic) cultures

(Ayman, 1993; Cox, 1993; Ensari and Murphy, 2003). These various research programs demonstrate how leaders' backgrounds—their cultural experiences and traditions—alter their leadership beliefs and actions. They also demonstrate how leadership is affected by the characteristics of different cultural contexts. Certain characteristics and behaviors have been found to be more universal such as honesty, motivation, dependability, and encouragement, whereas other qualities have been found to be culturally contingent such as ambition, autonomy, compassion, enthusiasm, orderliness, risk taking, or sensitivity. Several models of multicultural leadership have been proposed based on social and cross-cultural research (Den Hartog and others, 1999; Gerstner and Day, 1994; Hofstede, 1980; House and others, 2004).

Recent studies have applied findings from cultural and social leadership research to develop instruments for measuring leaders' cross-cultural knowledge to enhance leadership development programs and activities (McCauley and Van Velsor, 2003). They observe that assessment of and feedback on leaders' performance (usually in the form of surveys) are themselves affected by cultural norms about whether one can be open and honest with coworkers; the notion of criticizing is foreign in some cultures, and trust is often lacking in others. Because psychology, the discipline that develops the surveys, and survey methodology are considered more western approaches, they also suggest creating forms of development that fit better in the cultural context—for example, journaling. An important first step is for leaders to read about and become aware of cultural differences in their beliefs and behaviors so that they can act more appropriately in the context. Leaders are encouraged to learn the art of perspective taking, which involves listening to and absorbing information skillfully, recognizing that other people may view a situation differently, understanding that other people's assumptions may be different, and accepting the limitations of one's own point of view.

Critiques, Problems, and Issues

Some researchers believe research is minimal to support leadership differences based on gender and race (Chemers, 1997). These scholars acknowledge cultural variation in the ways that leadership relationships and behaviors are structured and interpreted but note that the "major functions of leadership have universal importance" (Chemers, 1997, p. 134). Nevertheless, researchers are mixed in their interpretation and view of how significant cultural and social categories are and their effect on leadership. Others believe that a danger exists of essentializing differences by focusing on group characteristics that may not represent individuals in these groups. These authors point out that some white men might operate in collaborative ways, while some African American woman might operate in hierarchical and top-down ways.

Another concern with cultural theories is that they tend to focus on leadership in a particular context and cannot be generalized to other settings or institutional cultures. If leadership is truly so context based, then research is limited in being able to guide leadership practice beyond helping leaders conduct analyses of their own environments. As leaders are left with little time to conduct detailed analysis of the history, values, and context of their own institutions, however, practitioners claim that this line of research is often not helpful in assisting them to improve leadership.

Summary of Social and Cultural Theories

Theoretical frameworks draw from postmodern, social constructivist, and critical paradigms of leadership.

The importance of values, meaning, interpretation, traditions, and symbolic elements of leadership is emphasized.

Leadership contexts are examined from a cultural rather than structural perspective.

Leadership processes are influenced by cultural contexts.

Attention is given to the gender, racial, and cross-cultural dimensions of leadership (for example, the collective and empowering nature of women's leadership).

Individual leadership beliefs and actions are shaped by cultural background.

Awareness is heightened of the role leaders' values play in shaping organizational culture and action.

Different Strokes for Different Folks: The Importance of Cultural Leadership

The outgoing and incoming chairs of the faculty senate committee on education policy are meeting for coffee this morning to discuss matters of leadership transition. Specifically, the new committee chair, Joan, a female faculty member in the department of sociology, is interested in gathering the former chair's perspective on the cultural dimensions of committee leadership. Perplexed by this line of questioning, the outgoing chair, Ted, a professor of psychology, asks Joan for additional clarification on cultural theories of leadership. Joan obliges by offering a compelling discussion of the gender and racial implications embedded in leadership, calling on her own Native American heritage to illustrate the cultural differences between Western notions of leadership centered on hierarchy and control and the Native American leadership principles of community, shared decision making, and spirituality. Throughout her discussion with Ted, Joan articulates a personal leadership philosophy centered on empowerment and collaboration that is heavily influenced by her cultural experiences as a Native American woman.

Although she is committed to enacting her own cultural values of leadership in the role of committee chair, Joan acknowledges to Ted that the committee's leadership context (and therefore her leadership actions) will be shaped by the cultural backgrounds of all committee members as well as the members' diverse interpretations of existing committee norms. For example, the education policy committee is notoriously dominated by male faculty members, most from the natural and physical sciences, who attempt to maintain their implicit control of the committee's policy agenda through strict adherence to committee norms that privilege the voices of senior (typically male) faculty members. Joan expects that several of the senior members of the committee will question her consensus-oriented leadership style but hopes that in time the group will begin to recognize the benefits associated with broader participation in committee deliberations.

Ted is initially offended by Joan's characterization of the committee (up to now he had attributed the committee's high degree of efficiency and productivity to the strong leadership of senior faculty members), but his discussion with Joan does highlight several committee norms and values that undermine the voices of female and junior faculty members. For example, although the twelve-member education policy committee usually has no more than three women on it, a female colleague is typically asked to assume responsibility for taking

(Continued)

Different Strokes for Different Folks (*Continued*)

minutes—a task that frequently limits her participation in committee discussions. In addition, returning committee members are always allowed to pick their preferred subcommittee assignments, while new members receive their assignments from the chair and are discouraged from advancing their own policy ideas until they are more familiar with the committee's established priorities and values. Ted did not question these norms when he assumed leadership of the committee, given that his personal framework of leadership is much more product oriented than process oriented, but Joan's explanation of the cultural leadership dynamics in the policy committee calls attention to the fact that many of Ted's leadership assumptions and behaviors are grounded in Western notions of hierarchy and control and thus are limited in their ability to meet the needs of culturally diverse leadership. Although he had intended to be the one doing most of the talking at this leadership transition meeting, Ted is thankful for the opportunity to listen and expresses his gratitude to Joan for introducing him to a new perspective on leadership. Despite the fact that his term as chair of the education policy committee is now coming to an end, Ted intends to draw on his emerging understanding of cultural leadership theory in his new role as chair of the psychology department, a diverse organization also struggling to reconcile multiple interpretations of effective leadership.

Rethinking Contingency Theories: Processual Leadership

Definition and Emergence

Emerging in the 1960s with a recognition that certain leadership activities might require a different style or approach, situational and contingency models examine the relationship between microaspects of the organizational context (such as task design and subordinate development) and leadership (Fiedler, 1997). Accumulated contingency research findings suggest that aspects of the organization and leadership task affect the leadership process. Newer theories such as processual theory focus more broadly on notions of context and how they affect leadership (Fiedler, 1997).

Assumptions and Contributions

Processual theory examines context from a constructivist rather than a functionalist paradigm (Dawson, 1994; Osborn, Hunt, and Jauch, 2002; Parry, 1998; Pettigrew, 1997; Pettigrew, Woodman, and Cameron, 2001). In other words, situations are not objective realities to which leaders respond. Instead, situations are interpreted and created by people in a setting. Moreover, leadership actions are not contingent on objective, fixed situational variables in the organization. Instead, situational aspects such as employee motivation or task design are interpreted by various people in the context.

In addition to focusing attention on context, processual leadership emphasizes the dynamic nature and process orientation of leadership. Processual leadership makes the importance of context more obvious by examining leadership over time and through a sequence of activities (Antonakis, Avolio, and Sivasubramaniam, 2003; Chaffee and Tierney, 1988; Chemers and Ayman, 1993: Dawson, 1994; Klenke, 1996; Neumann, 1995; Osborn, Hunt, and Jauch, 2002; Parry, 1998; Pettigrew, 1997; Pettigrew, Woodman, and Cameron, 2001; Shamir and Howell, 1999). Some have likened this approach to a shift from taking pictures or snapshots of leadership to developing a motion picture. Processual studies explore leadership development over long periods of time, highlighting the limitations of early psychologically oriented leadership studies that ignored context and process (Pettigrew, 1997). This line of research is more complex than administering a survey or conducting a few quick interviews. Processual research entails observation and prolonged engagement to address a question: How does a process of leadership emerge and change over time? Researchers look at a succession of tasks, events, crises, and other aspects of the process that help shed light on the leadership process as it unfolds. Accordingly, relationship development, collaboration, and social change (which can take a long time) are better understood through a processual approach.

Researchers also challenge the way context is defined in earlier contingency approaches that focus on microcontextual conditions (task design, employee motivation, leadership style) at the cost of ignoring macroissues such as institutional climate or culture, the larger society, and global economic conditions (Osborn, Hunt, and Jauch, 2002). In addition, processual researchers argue that views of context have been overly simplified, reduced to a set of six to eight variables that do not truly ascertain the complexity of how institutional contexts operate. Many of these studies emerge from anthropological and sociological approaches to the study of leadership, focusing on how organizations and societies have particular histories and cultures that affect organizational phenomena, including leadership.

These advances in contingency and situational theories of leadership provided in the processual approach are important and have helped to make this line of research stronger. The emergence of more complex views of leadership contexts has resulted in the identification of important concepts that warrant additional attention from leaders, including organizational history and culture and societal trends. In addition, similar to other theories reviewed earlier in this chapter, the importance of interpretation and perspective in the processual approach has added needed complexity.

Key Research and Insights

Several studies have demonstrated that context is socially constructed by individuals involved in a leadership process (Dawson, 1994; Neumann, 1995; Osborn, Hunt, and Jauch, 2002; Parry, 1998; Pettigrew, 1997; Pettigrew, Woodman, and Cameron, 2001). One person, for example, may perceive that a situation requires a task orientation while another may see this same situation as requiring a relational orientation. In addition, studies have demonstrated that leadership in some situations goes through cycles in which certain tasks, events, and issues tend to occur in regular sequences and are necessary for the leadership process to unfold (Dawson, 1994; Klenke, 1996; Osborn, Hunt, and Jauch, 2002; Parry, 1998; Pettigrew, 1997; Pettigrew, Woodman, and Cameron, 2001).

In addition to studies that challenge the objective and fixed character of situational and contingency models, other studies have expanded and reexamined the concept of context itself. Researchers are beginning to design studies of leadership context more complexly by examining macro (global economics), meso (institutional politics), and micro (employee motivation) conditions. For example, the major finding of Osborn, Hunt, and Jauch (2002) is that leadership is organizationally determined and that the culture and norms of organizations limit, enable, and affect the leadership processes. These authors demonstrate that people can go to training sessions to learn new leadership skills but will revert to the norms of the organization when they return. Organizations differ in many important conditions such as how people achieve positions of authority (elected, appointed, volunteer), how people influence one another in the organization, channels of communication, conditions of employment, and type of people employed (professionals, untrained workers, volunteers). As noted, every organization also has a distinctive organizational culture and history that further make the context unique.

Another line of research in this approach is the idea that leadership principles are specific to certain contexts and the specific aims of the leadership activity. Hargrove and Owens (2003) demonstrate that political leadership is distinct from leadership in business or educational settings. Leadership is illustrated to be inherently context bound. The skills, values, knowledge, attitudes, and behaviors required in one situation differ radically from those in another. Corporate managers, voluntary associations, and schools face different leadership needs and contexts. Thus, treating leadership as a universal phenomenon, as was usually the case in past research, is now considered problematic. Bensimon, Neumann, and Birnbaum (1989) also emphasized the importance of context and are among some of the first writers to focus on how the higher education setting requires a distinctive form of leadership, with different institutional types and divisions requiring different leadership.

Critique, Problems, and Issues

Many have begun to argue that context may be the most important factor affecting leadership and that it has largely been ignored over the years in leader-centric models focusing on traits, behaviors, power and influence strategies, and cognitive mind-sets. The importance of context is finally being acknowledged, yet many more studies need to be conducted to better understand the dynamics between the various levels of context. Most researchers lack a sustained research agenda to study leadership from this perspective over five or ten years, which makes it a less popular approach. In addition, tenure and promotion processes at universities often reward productivity in terms of yearly publications, and long-term studies often prevent researchers from meeting these institutional goals, which may deter some researchers from engaging in this form of research.

Summary of Processual Leadership

This framework extends existing situational and contingency models of leadership.

It examines the effect of context on leadership from a constructivist paradigm (that is, context is believed to be socially constructed by individuals involved in the leadership process).

It emphasizes the process orientation of leadership that unfolds over time.

It focuses on the relationships between macrocontextual conditions (institutional culture, the larger society, global economic conditions) and leadership processes.

Research is characterized by prolonged engagement in the setting to observe leadership dynamics over time.

Team or Relational Leadership

Definition and Emergence

In an update of his leadership textbook, Northouse (2004) notes a new approach or body of research in traditional leadership literature—team leadership. The notion of team leadership was foreshadowed by critiques of modern organizations as rigid, lacking in innovation, and bureaucratic—needing greater flexibility to work together. Traditional individualistic leadership was also critiqued by complexity theories that emphasize networks and group work. Studies of women and cross-cultural leaders demonstrate a preference for collective work. Given these many precursors, it is not surprising that the notion of team leadership emerged. Leadership teams serve many important institutional purposes, from planning and completing tasks to providing intellectual discourse and problem solving to drawing people together to provide support to identifying connections and ways groups can assist each other. This approach is described in two distinctive ways in the literature: one represents functionalist assumptions, the other social constructivist and critical theory assumptions.

In the first approach using functionalist assumptions, researchers study leadership teams to understand the best approach to fostering leadership in a team setting (Ilgen, Major, Hollenbeck and Sego, 1993; Kelly, 1998; Kinlaw,

1998). Much of this literature combines principles from other recent approaches to leadership cited earlier in this chapter. For example, leaders need to foster learning in teams, be aware of the mental models of team members, and help teams manage and negotiate complexity and systems problems. The research in this area mirrors much of the behavior, situational, and power and influence theories reviewed in Bensimon, Neumann, and Birnbaum's earlier report on leadership (1989). It maintains functionalist assumptions and outlines characteristics such as teams' having clear goals, developing a collaborative culture, building confidence among team members, fostering technical competence, setting priorities, and measuring performance (Northouse, 2004).

The other approach is to see leadership as an inherent team process; it has been labeled team, relational, shared, and multilevel leadership (Bensimon and Neumann, 1993; Bradford and Cohen, 1998; Hackman, 1990; Helgesen, 1990; LaFasto and Larson, 2001; Riggio, Murphy, and Pirozzolo, 2002). This approach to a team model evolves from the critical paradigm of leadership and feminist studies of women leaders. A review of studies of women leaders revealed the prominent role of teams in this group's conception of leadership. From this perspective, leadership is defined as a collective and collaborative process focused on relationships and networks. In this volume, we focus on the second definition of team leadership as it reflects the values of the leadership revolution.

Major Assumptions and Advantages

Researchers such as Bensimon and Neumann (1993) distinguish teams as a culture from the traditional athletic metaphor of teams. The focus in a team process is on interconnectedness and working collectively (culture) rather than emphasizing individual players and results (the athletic metaphor of teams). In addition, all members are equal and deserve respect. The teams-as-cultures concept assumes that differences exist among people; this approach attempts to actively tap into and affirm differences. The purpose is to enlarge each member's understandings of others' views. Earlier research on teams often focused on consensus and shared understandings. In this line of research, differences and various interpretations are seen as the advantage of teams and a way to develop cognitive complexity.

Interpretation and dialogue are also key elements in this model; different team members are encouraged to try to understand others' behavior and become more aware of perception and multiple interpretations. One way to better come to this understanding of the interpreted world is by engaging teams in dialogue. Much of the earlier research on teams focused on ways to make them more productive by emphasizing task efficiency. This new research on team leadership suggests that teams will not be effective unless they have ample time to build relationships and have significant dialogue before working on a task. The team as culture model also examines how the larger organization affects leadership, which is seen as a *process* rather than a person or group. Although it is assumed that the overall environment and context affect team leadership, research in this area has been limited.

A very similar model to the team approach is relational leadership, which emerged out of Rost's postindustrial model of leadership (1991) in which process and mutuality are emphasized over the individual leader or group. A relational view defines leadership as a process in which people working together attempt to accomplish change or make a difference to benefit the common good (Komives, Lucas, and McMahon, 1998). It has five primary components: leadership is inclusive of people and diverse points of view, empowers those involved, is purposeful and builds commitment toward common purposes, is ethical, and recognizes that all four of these elements are accomplished by being process oriented. The model is more complex than merely understanding and applying the five elements because each element entails learning knowledge, attitudes, and skills to successfully enact the elements. For example, Komives, Lucas, and McMahon (1998) note that to practice inclusiveness one needs to know oneself and others (knowledge), be open to difference and value all perspectives (attitude), and practice listening skills, building coalitions, and effective civil discourse (skills). This model emphasizes personal reflection, ethics, and inclusiveness. It also involves a commitment to understand organizational dynamics and thus how to build an inclusive and empowering environment, to motivate people and build coalitions, and to undertake a strong process focus.

Like the organizational learning approach to leadership, the benefits and advantages of team and relational approaches are prominent in the literature. For example, Bensimon and Neumann (1993) highlight how creative problem solving emerges among teams with diversely oriented minds. The other significant benefit of teams is smoothly implemented decisions by virtue of greater ownership by individuals throughout the organization.

The contribution from a research perspective is more difficult to ascertain. Viewing leadership as a collaborative and collective process is not unusual. A variety of theories reviewed earlier in this chapter suggest that leadership is collective and process oriented, and context was emphasized in our previous discussions of cultural and contingency theories. The main contributions of team leadership theory are identifying teams as the desired unit of analysis and focusing researchers' attention on the interpersonal dynamics of teams. Researchers in this tradition have asserted and tried to demonstrate that the team level is the critical level at which leadership can be understood. They acknowledge that societal and organizational context affects leadership but suggest that the key unit of analysis should be organizational and societal teams.

Key Research and Insights

Both conceptual and empirical scholarship underscore the inextricable relationship between leadership processes and team effectiveness. Indeed, Zaccaro, Rittman, and Marks (2001) assert that "effective leadership processes represent perhaps the most critical factor in the success of organizational teams" (p. 452). Drawing on previous studies of leadership and team performance, Zacarro, Rittman, and Marks document the important role individual leaders play in facilitating the cognitive, motivational, affective, and coordination processes of teams. For example, through the motivational leadership processes of setting goals, providing feedback, and developing individual team members, leaders foster team task cohesion and collective efficacy—two essential dimensions of teamwork. Rather than framing the relationship between team leadership processes and team effectiveness as a product of one-sided influence originating with the leader, these researchers posit a reciprocal relationship in which team processes also shape the leader's behavior, roles, and responsibilities.

Despite the fact that Zacarro, Rittman, and Marks (2001) acknowledge a mutual influence between leaders and their teams, their functional model of team leadership continues to conceptualize leadership as an individual attribute of formal team leaders. Day, Gronn, and Salas (2004) challenge such traditional "individual input" models of team leadership, arguing instead for a perspective that views leadership as an outcome of team processes focused on collaborative achievement of common goals. In this output-oriented team leadership framework, Day, Gronn, and Salas acknowledge that team members bring individual leadership abilities and knowledge to the group. What is of primary importance to these researchers, however, is understanding the team-level leadership that results from engaging in shared work. "It is not so much that leadership and team processes become indistinguishable but that leadership happens as an outcome of team processes, and this team-level leadership is then used as a resource in future processes and performance episodes" (p. 859).

The shift from input- to outcome-oriented notions of team leadership holds significant implications for researchers interested in examining effective team strategies. O'Connor and Quinn (2004) assert, "When leadership is viewed as a property of whole systems, as opposed to solely the property of individuals, effectiveness in leadership becomes more a product of those connections or relationships among parts than the result of any one part of that system (such as the leader)" (p. 423). Rather than focusing on the individual attributes and behaviors of team leaders, team leadership research seeks to describe and understand the relationships and processes that foster collective leadership. Of particular interest in this strand of scholarship are the processes and outcomes of team-level learning (Day, Gronn, and Salas, 2004). To effectively address and overcome the complex (adaptive) leadership challenges that characterize contemporary organizations (Heifetz, 1994), teams must increase their leadership capacity by engaging in team-level learning processes that expand the team's collective adaptability and cognitive complexity. Although research has examined the relationship between team learning and team performance and scholars have identified specific strategies individual leaders can employ to foster team learning (to be accessible, seek input, admit mistakes) (Edmondson, Bohmer, and Pisano, 2001), few researchers have explored the explicit connection between team learning and the emergence of team-level leadership. This gap in the literature will need to be addressed by those interested in advancing the team approach to understanding leadership.

Leadership in self-managing and virtual teams involves two similar but distinct strands of team leadership research that has also gained prominence in the last fifteen years (Bell and Kozlowski, 2002; Druskat and Wheeler, 2004; Hertel, Geister, and Konradt, 2005; Kayworth and Leidner, 2001/2002; Wageman, 2001). Both strands of scholarship investigate the specific leadership challenges and practices associated with team structures that exhibit greater autonomy and transparency of process as a result of rapid developments in information and communication technologies. Research on the leadership of self-managing teams, those teams with a designated leader (or manager) who is not a regular member of the team, has focused on the identification of effective leadership behaviors that maximize the team's performance (for example, coaching, team design, flexibility, empowerment) (Druskat and Wheeler, 2004; Wageman, 2001). Ironically, external team leaders, not the self-managing team members themselves, continue to be situated at the center of leadership research on self-managing teams.

Research on the leadership of virtual teams, "distributed work teams whose members predominately communicate and coordinate their work via electronic media" (Hertel, Geister, and Konradt, 2005, p. 69) has expanded in recent years in the context of rapid globalization and technological innovation. Rather than conceptualizing virtual teams as fundamentally different from "conventional" work teams, Hertel, Geister, and Konradt (2005) frame "virtuality" as one among many team attributes, with all teams falling somewhere on the virtual spectrum. A review of research on leadership in virtual teams (also called e-leadership) reveals that "virtual team leadership is typically not under the control of any one person, but is expressed through the interplay of team members and technology" (Zigurs, 2003, p. 348). In virtual teams, leadership roles shift among team members depending on the specific objectives and performance tasks occupying that particular moment in the team's life cycle. The challenges of virtual team leadership include overcoming cultural difference, logistical matters such as working in different time zones, technology issues, and limited opportunities for face-to-face interaction (Kayworth and Leidner, 2001/2002; Zigurs, 2003). Additional research findings on virtual team leadership underscore the importance of frequent positive communication, the need to dedicate more time to relational development in comparison with "conventional" teams, the benefits of initiating virtual teams with face-to-face interactions, and the importance of mentoring and empathy in virtual teams (Kayworth and Leidner, 2001/2002; Zigurs, 2003).

Minimal research supports relational leadership theory/approach, yet it is built on research from complexity, social/cultural, team, and organizational learning theories. Because it is so new, it may take some time for studies and research support to emerge specifically on the model. Another approach to shared or team leadership is termed *coleadership* or *multileadership* (Alston, 2002). Rather than leading in an established team, coleadership involves a set of leaders working informally but in tandem to provide leadership for an organization such as the principal, assistant principal, chief financial officer, and instructional leader. Little research has been conducted on this model as well.

Research on team leadership has been fairly conclusive. Teams are effective mechanisms for leadership and have many benefits but need to be structured and organized appropriately to reap the benefits (Bensimon and Neumann, 1993; Komives, Lucas, and McMahon, 1998). The references in this book provide ample guidelines to help practitioners build effective teams that will strengthen leadership capacity.

Critique, Problems, and Issues

Much of the literature from a team or relational perspective is conducted in an idealized way and does not address the challenges of developing a team or relational orientation in hierarchical and bureaucratic structures. Most organizations remain rigid bureaucracies and are limited in their flexibility. We need research that helps guide leaders in these environments to create pockets of collaboration that may eventually help transform the institution. Although leaders can work to transform organizations into ones that support collaboration and teamwork, it can take decades, particularly for large organizations such as colleges and universities. In general, this area of research needs greater exploration to enhance our understanding of how a shared leadership model can work, how empowerment can be fostered, and how leadership can be made more inclusive.

Summary of Team or Relational Leadership

Leadership is a collective and collaborative process.

One strand of the team leadership research is grounded in a functionalist paradigm and focuses on understanding how to foster leadership in team settings.

A second strand of the team leadership literature is framed by the paradigms of social constructivism and critical theory and views leadership as a relational, collaborative team process. In this framework of team leadership: (1) teams are viewed as cultures in which all members are believed equal and individual differences are affirmed; (2) dialogue among team members with multiple interpretations of the context is encouraged; (3) differences and specific interpretations in team settings are believed to advance cognitive complexity; (4) building relationships is emphasized; (5) relational views of leadership focus on the process of people working together to accomplish change or benefit the common good; and (6) reflection on personal leadership attributes as well as organizational dynamics is believed essential for building inclusive, empowering team environments.

Summary

Leadership research in recent years has taken a dramatic turn. Although bookshelves will continue to hold many titles that read "the eight most important traits for leaders" or "how you can influence people to follow you," the leadership research has been enriched by a variety of new perspectives. Leadership researchers and practitioners are now beginning to understand the incredible complexity of organizations and global societies where contemporary leadership takes place. The contemporary leadership scholars reviewed in this chapter have also underscored the need for more adaptive, systems-oriented approaches to leadership that enhance cognitive complexity through learning and team leadership. Researchers have called attention to the significance of leaders' being culturally intelligent and able to understand the perspective of those from different races, cultures, and ethnic backgrounds. Leaders need to hone their ability to work in groups and to become more artful at reading organizational and historical contexts. For many practitioners, many of these lessons will not be new because these ideas have been emerging over the last twenty years. But collectively, few practitioners or researchers will have thought about these massive changes in total. The goal of this chapter and this book is to synthesize these collective theoretical and research insights to expand the horizon of our views as both leadership researchers and practitioners.

Revolutionary Concepts of Leadership

THE APPLICATION OF NEW PARADIGMS and theories in leadership research has resulted in the emergence of new leadership concepts: ethics and spirituality, collaboration and partnering, empowerment, social change, emotions, globalization, entrepreneurialism, and accountability. These concepts reflect the new societal context in which leadership occurs, a context described as postindustrial by Rost (1991) and as postmodern by others (Palestini, 2003; Parry 1998). The increasingly global nature of society, characterized by frequent and extended interactions across different cultures, has made cultural issues more prominent in the work of leadership as well as raised interest in examining leadership cross-culturally. In addition, the increasingly competitive world brought on by economic and political globalization has made partnerships and alliances central to success. This interdependence is further reinforced by technology such as the Internet, which links people and makes collaboration across contexts easier.

Collaboration, networks, and the importance of culture are all important concepts in this new context of leadership. The collaboration and shared power of a global world economy encourage research on how to empower organizations. As decision making and authority move to all levels of the organization, individuals and groups can be more entrepreneurial in their approach. Yet in the wrong hands, sharing power can result in abuses. The many recent scandals in leadership have led to a renewed interest in ethics, spirituality, and accountability to ensure the process is fair and just.

Certain characteristics cross each of these concepts. For example, a focus on the individual, autonomous, and positional leader with formal authority has been replaced by a focus on the actions of collective groups and nonpositional leadership outside formal authority structures. Second, leadership is also now seen as value laden, so concepts such as emotions, spirituality, and ethics become prominent (Heifetz, 1994). Third, all the concepts reviewed in this chapter reinforce the importance of breaking down hierarchy and traditional bureaucratic organizational structures and processes. Although these concepts are described separately, the emerging concepts of leadership show a great deal of overlap and interactivity. For example, empowerment is often created through partnering and collaboration, leaders feel a need to empower to create entrepreneurialism, and accountability systems are initiated by leaders in response to commitments to engage in fair and socially just organizational activities.

The purpose of this chapter is to introduce the set of concepts by introducing their emergence, definitions, and key works. To fully understand the concepts will require further reading of literature cited in the section. As we review each concept below, we explain the emergence of the concept and its relationship to previous leadership research, present a definition of the concept, provide a few key examples, review relevant research, and describe the implications or contributions of this concept to the leadership research.

Ethics and Spirituality

As notions of power and leaders' intentions have come under examination through the paradigms of critical theory and postmodernism, ethics and morals have become a critical area of concern. Critical theorists and postmodernists have exposed how supposedly value-free assumptions of early leadership theories have resulted in disguising unequal power relations and reinforcing the status quo of organizations. As a result of illuminating this problem, they encourage seeing leadership as a social process that is value laden. In addition, cultural theories of leadership demonstrate that leaders have different values that they bring to the leadership process and that different groups engage morality and spirituality to greater and lesser degrees.

The word *ethics* usually refers to underlying beliefs, assumptions, principles, and values that support a moral way of life. Ethical leadership is an attempt to act from the principles, beliefs, assumptions, and values embedded in the leader's espoused system of ethics. It is often associated with character, authenticity, and credibility in the leadership literature. Trait, behavior, power or influence, situational, and cognitive theories, however, take a value-neutral approach to leadership (one exception is the transformational leadership theory). For example, these traditional leadership frameworks are not likely to question whether the selection of an authoritarian leadership style is an ethically sound decision or one that is likely to disempower individuals and groups. In value-free theories of leadership, a leader's behavior is dictated by the achievement of desired goals, not ethical considerations. If persuasion works, then it is the best tactic. If coercive power or rewards create an effective organization, then in most models of leadership the leader has made an accurate decision. In sharp contrast, interpretive, critical, and postmodern scholars question whether the ends justify the means and whether the ends themselves (typically meeting an organizational goal, effectiveness, or change) are worthwhile uses of leadership.

In response to the criticisms and questions raised by the revolution taking place in leadership research, scholars have begun to examine the ethical foundations of new approaches to understanding leadership. Robert Greenleaf's concept of servant leadership (1977) has had a revival and is perhaps more popular now than when it was originally introduced in the 1970s, given the explicit ethical orientation of Greenleaf's servant leaders. In addition, Noddings's ethic of care (1984) has been applied to the development of a moral foundation for leadership (Pellicer, 2003). Starratt (2004), for example, suggests that school leaders need to hold an ethic of care, an ethic of justice, and an ethic of critique, providing a multidimensional map of an ethical system of leadership. Certain helpful texts examine ethical issues such as authenticity, character, responsibility, stewardship, servant leadership, and responsibility to stakeholders (see Avolio and Gardner, 2005; Ciulla, 1998; Conger and others, 1994; Griffin, 2002; Hodgkinson, 1991; Palmer, 2000; Pellicer, 2003; Rabbin 1998). Avolio and Gardner (2005), for example, have defined the components of authentic leadership and differentiate it from transformational, charismatic, servant, and spiritual leadership. Authentic leadership has its roots in Greek philosophy and humanistic psychology and is related to Maslow's idea of self-actualization. They outline the following features of authentic leadership that need further study: positive psychological capital, positive moral perspective, leader's self-awareness, leader's self-regulation, personal and social identification, followers' self-awareness, followers' development, sustained performance beyond expectations, and positive organizational environment (open access to information, resources, support, and equal opportunity).

Another concept related to ethics has emerged in recent years—spirituality (Kyle, 1998; Palmer, 1998b, 2000; Spears, 1998). Ethics might be developed from professional standards, codes of conduct, and other guidelines developed by people. Some people believe, however, that an ethical code should be derived from a higher being or be based on transcendent principles that have held over time. These more metaphysically based notions of ethical conduct are referred to as *spirituality.* People often refer to spirituality rather than religion or morals to separate it from formal institutions such as the Roman Catholic Church. Certainly, Catholicism is a form of spirituality and can be used to guide an ethical life, but spirituality refers to a broader term that encompasses metaphysical beliefs that are included in formal institutions as well as beliefs that are not institutionalized into doctrine. Bolman and Deal's *Leading with Soul* (1995) is an example of a growing literature base that examines the way a spiritual foundation supports approaches to leadership that are more empowering. They describe the journey of a manager who believes in authority, control, power, individualism, and other characteristics associated with the traditional view of leadership. He has been given the advice to meet with a wise mentor who helps him undergo a process of reflection and spiritual growth by having him examine his own belief system and values. The manager is asked to look at things from not just his mind but also his heart and soul, to embrace the value of emotions in the leadership process, and to see the value in empowerment, collaboration, enriching people's spirits, and fostering a collective ethic.

Many of the leadership theories reviewed in the previous chapter emphasize an ethical dimension, for example, the relational and learning organization models. Wheatley's *Leadership and the New Science* (1999) and Senge's *The Fifth Discipline* (1990a) emphasize that the spiritual dimension of organizational life is critical to understanding ambiguity and complex problems.

Solutions to complex problems require all types of knowledge and thinking beyond data and rational linear thinking. They also suggest that leadership at its best is a spiritual journey in which people examine their motives, intentions, and relationships to other individuals and their place in the world. By answering these spiritual questions and through self-development, individuals are better prepared to be leaders and participate in a leadership process. Likewise, Palmer (1998b, 2000) has written about leadership as a spiritual calling. Books on spiritual leadership identify actions such as creating a presence, developing wisdom, using compassion, engaging in reflection, fostering self-development, building trust, and the like as important steps toward improving the leadership process.

Research in this area focuses on the human aspects of work. Rather than seeing people as mechanized workers serving the organization's interests, these individuals are viewed as holistic entities of mind, body, and spirit who make significant contributions to the process of leadership. Cross-cultural leadership research demonstrates that certain groups strongly affiliate leadership with spirituality—for example, African Americans, Native Americans, and East Asian Indians. Newer books such as Garner's *Contesting the Terrain of the Ivory Tower* (2004) describe how these women leaders use their spiritual experiences and background to enhance their leadership by providing an ethic of care, focusing on service and social justice, and recognizing interdependence by expanding leadership beyond the organization to the community and world. Empirical work in this area has tied moral and ethical leadership to greater organizational effectiveness and efficiency (Aronson, 2001). Dickson, Smith, Grojean, and Ehrhart's study (2001) demonstrates that ethical climates vary by organizational culture and that no one effective ethical leadership culture exists. Leaders should strive to develop a culture that people believe is ethical and sustain this environment because it leads to organizational effectiveness.

The major contribution of ethics and spirituality is to examine and critique a value-free representation of leadership that had become dominant in scientific views of leadership. It has also helped to bring a fuller or more comprehensive view of leadership into prominence that focuses on mind, body, and spirit, which had been important in earlier centuries before a scientific view of leadership.

Collaboration

Another major theme in recent leadership literature is collaboration, networks, and partnering (Bradford and Cohen, 1998; Ferren and Stanton, 2004; LaFasto and Larson, 2001; Riggio, Murphy, and Pirozzolo, 2002; Rubin, 2002; Shakeshaft, 1999; Tierney, 1993a). As noted earlier, critical theorists and interpretive scholars question traditional notions of authority, which view leadership as an individual attribute or possession. Research on women leaders demonstrated that many preferred to work collaboratively rather than alone in a leadership position. Simultaneous with this research on women leaders, traditional leadership scholars began to suggest that leadership was a process, emphasizing mutuality between leaders and followers (although still seeing a distinction). These scholars also began to note the importance of team, shared, and relational approaches to understanding leadership.

Collaboration is conceptualized or defined broadly as people working together. Some definitions of collaboration are much narrower, focusing on shared purpose and definition of roles. In the leadership literature it tends to be used more broadly. In general, the work of leadership is building a culture that encourages teamwork and collaboration and then redesigning organizational structures and processes accordingly in support of this culture. Certain leadership skills such as being interactive, inclusive, and addressing issues of the common good are highlighted in the collaboration literature, and several survey instruments have been developed for measuring these shared leadership abilities (LaFasto and Larson, 2001; Segil, Goldsmith, and Belasco, 2003). Leadership is considered a community activity, and some allude to the role of leaders in creating communities of practice that learn and lead together (Wenger, 1998). A related leadership approach is partnering or networking (for example, Segil, Goldsmith, and Belasco's *Partnering: The New Face of Leadership* [2003]). In a more global and interconnected world where power is increasingly distributed and leaders work in teams, organizations and groups are partnering, creating alliances as well as more collaborative arrangements. For educational organizations it might mean pooling shared resources among institutions or working more closely with the community. Creating networks with others is seen as indispensable to leadership in the new context of reduced funding and greater competition.

The research provides guidance for how to develop effective teams and advice on how to develop collaborative leadership. Strategies include redesigning organizational structures to promote group work, changing reward structures to deemphasize individual merit, initiating new forms of accountability, and revising mission, vision, and strategic documents to support collaborative work (Allen and Cherrey, 2000; Pearce and Conger, 2003).

A major contribution of the concept of collaboration is moving conceptualizations of leadership from being leader centric to being process focused. Collaboration inherently involves many different individuals and begins to make the unit of analysis for leadership broader and perhaps more complex. In relation to complexity, research on learning such as Gardner's *Multiple Intelligences* (1993) suggests that any single individual will be limited in the skills and competencies that he or she can bring to a leadership process or situation and that the more individuals involved, the more likely a successful resolution can be developed. Therefore, collaboration may create a more effective approach to leadership.

Empowerment

With an emphasis on shared and team models of leadership, the notion of empowerment has become a critical area of focus in the leadership literature (Astin and Leland, 1991; Brown and Mazza, 1997; Rubin, 2002; Shakeshaft, 1999; Shapiro, 2003; Shaver, 2004). Empowerment refers to or is defined as the practice of sharing power and enabling organizational constituents to act on issues they feel are important and relevant. Because organizations have traditionally been structured to reinforce hierarchy, social control, and the concentration of power in positional leaders, empowerment or the sharing of power has not come easily (Shaver, 2004).

Two helpful illustrations of the importance of empowerment are found in the social change model of leadership (Higher Education Research Institute, 1996) and in the relational approach by Komives, Lucas, and McMahon (1998). In the social change model, leadership is defined as a group process, emphasizing empowerment and working synergistically toward a common goal. This model deemphasizes the central role of the leader and does not define the leader as someone in a position of authority. Interdependence is central, and power is energy, not control. The leader is a facilitator who enables others to act collectively toward a goal. Leadership is relational, and reciprocal relationships are used to help define mutual goals rather than leader-subordinate relationships, which emphasize differences between people. The chain of influence proceeds between people instead of passing through the hierarchy. This approach builds on the network and collaboration theme just described. By following the principles of the social change model, organizations can create empowering environments.

As noted earlier, Komives, Lucas, and McMahon (1998) describe five primary aspects in the relational approach to leadership. Similar to Astin and Leland (1991), empowerment is one of the most significant parts of their model. All the other concepts are also directly tied to supporting or creating empowerment. For example, framing leadership as inclusive of people and their diverse points of view is a way to build empowerment. A commitment to ethics can keep power and control structures in check (Shapiro, 2003).

The majority of the literature on empowerment provides techniques and models for breaking down hierarchical structures through the delegation of authority, creation of teams, and destruction of political cultures. The importance of developing a culture of trust is a prominent strategy highlighted in the literature; it is also a key strategy for creating learning. Other important variables that lead to empowerment are contextual. Environments that foster democratic practices and autonomy are directly linked to empowerment. Organizations that are led in ways that promote community and commitment experience increased learning and empowerment at the individual level. These elements directly contribute to organizational strength and progress.

Not all research on empowerment is focused on social justice, however. Empowerment has also been used as a tool to increase productivity, effectiveness, and group development (Conger and Kanungo, 1988). Business fads such as Total Quality Management emphasize empowering forms of leadership, moving decision making down to a more decentralized level, with the appearance of sharing power and authority. Most critiques, however, demonstrate that workers get more responsibility but without the added authority and power (Neumann and Pallas, 2005).

A major contribution of the research on empowerment is that it helps to distinguish leadership from authority and hierarchy, expanding the unit of analysis and the way that people conceptualize leadership.

Empowered Leaders Everywhere: The Democratic Distribution of Power

The Orpheus Chamber Orchestra, a world-renowned self-governing musical ensemble that rehearses, records, and performs without a conductor, is a prime and compelling example of empowerment-oriented leadership. Rather than endowing one individual, the conductor, with centralized artistic and organizational authority over the orchestra, Orpheus musicians share and rotate leadership roles, taking turns assuming responsibility for the creative development and execution of each musical work. The members of Orpheus understand that both musical performance and leadership are collaborative processes that require a shared vision of excellence, a common set of guiding values, and the active engagement of all organizational members, not just those individuals in possession of hierarchical leadership titles. Inspired by the common goal of making beautiful music, the musicians recognize the value of democratic leadership practices for cultivating a sense of responsibility and commitment among all orchestra members. Although artistic differences arise among orchestra members, the empowering nature of the ensemble's creative process provides a space for all members of the group to express their views and achieve consensus on appropriate strategies for seeking resolution. In addition to creating music that is celebrated around the world, the Orpheus Chamber Orchestra is also recognized for the important role it plays in advancing the principles and practices of empowering leadership.

Fortunately, the principles of empowerment and collaboration modeled by the Orpheus Chamber Orchestra can also be applied in higher education settings. Take, for example, the Fairmont College Staff Environmental Coalition (SEC). Started three years ago by two administrative assistants who shared a concern for the lack of environmental awareness displayed by faculty, staff, and students in the School of Arts and Sciences, this staff network now includes approximately thirty regular participants and was recently honored with the Fairmont "Leadership for Change" award as a result of their outstanding efforts to promote environmental activism on campus.

(Continued)

Empowered Leaders Everywhere (*Continued*)

Although the SEC founders, Jerome and Cassandra, did not originally intend to establish a formal coalition, they were optimistic that their individual efforts to increase recycling and reduce the amount of paper consumed in their respective offices could have a broader impact on the college. To raise awareness of their environmental efforts and recruit additional participants, Jerome and Cassandra decided to develop and circulate a biweekly e-mail update that provided recipients with information on campus recycling, tips for conserving natural resources in the office and at home, and a trivia question or information bulletin item that educated their colleagues on key environmental issues. After sending out an electronic update that featured a particularly compelling information item regarding the local landfill, Diana, an academic adviser in the School of Arts and Sciences, approached Jerome and Cassandra about the possibility of organizing a brown-bag seminar to discuss the issue. Excited at the prospect of expanding their informal environmental network, Jerome and Cassandra quickly agreed to collaborate with Diana. Although turnout for the seminar was slightly less than expected (a total of eight staff attended in addition to the three organizers), the conversation was lively, and several of the participants expressed interest in continuing the dialogue. Despite the fact that Jerome and Cassandra were the individuals responsible for organizing the initial environmental campaign, neither one was comfortable assuming a formal leadership role in the group, given their interest in cultivating an inclusive organization that represented the interests and goals of the new participants. Cassandra suggested the network adopt a collaborative leadership model in which members shared responsibility for creating and implementing the group's vision. Diana volunteered to coordinate the next coalition meeting, which would focus on establishing organizational goals as well developing a plan of action for the next semester.

Two weeks later, six Arts and Science staff members attended the environmental coalition meeting facilitated by Diana. The meeting started with a group discussion of their individual and collective goals. Next, Diana asked the staff members to share their ideas about the environmental awareness projects the group might tackle in the spring semester. At the end of the hour-long lunch meeting, the group had developed a list of priorities: (1) continue biweekly e-mail updates in the School of Arts and Sciences and seek to expand circulation by contacting colleagues in other academic departments, (2) submit an application for a small grant to fund three environmental awareness "lunch and learn" seminars each semester, and (3) seek out opportunities to collaborate with the undergraduate and graduate environmental student organizations at Fairmont. Based on their individual interests, skills, and institutional networks, staff members formed project teams for each action agenda item. To keep the coalition's momentum moving forward, the group decided to meet over lunch every two weeks, with responsibility for organizing and facilitating the meetings rotating every month to a different action team.

Although the SEC started as the brainchild of two Fairmont College staff members, the mission and vision of the coalition has expanded quite a bit to recognize the diverse interests and talents of new members. Rather than becoming a static organization with a narrow agenda for action, SEC members are encouraged to voice new ideas and concerns in the group. The collaborative leadership model that serves as the foundation for the coalition has fostered an ethic of empowerment in the organization that promotes mutual respect, trust, and innovative thinking.

Social Change and Social Movements

Historically, leadership has served the role of social control. From Plato to Machiavelli to modern military and business notions of leadership, the goal was to maintain the status quo (Gordon, 2000; Rost, 1991). Rost (1991) noted that social control has so long been associated with leadership that to think about leadership for change can be difficult. This is not to say that leaders have not created change in the recent past but that the goals were often quite conservative and focused on serving the interests of elites. As critical theorists and postmodernists questioned the motives of traditional leaders and assumptions of traditional leadership models, they also began to posit more appropriate goals or outcomes for leadership (Shakeshaft, 1999). For example, the emphasis in many of the newer theories and writings on leadership is social change. By social change, they refer to efforts that create greater equity and are focused on justice, care, and compassion.

For example, Astin and Leland (1991) conducted a study of leaders of the women's movement and discovered that the vision of these leaders was quite different; it was focused on social change. Heavier emphasis was placed on agenda development and outcomes than in other leadership models. In fact, many of the women in their study would not feel they had been a successful leader or part of a successful process if some form of social change had not occurred. Studies of leaders of color have also found social change to be a key theme (Garner, 2004). Over the last decade many other leadership models and books have emerged with an emphasis on social change (see also Gordon, 2000).

This literature also draws on the sociological research of social movements to understand leadership, an underrepresented perspective compared with the business, organizational psychology, and political science models that tend to dominate the field. In this perspective, leadership is seen as less commonplace and more episodic, requiring many conditions to be in place such as an agenda, common values, resource networks, communication, and the like. Social movement leadership is often considered outside institutional channels and viewed more as a process of grassroots action (Scully and Segal, 2002). Some social movement theorists question whether institutional channels can or should be used for leadership purposes. In addition, new social movement theories emphasize a blurring of the boundaries between individual and collective resistance (that is, contemporary social movements are frequently advanced through individual acts of resistance as opposed to mass mobilization). New social movement theorists also highlight the prominent role of marginalized social identities (the gay rights movement, for example), not class-based economic interests, as the impetus for collection action (Larana, Johnston, and Gusfield, 1994).

Drawing on new developments in the study of social movements and leadership for social change, Meyerson and Scully (1995) identified a new group of leaders they call "tempered radicals," who patiently and persistently advance an agenda of social change in their organizations or the society at large. As described by Meyerson and Scully, tempered radicals are "individuals who identify with and are committed to their organizations, and are also committed to a cause, community, or ideology that is fundamentally different from, and possibly at odds with the dominant culture of their organization" (p. 586).

Building on her original collaboration with Scully, Meyerson paints a compelling and complex portrait of tempered radicals as organizational leaders in *Tempered Radicals: How Everyday Leaders Inspire Change at Work* (2003). Meyerson draws on interviews with more than 230 individuals working in a variety of professional fields and corporate settings to construct a framework of leadership for social change that is characterized by moderate, incremental actions intended to challenge the status quo of oppressive and discriminatory organizational norms. Rather than relying on positional leaders possessing formal authority to lead the charge for change, Meyerson observed tempered radicals working at all levels of the organizational hierarchy to foster a more just, humane, and empowering organizational culture. By choosing among a range of strategies for fostering change that differs on dimensions of intent (such as exhibiting personal congruence versus bringing about broader organizational change) and scope of impact (such as influencing a small number of individuals versus swaying the opinions and attitudes of many organizational members), tempered radicals are able to construct a personalized and contextualized framework for change that matches their identities and goals.

Meyerson (2003) identified three conditions essential to fostering collective action and positive change. First, tempered radicals were able to identify and articulate the existence of an immediate political threat or opportunity that required collective action. Second, tempered radicals strategically used organizational structures and resources to foster collaboration (for example, lobbying the human resources department to officially sanction and support identity-based employee groups such as a Latino or Latina employee network). Third, tempered radicals were able to successfully frame the issue (for example, unhealthy company expectations concerning work-family balance) as a matter of shared concern that required collective action. As Meyerson (2003) notes, "Tempered Radicals reflect important aspects of leadership that are absent in the more traditional portraits. It is leadership that tends to be less visible, less coordinated, and less vested with formal authority; it is also more local, more diffuse, more opportunistic, and more humble than the activity attributed to the modern-day hero. This version of leadership depends not on charismatic flair, instant success, or inspirational visions, but on qualities such as patience, self-knowledge, humility, flexibility, idealism vigilance, and commitment" (p. 171).

Although the work of the leadership scholars cited in this section represents an important advance in our understanding of the inextricable connection between leadership and social change, much more research is needed to develop a comprehensive understanding of the individual experiences and organizational processes that foster and sustain social change leadership. Although limited empirical research exists, this new way of conceptualizing leadership has made many important contributions, including challenging leadership in its reinforcement of the status quo and making leadership more outcomes focused, unembedding leadership from elite interests, seeing everyday people as leaders, opening up leadership to be seen as a social movement and further emphasizing the collective nature of leadership, labeling resistance and actions outside institutional channels as leadership, and blurring the boundaries among individual and collective actions.

Emotions

In recent years, the importance of emotions in leadership has blossomed, with some suggesting that emotions have emerged as the heart of leadership. In referring to emotions, leadership scholars refer to the affective dimensions of human nature. This trend is related to critical theorists' questioning the value-free nature of leadership as well as the growth of symbolic and cultural theories that emphasize values (Caruso and Salovey, 2004; Kyle, 1998; Schein, 1985, 1992). Certainly emotions are not new to the study of leadership. Charisma, a term long associated with leadership, focuses on emotions, but scientific management theories had neglected this area (Burns, 1978). Emotions reemerged with the concept of transformational leadership; one of the four qualities of a transformational leader is charisma, which is considered an emotional result of interaction between leader and follower. Although earlier human relations theories (from the 1940s and 1950s) often referred to the role of leaders in understanding employees' needs and interests as well as highlighted the importance of working to create a self-actualizing work environment, these theories have fallen out of favor in recent years.

Daniel Goleman's work (1995, 1998) on emotional intelligence is one of the key works to synthesize this research and examine the implications for leadership (Caruso and Salovey, 2004). Earlier cognitive theories of leadership view leadership as a process of rational thinking, ignoring how emotions affect leaders and how leaders can use emotions to motivate, persuade, and create social change. In addition, the work on emotional intelligence suggests new skills for leaders. For example, learning to harness one's intuition in the decision-making process is a critical leadership skill. Goleman (1998) suggests that leaders need to first understand their own emotions, learning to assess, negotiate, and manage feelings effectively so that when they interact with others, they create the right environment.

Goleman (1998) notes that people with emotional awareness have several qualities: they know which emotions they are feeling and why; they realize the links between their feelings and what they think, do, and say; they recognize how their feelings affect their performance; and they have a guiding awareness of their values and goals. Leaders use reflection skills to listen to the quiet inner voice. Self-control is another important characteristic of leadership, as many people get angry and frustrated in stressful leadership situations. Instead, they need to manage their impulsive feelings, stay composed, be positive and unflappable even in trying moments, and think clearly and stay focused under pressure. But self-control is merely the first level; leaders also need to learn other emotional tendencies such as trustworthiness, conscientiousness, adaptability, and innovation. After the leader has worked on understanding her or his own feelings, she or he also must be able to understand others by being attentive to emotional cues and listening well, showing sensitivity and understanding for the perspectives of others, helping out based on other people's needs, and being attentive to stakeholders as well as inside and outside social and political cues. As one builds both internal and external emotional intelligence, one can exercise greater leadership capacity in terms of communication, motivation, negotiation, conflict management, and the building of effective teams. It is important to note that Goleman's book summarizes the work of other scientists and that he has not actually conducted these studies. His book provides a helpful summary and bibliography for examining the original studies.

The work relating emotions to leadership has helped expand the capacities and skills needed to be a successful leader. Like spirituality, it has helped create a more comprehensive view of the work of leaders and the necessary areas that should be the focus of a leadership process.

Globalization

Global economic restructuring (for example, the economic, cultural, and political dominance of multinational corporations, the blurring of nation-state boundaries, and the internationalization of trade) along with the proliferation of research on cross-cultural differences in interpersonal and organizational behavior has resulted in a focus on leadership in a globalized context. One of the main assumptions of a global economy is that a high degree of interdependence results in the necessity to share information, objectives, activities, resources, and power (Goldsmith, Greenberg, Robertson, and Hu-Chan, 2003). In what is termed a "shared power world," leadership involves high levels of negotiation, bargaining, and interplay among interest groups; conflict is seen as legitimate and expected; and interest groups and coalitions can change fluidly and quickly (Crosby, 1999). Because the shared power world is largely political, leaders need to use forums, arenas, and courts effectively. This area of research builds from contingency views of leadership in which leadership needs to be modified based on the context.

In addition to honing skills with power, several other leadership competencies have been identified as salient to the practice of leadership in global contexts. Based on conversations with more than two hundred future global leaders working at 120 international companies, Goldsmith, Greenberg, Robertson, and Hu-Chan (2003) posit that abilities related to thinking globally, appreciating cultural diversity, developing technological savvy, and building strategic alliances are essential for successful global leadership. Similarly, Mendenhall (2001) presents a list of global leadership competencies drawn from a review of exploratory research in the field of international management. These competencies include, among others, integrity, change agentry, management of uncertainty, negotiation skills, improvisation, and courage. The identification of global leadership competencies is a rapidly expanding area of leadership research focused on understanding the most effective forms of leadership in a global environment. One limitation in this line of research, however, is a rather narrow focus on global leadership in the context of multinational corporations.

To date, the majority of empirical research on global leadership is cross-cultural in nature, focused on comparing and contrasting the traits and behaviors of business leaders in diverse cultural and geographic contexts. A prime example of this strand of research is the Global Leadership and Organizational Effectiveness Research (GLOBE) program, a network of more than 150 social scientists in sixty-two countries working collaboratively to identify both universally endorsed leadership attributes (leadership traits identified as essential for effective leadership in multiple and diverse cultural contexts) and culturally contingent leadership traits that reflect a culture's interpersonal and organizational norms (House and others, 2004, described earlier). During the course of this ten-year collaboration, GLOBE researchers surveyed more than eighteen thousand middle managers in sixty-two countries, collecting data on nine cultural dimensions (assertiveness, gender differentiation, institutional emphasis on collectivism versus individualism, for example) and six leadership dimensions (charismatic or value based, team oriented, humane, for example). An analysis of the GLOBE leadership data by Den Hartog and others (1999) confirmed universally endorsed leadership characteristics. Although not an exhaustive list, the universally endorsed attributes associated with leadership include foresight, trustworthiness, and the abilities to encourage, motivate, build others' confidence, and communicate. The study also identified culturally contingent charismatic leadership attributes that were ascribed varying levels of effectiveness by participants from different countries (risk taking, ambition, sincerity, sensitivity, and compassion). Although the authors note that the apparent global appeal of charismatic or transformational leadership does not mean that these attributes are enacted or interpreted identically across cultural contexts, their research findings suggest the existence of global leadership practices that transcend geographic and cultural boundaries and may contribute to the increased effectiveness of individuals charged with leading in global contexts. Although the GLOBE research project examines leadership from a global perspective, the project's emphasis on identifying universal leadership behaviors and characteristics is clearly informed by the assumptions of traditional trait and behavior theories of leadership. Accordingly, we do not characterize this strand of research as particularly "revolutionary" but include it in our discussion of globalization and leadership to illustrate the continued prominence of traditional leadership theories in revolutionary contexts.

In an attempt to move beyond global leadership frameworks that merely seek to compare and contrast the behaviors and traits of leaders in different countries, Adler (2001b) calls for a theory of global leadership concerned with the interaction of people and ideas across cultural and geographic boundaries. She critiques the existing literature on globalization for focusing exclusively on male leaders. Adler's framework is grounded in research underscoring the feminization of global leadership—"the spread of traits and qualities generally associated with women to the process of leading organizations with worldwide influence" (p. 81). Examples of these globalized feminine leadership traits include empathy, caring, interpersonal sensitivity, a collective orientation, and the cultivation of cooperative relationships. Adler asserts that given their emergence as a prominent leadership group during a distinctive moment in history—the transition from domestic to global political leadership—global women leaders now find themselves "at the forefront of learning how to move beyond a domestic focus to communicate on the world stage to a global audience" (p. 96). As a result of this position, global women leaders provide excellent models for understanding leadership in the context of globalization.

Embedded in Adler's feminine framework of global leadership is an explicit recognition of the increased social responsibility that must be shouldered by individuals, both men and women, exercising leadership on a global stage. Adler (2001a) asserts, "Given their global influence, which by definition, transcends national borders, global leaders have a responsibility for the well-being of society that far exceeds that of their domestic counterparts of yesteryear. Since no government body can regulate companies that span the globe, the social-responsibility function must be internalized by the company and its leaders in ways that have never been needed or seen before" (p. 259).

The ethical dimension of global leadership articulated by Adler is echoed in Crosby's description (1999) of leadership for global citizenship. Grounded in a desire to cultivate the leadership skills necessary to mobilize citizens in response to pressing global concerns, Crosby outlines seven qualities of leadership for global citizenship: leadership must take into account the social, political, economic, and technological contexts; personal leadership, which is understanding the people involved, especially oneself; team leadership; organizational leadership, which is nurturing effective human communities; visionary leadership, which is creating meaning in forums; political leadership in the negotiation of various policy arenas; and ethical leadership in terms of sanctioning conduct and managing residual conflicts. In the frameworks of global leadership discussed above, the processes and practices of globalization are inextricably tied to issues of ethics and morality. As a result of recognizing these new ethical dilemmas, leaders are spending more time considering ethical frameworks as part of leadership (Rantz, 2002).

As this discussion of globalization and leadership has demonstrated, the bulk of empirical research on leadership in global contexts is characterized by the search for a definitive list of leadership competencies and traits essential for managing multinational corporations that span geographic and cultural boundaries. Although the work of Adler (2001a, 2001b) and Crosby (1999) calls attention to the important ethical and social justice implications embedded in global leadership, additional research situated in diverse leadership contexts and informed by the tenets of critical theory and postmodernism is needed to develop a more comprehensive understanding of global leadership. In terms of the contributions of this research, it has helped draw attention to the ways that interdependence, power sharing, cross-cultural skills, and ethics and social responsibility will be important to future leaders.

Cultivating Global Student Leaders: Multiple Perspectives on Leadership for a Changing World

This afternoon members of the Valley College Leadership Team (VCLT), a group of undergraduate peer educators committed to fostering student leadership and campus involvement, are meeting to discuss plans for the upcoming fifth annual Student Leadership Conference. VCLT members are responsible for designing and facilitating the conference opening session, an interactive two-hour program centered on introducing the conference theme and promoting dialogue among participants. This year's conference theme, Cultivating Global Leadership, was unanimously endorsed by the conference planning team; however, *(Continued)*

Cultivating Global Student Leaders (*Continued*)

the VCLT members are struggling to reach consensus on the format and content of the opening session. Scribbled on the dry erase board at the front of the meeting room are two key brainstorming questions: What is global leadership? Why should Valley College students care about global leadership? After nearly forty-five minutes of discussion, the peer education team has still not settled on a program format. At the heart of their debate is a disagreement over the meaning of global leadership. Half the peer educators are interested in focusing the program on a discussion of the leadership competencies essential for achieving professional success in today's global economy, while the other half is committed to fostering a conference dialogue on the importance of confronting global challenges with socially responsible leadership.

Ben, a senior peer educator interested in pursuing a career in international finance, has emerged as the most vocal advocate for a competency-based program. After spending the previous summer in Japan working as an intern for a multinational telecommunications corporation, Ben possesses firsthand knowledge of the cross-cultural leadership challenges (such as communication barriers and differences in interpersonal norms and organizational values) that Valley College students interested in climbing the global corporate ladder must address and overcome. Ben proposes that the program format include a prominent keynote speaker (perhaps his uncle, a vice president of international marketing for a pharmaceutical corporation), followed by a panel discussion with Valley College students who have recently returned from international internship experiences. The purpose of the speech and panel, explains Ben, is to provide conference participants with personal insight on the skills and strategies of effective global leadership. To facilitate dialogue among the conference participants, Ben suggests ending the introductory session with a small-group case study activity that highlights the challenges of cross-cultural leadership. Each small group will be presented with a global leadership dilemma (such as cross-cultural differences in work habits, or conflicting professional values) and challenged to collaborate on the development of potential strategies for overcoming these barriers.

Although Susan, a sophomore member of the leadership team, appreciates Ben's enthusiasm and understands the importance of cultivating global leadership competencies such as building strategic alliances and managing uncertainty, she is less enthusiastic about focusing the annual leadership conference on cultivating global leadership in the context of multinational corporations that emphasize profit over principles. Inspired by the global leadership efforts of Anita Roddick, founder of the Body Shop, an international hair and skin product retail chain committed to the pursuit of social justice and environmental change, Susan believes the peer education team should design and facilitate an opening conference session that introduces Valley College students to the values and strategies of socially responsible global leadership. Rather than selecting a keynote speaker who will frame global leadership as a matter of economic necessity and strategic dominance, Susan suggests inviting the director of an international human rights organization based in Valley City to speak at the opening session. In addition to drawing on her travels around the globe to offer insight on cross-cultural leadership differences, the director can illustrate the connection between leadership and the social responsibilities associated with citizenship in a global society. Susan also likes Ben's idea of a student panel discussion on global leadership but suggests that in addition to internship participants, the panel include Valley College students who are currently participating in international campaigns to provide support for victims of the South Asia tsunami and human rights atrocities in Sudan. Finally, Susan also proposes to conclude the program with a small-group activity but suggests that the global leadership issues raised in the case studies challenge conference participants to reflect on the ethical and moral dimensions of global leadership rather than merely fostering student dialogue on strategic and logistical matters.

Although Ben is initially hesitant to endorse Susan's program design, he is soon convinced to adopt a broader global leadership framework that encompasses a commitment to social values as well as the cultivation of specific leadership skills. Rather than summarily dismissing Ben's interests in global finance and international management as fuel for transnational corporate greed, Susan's proposed program underscores the relevance of global leadership for a diverse range of Valley College students as well as highlights numerous opportunities for cultivating global leadership on campus.

Entrepreneurialism

In response to the more constrained financial environment for organizations and increased competition (as a result of the decline of many American businesses in the late 1980s and early 1990s), recent leadership literature also

---

focuses on two concepts to address this situation: entrepreneurialism and accountability. The concept of entrepreneurialism suggests that leaders need to do more than maintain the status quo, which was often the way leadership was portrayed in managerial versions of leadership. Leadership is about creating opportunities for organizations and in some cases generating profits (Cornwall, 2003; Fisher and Koch, 2004). In addition, entrepreneurialism works in the new distributed and empowerment notions of leadership, as it is based on a more grassroots or bottom-up approach to leadership. Entrepreneurial leaders are best created at the local level where decisions and innovations happen (Eggert, 1998). Entrepreneurial leadership is focused on cultivating leaders throughout the organization as a means to enhance opportunities for innovation and growth. Hierarchy tends to limit available options, the possibility of innovations, and the number of perspectives brought to bear on a problem. In the more competitive environment where organizations find themselves, they need as many avenues for growth as possible. Entrepreneurialism is similar to team or shared leadership in many ways: it is supported by the same decentralized, grassroots approach yet focuses more on the role of individuals than groups.

Key works on entrepreneurial leadership identify ten key actions or roles as essential (Dess and others, 2003; Eggert, 1998; Harrison and Leitch, 1994). These leaders are individuals who make a significant difference, are creative and innovative, spot and exploit opportunities, find the resources and competencies required to translate opportunity into action, are good team builders and networkers, are determined in the face of adversity and competition, engage change and risk, have control of the organization, put stakeholders first, and create capital. Many of these qualities overlap with concepts already reviewed such as the importance of collaboration and partnering and the importance of change, but many of the qualities of an entrepreneurial leader are distinct from previous orientations in the literature, particularly the emphasis on creativity and innovation, risk taking, competition, and the exploitation of opportunities.

One of the main concepts emphasized in entrepreneurialism is creativity (Eggert, 1998). Because entrepreneurialism has been associated with starting new businesses and creating initiatives from the ground up, the notion of creating something is directly related to entrepreneurship. In this sense, entrepreneurial leaders are expected not only to facilitate other people's growth, encourage teams to work together, and move people toward a common purpose but also to create something wholly new. Entrepreneurial leaders provide recognition for those in the organization who are creative and help develop new products or innovations. In addition, innovation and risk taking are often cited in the literature. Strategy becomes critical in an entrepreneurial view of leadership. Leaders help organizations to recognize their niche and differentiate their activities from other organizations, creating greater success in the marketplace. Entrepreneurial leaders also focus on discovering the strength of individuals in their organizations and fostering those skills rather than a generic set of management or technical skills. People will be more creative and innovative and take more risks if they work in an area where they feel particularly adept or strong (Harrison and Leitch, 1994).

Entrepreneurialism entails a strong focus on accountability as well (Harrison and Leitch, 1994). Some scholars suggest that accountability systems in collaborative environments are difficult to define and uphold. They also worry about the time constraints associated with building and managing teams in the complex and changing world. Thus, they see the need to make many of the changes advocated in the postindustrial paradigm but emphasize slightly different solutions, building many individual leaders throughout the organization. In addition, entrepreneurial leaders are cited for taking responsibility for failed innovations and misdirection in their work teams. This approach moves away from the scapegoatism that characterized earlier forms of bureaucratic organizations.

Research demonstrates that individuals who are entrepreneurial leaders do indeed create more innovation and risk taking in their organizations (Entrialgo, Fernandez, and Vazquez, 2000). They are also likely to have an organization with a stronger niche and strategic set of objectives. In addition, the locus of planning is distributed throughout the organization, and individuals report a greater sense of creativity and autonomy (Entrialgo, Fernandez, and Vazquez, 2000). The major contribution of this line of research is a focus on creativity. It also reinforces breaking down hierarchy, risk taking, and learning—three dimensions of leadership underscored throughout this book.

Accountability

In recent years accountability has become popular as a way to ensure that institutions maintain the public trust (O'Day, 2002; Ulrich, Zenger, and Smallwood, 1999). As people have become disillusioned with political and business leaders and scandals are reported daily, leadership scholars have begun to wrestle with the importance of accountability for leadership. Additionally, the leadership literature focuses on creating change and demonstrating outcomes, creating a decidedly strong interest in accountability. Accountable leaders accept responsibility for their actions. Accountability is broader than just demonstrating results, however; it is a commitment to an ethical standard as well. The leadership literature now wrestles with a new set of questions: To whom are leaders or the leadership process accountable? What does accountability look like in a group or collaborative environment? For what are leaders accountable?

These types of questions help leaders to expand their view of accountability from merely meeting organizational goals to considering stakeholders and thinking about principles used in the leadership process. Leaders are asked to examine not just ends but means as well and whether the leadership process has been responsible to all parties involved. The result of this comprehensive view of accountability is that groups now spend more time up front carefully examining goals and ways to measure progress, ask for input on goals and plans, and develop ground rules to ensure people act in principled ways toward each other. Accountability is not just a summation of goals achieved by a leadership group—although this outcome is important—but also entails an examination of the process and reflection on ways to improve it. Accountability has a learning focus, emphasizing questions such as how to do better next time and not repeat mistakes. Connors, Smith, and Hickman (1994) underscore the individual and organizational benefits associated with adopting a learning and future-oriented model of accountability, asserting that "when you combine the notion of accountability with the objective of accomplishing better results, you create an empowering and guiding beacon for both personal and organizational activity" (pp. 171–172).

Despite the growing demand for leadership accountability, Wood and Winston (2005) report that "no statistically reliable or valid methods for empirically measuring leader accountability have appeared in the growing body of literature on this subject" (p. 84). In their article, the authors attempt to pave the way for future research by developing a more coherent and conceptually distinct definition of leadership accountability. Wood and Winston begin by presenting an extensive review of the multiple accountability metaphors and definitions that frame contemporary accountability scholarship (such as stewardship, obligation, or responsibility). In the accountability as stewardship metaphor, leaders place the well-being of their organizations above their need for control and the pursuit of self-interests. Rather than merely being accountable for the financial health and efficiency of their organizations, stewards "exercise accountability and activism in service to their followers" (Fairholm, 2001, p. 190). Wood and Winston point out the practical differences between the concepts of accountability and obligation, although they are often used interchangeably. Obligations are often established through the use of formal contracts to explicitly identify expected actions and outcomes, while accountability structures are typically characterized by voluntary acceptance of responsibility and transparency of actions. Wood and Winston (2005) note that "while accountability may involve authority structures in organizational life, it is possible to be obligated without being accountable, and vice-versa" (p. 86). Similarly, Wood and Winston address the subtle conceptual differences between leadership responsibility and accountability. Responsibility is ascribed to individuals who hold specific offices of trust in organizations and as a result can be called on to explain and assume liability for organizational actions. Accountability, on the other hand, is "an individually held sense of duty to provide answers, justifications, and reasons for behavior and communication" (p. 86).

In an attempt to synthesize the rapidly expanding body of leadership accountability literature, Wood and Winston (2005) identify and elaborate on three defining elements of leadership accountability: (1) acceptance, (2) disclosure, and (3) justification. First, accountability requires that leaders accept responsibility for serving in the best interests of the organization. Second, accountability entails an expectation on behalf of both leaders and their constituents that the leaders' actions and words will be publicly disclosed and subject to scrutiny. Third, accountability requires that leaders be prepared to explain and justify their decisions, beliefs, and actions if called on to do so by their constituents. The process of public accountability is especially important in situations where leadership choices and outcomes do not match the expectations of stakeholders or fall short of organizational goals. As Wood and Winston (2005) note, "The nature of accountability assumes the potential for failure. Credible and accountable leaders are not flawless. They distinguish themselves, however, by their ability to respond to poor choices in ways that restore credibility and organizational strength" (p. 90).

Despite the lack of conceptual clarity identified by Wood and Winston (2005), a number of scholars, particularly in the fields of cognitive and social psychology, have researched the implications of accountability on individual behavior and decision making. For example, after conducting an extensive review of research on accountability and decisions, Lerner and Tetlock (1999) assert, "Accountability is a logically complex construct that interacts with characteristics of decision makers and properties of the task environment to produce an array of effects—only some of which are beneficial" (p. 270). Accountability variables found to influence the decision-making process include whether the accountability audience was known or unknown (increased cognitive complexity was demonstrated with an unknown audience), legitimate versus illegitimate accountability structures (excessive stress and a decline in intrinsic motivation were common responses to perceptions of illegitimate accountability structures), and outcome versus process accountability (outcome accountability increased commitment to determined courses of action, while process accountability was associated with a more thorough evaluation of alternatives and a higher degree of correspondence between judgment accuracy and self-confidence). Rather than viewing and operationalizing accountability as a monolithic construct that inevitably improves leader and organizational effectiveness, Lerner and Tetlock's review of empirical accountability research highlights the need to develop and implement a more complex and contextualized framework of leadership accountability.

In the interest of examining the connection between accountability and organizational actions in matters of moral, social, and environmental significance, Petrick and Quinn (2001) demonstrate the strategic competitive value that accompanies establishing leaders' accountability for organizational integrity capacity, the ability of the organization to align "moral awareness, deliberation, character and conduct" (Petrick and Quinn, 2001, p. 332). To cultivate leaders' accountability for this dimension of ethical decision making, Petrick and Quinn suggest using business leadership education to increase leaders' and stakeholders' awareness of the strategic assets embedded in integrity capacity and identify the implementation of social and environmental auditing practices that necessitate public disclosure of the organization's ethical track record as a second means of fostering leaders' accountability.

Despite the rapid expansion of research on leadership and accountability, a number of questions remain. For example, Wood and Winston (2005) highlight the need for empirical research to validate the three subconstructs (acceptance, disclosure, and justification) that make up their accountability framework as well as raise questions about the implications of accountability on team performance, corporate profit, and employees' satisfaction. In addition to expanding our knowledge of the relationship between leaders' accountability and organizational performance, researchers must also examine the implications of accountability structures for external constituents, particularly those groups historically marginalized and disempowered when leaders prioritize profit over people. Finally, although Petrick and Quinn (2001) identify two possible strategies for promoting leaders' accountability, we have a great deal more to learn about the processes and practices linked to the successful cultivation of individual accountability. Is knowledge of the benefits associated with the concept of accountability enough to generate commitment to the practices of accountability?

The research focused on accountability has contributed to our understanding of leadership in several ways. First, it provides a tool for ensuring an ethical dimension or sense of integrity to the leadership process. It moves beyond earlier views of simply trusting a leader and provides more power for stakeholders and interest groups. Second, it provides more focus on interest groups and shareholders than past views of leadership. Third, it helps focus on transparency and justification of leaders' actions, which have not been a major focus in earlier theories, particularly power and influence theories, cultural theories, or behavioral theories. Last, it is reminiscent of servant leadership and notions of stewardship that have long been emphasized in the history of leadership.

Accountability for the Greater Good: The Value of Mutually Beneficial Alliances

Although quite familiar with traditional accountability frameworks that prioritize public disclosure of measurable outcomes (such as expenditures per student, time to degree, faculty productivity, and enrollment demographics), higher education leaders are beginning to reconceptualize the processes and objectives associated with accountability to achieve congruence between institutional actions and their emerging commitment to the principles of ethical decision making, organizational learning, empowerment, and socially responsible leadership. For example, rather than continuing to focus on the bottom line of objective organizational outcomes, the vice president of alumni relations at Sunbelt College has initiated a process-oriented accountability framework that seeks to engage her staff in the reflective practice of double-loop learning (learning that challenges deeply held assumptions and beliefs). In addition to documenting institutional progress toward the achievement of predetermined organizational goals (such as the diversity of alumni volunteers and undergraduate alumni memberships), the vice president also engages her staff in a second reflective loop that examines the ethical foundations of institutional actions as well as the continued relevance of the established goals themselves. Rather than merely focusing on whether or not the alumni relations office reached a predetermined numerical target for the number of African American and Asian alumni volunteers, the vice president's end-of-year report demonstrates a commitment to process-oriented accountability, highlighting both the organization's objective achievements as well as the department's ongoing efforts to better meet the needs and interests of the college's diverse alumni stakeholders. By creating accountability processes that focus staff efforts on cultivating mutually beneficial relationships with alumni as opposed to the pursuit of fixed numerical targets, the vice president is confident her department will not only achieve the desired goal of increased diversity but also, and more importantly, reach that objective through a means that advances the greater good by cultivating strong, collaborative relationships with Sunbelt alumni.

Summary

Leaders find themselves in a new and changed world, which requires novel ways to approach leadership. Although some things change, some things remain the same. The importance of leaders' reflecting on their interactions and behaviors and realizing the importance of ethics and morality is an age-old lesson that leadership researchers have come to embrace again. Spirituality has long helped to drive leaders and provide a foundation for understanding leadership. Emotions have also long been a part of leadership as one of the key ways to influence and connect with people. What is new is the emphasis on studying and providing empirical evidence of the importance of ethics and emotions for leaders. For example, we now have evidence to support that a leader with integrity actually creates better morale among staff and improves the effectiveness and efficiency of a workplace. Moreover, conceptualizing leadership as aligned with social movements also has a long history (even if this history has not been emphasized in recent years), as it does not support the prevailing dominant ideology of the profit-making sector and industrial military complex. Leadership has always been part of the great story of social evolution, helping to empower individuals and create social change, yet the emphasis on empowerment and social change in organizations and colleges and universities is a newer affiliation.

Although people disagree as to whether globalization is a wholly new concept, today's world does seem to represent some new challenges for leaders who may find themselves in situations where they interact with people from many different cultures and where power is distributed differently among countries. Leaders throughout history have been entrepreneurial, taken risks, and worked toward transformation. What is new is that leaders more generally are being called on to be entrepreneurial as well as accountable to a broader set of stakeholders. It is hoped that this chapter has demonstrated that current leadership research is actually embracing the history of the concept of leadership, being more rigorous by delving into earlier meanings and understandings. We believe that part of the revolution that has occurred in the last twenty years through the research of leadership scholars using social constructivism, critical theory, and postmodernism is a richer understanding of leadership that places more recent scientific management conceptualizations in a broader historical context. Old and new conceptualizations have merged into wholly new and evolving understandings of leadership.

Higher Education Leadership in the New World

THE PREVIOUS THREE CHAPTERS REVIEWED the revolution in leadership research; the following chapters examine whether higher education leadership research has experienced a similar revolution in theoretical and conceptual focus. Certainly each field and discipline represented in the leadership literature (psychology, management, political science, education, for example) emphasize different paradigms, concepts, and theories and as a result have embraced these new "revolutionary" leadership ideas with uneven enthusiasm. It may be that certain theories, concepts, and paradigms fit better in some disciplines and fields, or it may be that certain fields and disciplines are more open to the new ideas that have been used to shape and understand leadership. Yet gaps in application of these new theories in higher education may represent important areas for future research. This chapter also presents the major findings of leadership studies in higher education from the last fifteen years, synthesizing for practitioners the latest insights on improving leadership practice.[2]

Changes in the Landscape of Higher Education Leadership Research

The leadership literature in higher education has changed in a few meaningful ways in the last fifteen years. First, earlier research focused primarily on the college president, but in the last fifteen years, much of the research has focused on leaders throughout the institution—deans, department chairs, and directors. The notion of a more collective approach to the practice and study of leadership has clearly taken root in higher education. In addition, leadership studies have started to view people who do not hold positions of authority or power as being part of the leadership process. More advice is now available for leaders throughout the institution, providing deans, faculty, directors, and department chairs with data to guide their actions.

A second change is that the research paradigms applied to higher education have expanded. Almost all research until 1990 used a functional perspective of leadership (exceptions include Tierney, 1988; Chaffee and Tierney, 1988). More recent studies have embraced a social constructivist view of leadership, in particular research from a cultural and symbolic perspective and work in a cognitive framework. For example, the largest project on leadership—the institutional leadership project—used a social constructivist perspective (Birnbaum, 1992). Few studies have been conducted from a critical or postmodern perspective, which remains an important area of needed focus in the higher education leadership literature. In the limited body of work on critical leadership in higher education, the main area of research is studies that explore the experiences of women leaders and leaders of color, documenting how their approaches to leadership are not represented in earlier leadership research that focused almost exclusively on white male samples (because most earlier studies were of college presidents, who were almost exclusively white males). This research is described in greater detail below in the discussion of social and cultural theories of leadership. The one or two studies of higher education leadership conducted from a postmodern perspective are also highlighted in this chapter.

A third change evident in higher education leadership research conducted over the last fifteen years concerns the representation of successful leaders. Early descriptions of effective leaders projected heroic images of individuals who were distant from their followers, acquired resources, wielded power and influence, and acted in political ways. In more recent years, effective leaders are seen as individuals who work for the shared good of their organizations by collaborating with others and sharing power, balancing their orientation to people and tasks, and working to interpret and make meaning in the organization.

Much of the higher education leadership research is being conducted with regard to the newer theories described in the second chapter—power and influence, cognitive, cultural, learning, and teams—although studies continue to be conducted from the traditional trait, style, and behavioral approaches to leadership. New insights in these traditional perspectives are reviewed first before a more lengthy discussion of the new research areas. Rather than repeat information presented earlier on the emergence, definition, and major assumptions of each theory, we limit our discussion in this chapter to a synthesis of the key scholars, texts, and research findings that have advanced our knowledge of higher education leadership over the past fifteen years. Like the earlier discussion, disparities in the volume and depth of information presented for each theory reflect differences in the extent to which scholars have adopted a particular theory or approach (for example, relatively few higher education scholars have conducted research using chaos theory compared with the large number investigating leadership from a cognitive perspective). Again, a summary at the end of each section emphasizes key insights and research findings. To complement this chapter, the book's appendix includes a set of higher education case studies that illustrate the value of new leadership theories in addressing contemporary institutional dilemmas such as diversity, assessment, and leadership succession. Analytical questions at the end of each case provide an opportunity to translate these new leadership theories into practice.

Trait and Behavior Theories

In 1989, Bensimon, Neumann, and Birnbaum noted that studies of leaders tended to find certain traits associated with leadership: courage, confidence, strength, social distance, intelligence, to name a few. The authors note that the "prototypical effective president was self described as a 'strong, risk-taking, loner with a dream' who was less likely to form close collegial relationships than typical presidents, worked longer hours, made decisions easily, and confided less frequently in other presidents" (p. 36). More recent studies of college presidents and other leaders have found that the image of leadership no longer is salient. In the contemporary leadership research, the characteristics and traits associated with leaders (both self-reported traits as well as those expected by followers) now focus on a broader set of characteristics that include both male and female traits (see Table 1 for a review of the trait theory of leadership). For example, research has found that relational, caring, and collaborative traits are important to successful leaders (Astin and Leland, 1991). In addition, several different studies have examined the leadership styles of presidents, deans, and administrators, revealing the importance of balancing relational and task orientations and examining them in relation to leadership outcomes (McKee, 1991; Neumann and Neumann, 1999; Wen, 1999). These findings are distinctive from those reported in 1989 in which a task orientation was seen as more important (Bensimon, Neumann, and Birnbaum, 1989).

In terms of behavioral theories of leadership, early studies showed presidents focused on goals, vision, planning, and motivating people to action. Presidents perceived effectiveness as being related to directing others and focusing on getting things done (Birnbaum, 1989). Much has changed from these directive, task-oriented, and narrow views of successful leaders. As noted earlier, relational and interactive behaviors are seen as much more important for being an effective leader at all levels of higher education (Fagin, 1997; Martin and Samels, 2003; Montez, 2003; Wolverton, Gmelch, Wolverton, and Sarros, 1999). Birnbaum (1992) found that college presidents were seen as effective when they were perceived to be competent, legitimate, value driven, of complex mind, respectful listeners, and open to influence. The focus on listening, being value driven, and open to influence differs from earlier research.

In addition to the change in nature in the way behaviors are characterized, a plethora of studies have examined specific behavioral dimensions in leadership such as roles and responsibilities focused on competence around financial issues, fundraising, balancing academic and administrative roles, reconciling internal and external roles, strategic planning, and collaboration (Fagin, 1997; Martin and Samels, 2003; Montez, 2003; Wolverton, Gmelch, Wolverton, and Sarros, 1999). These studies are important because little of the earlier leadership research examined behavioral dimensions among particular groups of leaders such as deans, provosts, or student affairs officers. Research findings suggest that successful leadership in different roles requires distinctive approaches and skills. For example, one study identifies four behavioral orientations among department chairs: leader chairs, scholar chairs, faculty developer chairs, and manager chairs (Carroll and Gmelch, 1992). Insights on behavioral orientations have been helpful for leaders in conducting self-assessment and in building their skills, developing more multidimensional leadership roles.

An important contribution to the behavioral line of research is the work by Montez (2003) to develop an instrument for assessing five dimensions of leadership behaviors and competencies in higher education: (1) integral, which captures the practices and behaviors that are necessary to enhance the organizational relationships in the administration of shared governance such as inclusion, interdependence, and shared authority; (2) relational, which captures the practices and behaviors associated with leaders' relationships on a personal level with members of higher education institutions such as mentoring, inspiration, caring, and interpersonal skills; (3) credibility, which includes value-based behaviors such as accountability, clarity of values, and confidence; (4) competence, which defines the work ethic of leaders and includes hard work, distributed wisdom, and balance; and (5) direction or guidance, which exemplifies leaders' behaviors that direct the course of the institution, including such behaviors as visioning and challenging the status quo.

Montez's instrument (2003) builds on the literature in higher education leadership and is distinctive from other assessment tools developed in the business and nonprofit sectors. The instrument was tested among higher education leaders to see whether they perceived that they were the main skills and behaviors necessary to be a leader; it was shown to be an effective instrument that will continue to be developed. This area of research is important, given the lack of instruments and tools designed specifically to allow higher education leaders to examine their own behaviors. Additionally, the behaviors represented on the instrument demonstrate the shift that has taken place in behavioral research. Instead of focusing on traditionally male behaviors, the instrument includes behaviors that have more recently been associated with effective leadership such as being relational and fulfilling the role of integrator.

Key Insights

Leaders need to balance a relational and task orientation.

Leaders should work with people, recognize the shared governance environment, listen, and be open to influence.

Leaders must be clear about their values and act authentically.

Leaders must focus on direction setting and vision.

Leadership in different units and levels requires distinctive leadership approaches.

New leadership instruments provide a helpful tool for examining traits, behaviors, and characteristics that are associated with successful leadership in higher education.

Power and Influence Theories

Much has changed since 1989 when studies of power and influence focused on presidents and their directive forms of leadership represented through social power theory. As Bensimon, Neumann, and Birnbaum (1989) commented, "Concepts of social power appeared to be an important influence in shaping presidents' implicit theories of leadership in one study. When asked to explain what leadership meant to them, most of the presidents participating in an extensive study of institutional leadership provided definitions describing leadership as a one-way process, with the leader's function depicted as getting others to follow or accept their directives" (p. 37).

In recent years, the type of power and influence approaches used and seen as effective in higher education have shifted from directive to mutual and two-way power and influence processes. In addition, power and influence processes are studied among various individuals and groups on campus, not just the college president as they were before 1989. One notable exception to this trend, however, is Fisher and Koch's *Presidential Leadership: Making a Difference* (1996). Frustrated by a perceived lack of substantive and methodologically rigorous research on the college presidency, Fisher and Koch reviewed empirical studies of power, leadership, and management and developed a portrait of effective college presidents that draws heavily from social power theory. Grounding their assertions in the power typology developed by French and Raven (1959) (coercive, reward, legitimate, expert, and referent [charisma] power), Fisher and Koch assert, "A president who possesses legitimate power, judiciously punishes and rewards, demonstrates expertise, maintains appropriate distance, and develops charisma and public presence is especially likely to be a success" (p. 333). Articulating a belief in the ability of college and university presidents to effect transformational change on campus, Fisher and Koch dedicate the remainder of the book to a discussion of practical strategies for using presidential power to advance a leadership agenda.

Studying power and influence as a two-way process throughout the organization, Rosser, Johnsrud, and Heck (2000) examined the role of deans and directors in negotiating power as a result of their location between central and decentralized administration. The research in general showed a trend to understand and describe the way midlevel administrators acted as negotiators, coalition builders, and facilitators in a college environment characterized by conflict and power dynamics. Several books, including Rosenzweig (1998), have examined the increasingly political nature of colleges and universities and its effect on leadership. These works examine the rise of activist trustees and the increasing role played by external groups in campus decision making and leadership to understand the potentially decreasing role or potential of internal leadership on college campuses as external power forces and leadership emerge. In this environment, leaders are encouraged to develop their political skills and their abilities to negotiate, build alliances, manage conflict, and influence these new stakeholders. Studies of leaders demonstrate how stronger political skills have been shown to be more effective in terms of reaching goals and being seen as effective by groups on and off campus in these more political environments (LaRocque and Coleman, 1993; Seagren, 1993).

A variety of studies from social constructivist perspective have examined how power and influence processes are affected by contextual conditions such as leadership succession at the institution, institutional history, and life stage of the organization (Birnbaum, 1992; Levin, 1998). For example, if earlier leadership transition processes have gone smoothly, then new leaders are usually able to influence campus stakeholders with greater ease, while previous difficult leadership transitions result in the leader's having to prove himself more to campus stakeholders (Birnbaum, 1992). Campuses that are experiencing some level of crisis are more open to influence and leaders with risk-taking ideas, while stable campuses are usually less likely to be open to influence processes from leaders (Birnbaum, 1992; Levin, 1998).

In a study of presidential influence, leadership succession, and organizational change in community colleges, Levin (1998) found "in all cases, institutional context is equally or more important than the perception of presidential influence in contributing to organizational actions and outcomes. . . . Presidents who are perceived as the most influential are those who fit into the socially constructed story of the institution" (p. 420). In addition to insights on the relationship between institutional context and perceptions of leaders' influence, Levin's research documents the strong role organizational position and affiliation play in shaping perceptions of presidential leadership. "Because of their institutional position, administrators, faculty, support staff, and board members—all organizational members—have selective perceptions and indeed biased judgment of the chief executive officer" (Levin, 1998, p. 422).

Key Insights

Midlevel leaders end up as negotiators and are constrained more by power and conflict.

Leaders need to develop their political skills in environments where power is being centralized such as with activist trustees.

Understanding historical patterns of power and conflict is essential to becoming an effective leader.

Faculty, unions, and trustees all play a significant role in shaping the power dynamics that affect leadership processes and need to be given special attention.

Transformational Leadership

Mirroring the general leadership literature, transformational and transactional studies of leadership remain an important area of inquiry in higher education.[3] In 1989, Bensimon, Neumann, and Birnbaum asserted that transactional leadership may play a greater role than transformational leadership in higher education leadership. Given the ambiguity of goals and decentralized structure, transformational leadership may not be possible in the same ways it would be in another organizational structure. The authors believed that transactional theories focused on social exchange may be more characteristic of leadership on campuses, noting that "college and university presidents can accumulate and exert power by controlling access to information, controlling the budgetary process, allocating resources to preferred projects, and assessing major faculty and administrative appointments" (p. 39) but doing so in the context of shared governance and consultation and the image of the president as first among equals that is part of the normative values of academic organizations.

Studies have followed up on this assertion, examining the degrees to which leaders use transactional versus transformational approaches. Gmelch and Wolverton's study of leadership among deans (2002) suggests that the hierarchical structure, reward systems, and tenure and promotion processes favor a transactional approach to leadership. Their study supports the view, however, that deans use both transformational and transactional forms of leadership to be effective in their roles. Deans set direction and empower others, actions clearly embedded in transformational leadership constructs. Some of the transformational aspects of leadership such as direction setting can often take their toll, resulting in great stress for the deans participating in the study. Thus, some leaders may be inclined to use transactional leadership because it is less stressful and easier.

Gmelch and Wolverton (2002) also found that institutional type had a significant effect on deans' abilities to play the role of transformational leaders. For example, deans at research universities found it quite difficult to build community and to operate as a transformational leader compared with deans at comprehensive universities. Therefore, research findings demonstrate a more complicated picture in which pockets of transformational leadership may occur among certain positional leaders or change agents in particular institutions. As earlier authors posited, however, transactional leadership characterizes much of the leadership in higher education.

Bensimon (1993) examined differences in effect between the transformational and transactional leadership style of presidents. Like Gmelch and

Wolverton (2002), Bensimon found that a blend of the two approaches appeared to be most effective. Transformational leadership helped build satisfaction among staff and faculty and increased morale, while transactional leadership helped build the infrastructure of the organization and build capacity and resources. Other studies have examined the success of using transformational and transactional leadership in other positions (hall directors, deans, faculty) and found similar results about the importance of blending both approaches (Komives, 1991a).

Research also suggests, however, that leadership around certain issues may require more transformational forms of leadership. For example, Aguirre and Martinez (2002) examined the role of leaders in diversifying college campuses. They found that leaders that embrace a more transformational view of leadership—seeking to empower others, develop trust, create motivation, and work to transform the values and preferences of the organizational culture— were better able to provide leadership for diversity. Although studies have not been done around the area of technology or assessment, this same research finding may hold for other areas that entail fundamental change to colleges and universities. Tierney (1991) also argued for the importance of transformational leadership for moving higher education out of the status quo and for making many of the changes needed so that it can serve a more diverse student body, create greater access, and embrace assessment and technology. Research to date suggests that the earlier belief that transformational leadership was of limited importance to and had limited efficacy in higher education is not accurate and that a variety of leadership issues and contexts need and benefit from transformational leadership. Most research supports the idea that a combination of transactional and transformational leadership is needed in various leadership roles and institutional contexts and with different leadership issues.

Key Insights

Transactional and transformational leadership are both important, and leaders need to identify the appropriate approach for different situations.

Transformational leadership is particularly important for issues that challenge the status quo such as equity, diversity, technology, and assessment.

Complexity and Chaos Theory

Few researchers in higher education have examined leadership from the perspective of chaos theory. Because colleges and universities have long been noted as organizations with ambiguous goals and purpose, diffused power, and decentralized systems, perhaps some of the ideas from chaos theory did not seem as revolutionary as they did in the more bureaucratic institutions of the corporate and nonprofit sectors. Cohen and March's *Leadership and Ambiguity* (1974) has long been a classic in higher education, underscoring the need for leaders to work in a complex, nonlinear system where the direct results of leaders' actions are almost never readily apparent. As a leader, one is encouraged to support grassroots efforts, set up feedback loops for problems, and exert minimal direct control because such efforts are likely to be met with resistance or redirected in the system (Birnbaum, 1988). The notion of organized anarchy in their book foreshadows the application of chaos theory to organizations fifteen years later. Researchers in higher education have long recognized that higher education operates as a loosely coupled system, meaning that it is heavily decentralized and has few accountability systems and controls.

Marc Cutright (2001) builds off the earlier work done by authors such as Cohen and March (1974) (ambiguous leadership in higher education and the notion of the organized anarchy) and Weick (1976) (loose coupling), suggesting that we can reexamine earlier work on leadership through the lens of chaos or complexity theory. Throughout the 1980s and 1990s, many leadership advocates and researchers were concerned with the image that leaders have little direct control, that change from the top down is often met with resistance, and that leaders should get out of the way of the institution (Fisher and Koch, 2004; Fisher, Tack, and Wheeler, 1988; Kerr and Gade, 1986). Instead, Cutright (2001) and the other authors in this edited volume suggest that loose coupling and organized anarchy, characteristics of higher education institutions, should not be viewed as hindrances to directive leadership but embraced as elements of flexibility and adaptability that are particularly important in meeting external demands. The authors in this volume also emphasize that chaos is not random activity and that complex, replicated patterns underlie organizations, including colleges and universities. Yet in this book, the implications of chaos theory for leadership are examined only in conjunction with new models of strategic planning that are less linear in orientation. More research and conceptualization are needed in this area.

One book directly links higher education, chaos theory, and leadership—Allen and Cherrey's *Systemic Leadership: Enriching the Meaning of Our Work* (2000) and reinforces Cutright's call to embrace complexity. Each leadership task noted in their model is designed to make sense of a networked world consisting of increasingly interconnected organizations. The first skill Allen and Cherrey (2000) mention entails accepting new networks (across organizational boundaries) and understanding them differently (working with several groups simultaneously, for example). The second skill leaders need to practice systemic leadership is new ways of influencing change. Rather than mandating or creating change from the top down, leaders in networked organizations are limited in their ability to produce change and must approach organizational transformation differently. Change and communication in networks can originate at almost any level in organizations and are gradual processes. Leaders using this approach must be patient and respect their limited ability to influence change. A third skill associated with leading systemically that also relates to transformation is learning. Leaders must learn to think macroscopically, considering the entire system. New ways of learning also serve to challenge accepted organizational norms and assumptions and to assist leaders in identifying ways in which their organizations are interrelated.

The "pervasive leadership" framework introduced by Love and Estanek (2004) in *Rethinking Student Affairs Practice* is also heavily influenced by the principles and processes of chaos theory. Recognizing the need to reconceptualize professional practices and processes to successfully meet the challenges of working in an increasingly unpredictable, interdependent, and complex world, Love and Estanek advance a leadership framework that is built on trust, comfort with ambiguity, grassroots activism, learning, and authentic relationships. Rather than operating from the assumption that leadership is a function of formal authority or designated title, persuasive leaders are guided by a belief that everyone in the organization, regardless of his or her position in the administrative hierarchy, can and should engage in leadership. Accordingly, Love and Estanek define pervasive leadership as "individually generated relationships and actions among members throughout an organization focused on struggling together to influence and promote organizational learning and accomplish positive changes to benefit the common good" (p. 38). By emphasizing the dynamic, relational, and self-organizing dimensions of leadership in chaotic and complex organizations, Love and Estanek seek to empower student affairs organizations and professionals that demonstrate vision, innovation, and continuous learning. To aid in the translation of pervasive leadership principles to action, they discuss strategies for exhibiting pervasive leadership when addressing critical campus issues such as assessment, resource management, technology, and globalization.

Recognizing that contemporary higher education institutions and student affairs organizations are simultaneously influenced by the traditional and emerging views of leadership (administrative hierarchies still dominate college and university campuses despite the heightened value placed on collaborative networks), Love and Estanek encourage student affairs administrators to develop and implement a framework of leadership and professional practice that draws on the principles from both perspectives. According to Love and Estanek, to successfully carry out the challenge of fundamentally rethinking the nature of their work, student affairs administrators must learn to (1) value dualisms (described as exhibiting "both-and" thinking rather than an "either-or" cognitive model); (2) demonstrate paradigm transcendence (that is, accept the coexistence of multiple views and understand that the relevance of a particular paradigm is informed by context); (3) recognize connectedness as a defining feature of organizational life; and (4) embrace paradox, described by Love and Estanek as the ability to "hold contradictory or apparently contradictory assertions or beliefs in their minds" (p. 23).

Cooper and Ideta (1994) also examine the implications of complexity theory for higher education leadership. They conducted a qualitative study of women and minority higher education leaders, examining their perspective on how to enact leadership in a complex and multicultural world. Leaders in complex environments spend more time listening and gathering information from individuals who are on the margins before making decisions. In addition, these leaders clearly saw the value of different voices in their institutions. Some leaders collected these voices to effect a shift in power from the privileged to those groups struggling to gain a measure of control over their lives (Cooper and Ideta, 1994). Leaders made sense of a variety of voices instead of acting on the authority or voices of only a few. They also were committed to protecting groups in the organization that had been disempowered because of domination. For example, adjunct faculty, who have extremely high teaching loads, became a focus for these leaders, trying to find ways to balance the institutional demands on these groups. They also listened more to students, particularly student groups that have been ignored.

The research on cognitive frames discussed in the next section could be considered an attempt to examine complexity through the notion of cognitive complexity. One of the main concepts that Birnbaum (1992) explored in the institutional leadership project was the notion of cognitive complexity; he hypothesized that the more perspectives leaders brought to bear on an issue, the more likely the leaders were to develop an effective approach or solution. The institutional leadership project examined a variety of perspectives that leaders used to analyze a situation, but it did not explore whether a more thorough analysis culminated in a better solution. Over the years, higher education researchers have explored the notion of cognitive complexity in fairly great detail, trying to identify whether leaders take a cognitively complex approach. The notion of complexity could be studied from other angles as well, including the complexity of the problems and the complexity of the context or organizations, and whether a complex analysis results in a complex solution.

It is unclear why so few researchers have examined the implications of chaos and complexity theory for understanding leadership in higher education. We have suggested that some earlier research by Cohen and March (1974) on the role of ambiguity in leadership, nonlinear processes, irrationality, and the importance of interpretation to leaders' effectiveness may have made this line of research seem less revolutionary.

Key Insights

Colleges and universities have ambiguous goals and purposes and diffuse power, making notions of complexity and chaos critical.

Leaders are more successful if they develop networks (key individuals with expertise or resources) to guide the leadership process. Networks become increasingly important as organizations change.

Leadership processes are enhanced when they include ways to foster learning.

Leaders should embrace higher education institutions as loosely coupled systems that are inherently flexible and can be responsive to change.

Listening to people on the margins and gathering additional data are keys for making effective and ethical cognitively complex decisions.

Using multiple cognitive lenses is one way to address complexity.

Cognitive Theory: Cognitive Frames and Organizational Learning

In higher education, cognitive approaches to the study of leadership have been the most used in the past fifteen years—a marked change from 1989 when Bensimon, Neumann, and Birnbaum could cite only one or two studies that had been conducted using this theoretical approach. As a reminder, cognitive theories of leadership focus on the thought processes of individuals involved in leadership, seek to understand how individuals attribute actions and outcomes to leaders, and underscore the importance of perception and cognition in general to leadership. Given the large number of studies in this area, only a few general trends can be reviewed.

Leaders' Cognitive Frameworks

One of the largest studies of higher education leadership, the institutional leadership project (Birnbaum, 1992), was structured largely around the notion of cognitive frames. The institutional leadership project was a five-year study (1985–1990) funded by the Department of Education to examine leadership across various sectors of higher education, focusing in particular on presidential leadership. The study examined how presidents conceptualized their roles as leaders and the assumptions and beliefs they brought to this role, using four frameworks to capture their perspectives: bureaucratic, collegial, political, and symbolic. This research mirrors the work of Bolman and Deal's *Reframing Organizations* (2003). Leaders using the bureaucratic frame focused on the institution's structure and organization, paying particular attention to goals, priorities, the organizational chart, authority, and control. Leaders using a collegial frame focused on the achievement of goals through collective action, consensus, team building, loyalty, and commitment. Leaders using the political frame examined the internal and external environments and tried to mobilize coalitions, negotiate, engage conflict, and focus on scarce resources. And leaders using a symbolic frame focused on values, beliefs, and the history of the institution and employed symbols, rituals, stories, and myths.

Birnbaum (1992) found that leaders were considered more effective when they developed cognitive complexity and used all four frames simultaneously or used more than one frame to analyze a situation. Presidents can increase their cognitive complexity by broadly consulting multiple views, examining multiple sources of data, remaining open to evidence that disconfirms their own views, and actively seeking information about campus functioning. Yet most presidents tend to emphasize bureaucratic cognitive frames and use linear strategies. Bensimon (1989b) found that few presidents use a multiframe orientation and that community college presidents are likely to use a single frame. Newer presidents are also likely to use a single frame, while more experienced presidents tend to use multiple frames. Researchers have also examined presidents' implicit leadership theories (trait, behavior, power and influence, contingency, and symbolic) and how these views affect their leadership (Birnbaum, 1989). Most college presidents have a power and influence or behavioral view of leadership, meaning that they conceptualize the task with limited complexity and are not embracing the plethora of concepts necessary to be successful as a leader.

Cognitive framing affects the way leaders approach various tasks (Eddy, 2003). A study of change strategies of two different community college presidents, one exhibiting visionary framing (focusing on the future direction and potential of the campus) and the other using operational framing (challenges presented as a series of problems to solve), confirmed that the presidents' cognitive framing of organizational change influenced the selection of specific change goals and sources of power called on to facilitate the change process. The president with a visionary frame of change used strategic planning, symbolic meaning making, and collegial relationships to communicate long-range plans for change and foster campus commitment. In contrast, the president with an operational frame of change relied primarily on formal authority, organizational structures, and rules to articulate a plan for change centered on short-term, incremental goals.

Investigating the relevance of cognitive frame research to leadership outside the president's office, various studies have attempted to identify the cognitive orientations of staff subcultures in different institutional roles and divisions (student affairs and academic affairs, for example). The findings of this research suggest that areas such as student affairs and continuing education tend to have a preponderance of individuals from the human resources frame (Palestini, 1999). Kekale (2001) and Kezar (2001a) examined how the disciplinary background of academic leaders shaped their cognitive framework for leading, demonstrating that the hard sciences, social sciences, and humanities differ significantly. For example, individuals in the humanities are much more likely to describe leadership in terms of collaboration, while leaders in the sciences are more likely to take a bureaucratic approach. Distinctions also exist in specific disciplines; for example, historians tend to work in more individualistic ways and have a difficult time engaging in teamwork. A professor of sociology is likely to take a critical perspective of leadership, an anthropologist may assume a constructivist approach, and a business faculty member will likely adopt a functionalist perspective. Yet generalizations are hard to make, as differences exist among sociologists and business professors. Because most academic leaders emerge from a disciplinary perspective, these differences are extremely important for understanding the cognitive orientations of leaders and the leadership process in colleges and universities.

Followers' Cognitive Frameworks

Another trend in this line of research is examining the perception of followers, the interaction of leader and followers, and attributes of leadership. In examining people's perceptions of why they considered someone to be a leader, Birnbaum (1992) identified a relationship between the way individuals view the organization from a structural, collegial, political, or symbolic perspective and whom they label as leaders. Those in a structural frame tended to see people in the hierarchy of an institution or people who possessed power as leaders; almost half of those in the study were from a structural frame, although those who had a more political frame identified those who made things happen as leaders. Individuals who examined the world from a collegial frame tended to see leaders as those who were team players, encouraged others to participate, and had a more personal approach. And campus employees who viewed leadership from a symbolic frame identified leaders as individuals who had vision and reflected the values and purpose of the institution. Therefore, people's cognitive frames of reference affect whom they define as leaders, whom they see as effective, and how successful they think leadership is on a given campus. Birnbaum notes that "presidents are considered effective leaders to the extent that they are seen to exhibit leadership and do what others consider good presidents should do" (p. 18). He elaborates that because people tend to see leadership as part of the campus hierarchy, it gives these individuals visibility and power and allows them to do things that other individuals may not be able to do. It also means, however, that if our view of who is important and salient changes, then others can be empowered in the same way for action.

Neumann (1990) conducted a case study project of two campuses in financial crisis examining followers' and the leaders' (college presidents') perceptions and interaction. The study identified how the leaders' actions and perspectives affected followers' perceptions. The results show a contrast between one college president, who in times of financial strain focused on what she thought mattered most to faculty (good teaching) rather than placing fundraising and expenditures at the heart of her leadership, and a second college president, who focused more specifically on the financial hardship. She demonstrates that how people understand their resource condition, including the role of leadership in mediating their understanding, is more closely related to morale on campus than the objective financial situation. Therefore, leaders need to consider people's understandings and commitments, not just the "objective" problem at hand. Leaders can foster hope by attending to what people believe and feel and by focusing on the meaning of their collective work. The study demonstrates the importance of understanding followers' cognitive orientations and maps.

Another study examined presidents' views of their leadership compared with others on campus (Bensimon, 1990). A discrepancy was apparent when leaders used both a bureaucratic and collegial or bureaucratic and symbolic approach. When leaders used a combination of approaches to leadership, the community tended to see only the bureaucratic orientation, and the collegial and symbolic orientation became lost. Bensimon suggests that presidents should consider how they want to be perceived: if they want to be perceived as collegial or symbolic, than they have to rely much less on the bureaucratic orientation.

Another study examined the sense-making process of followers in a work team around the notion of participation, noting how the leader's communication affects the ways in which followers participate. Leaders who were poor in communicating the charge of the group, assigning tasks and priorities, and providing direction about process ended up with frustrated followers who could not find meaningful ways to participate (Erb, 1991). As the studies reviewed in this section demonstrate, over time interest has been greater in studying the understanding and frameworks of followers, not just leaders. These studies also suggest that the notion of effectiveness is socially constructed and related to similarity of perspective between leader and follower.

Learning

Although not a major area of research, studies have examined the importance of learning for improving leadership in higher education. For example, researchers have examined how presidents who identify and learn from their mistakes develop greater cognitive complexity (Birnbaum, 1986; Neumann, 1990). Leaders make mistakes, but those who have been more successful over time in their presidency and their career as college presidents are those who have strong recognition when they have made a mistake, reflect on the experience, and identify what can be learned from the situation (Birnbaum, 1986; Neumann, 1990). Kempner (2003) also studied the cognitive maps of various leaders. Rather than focusing on mistakes, however, he followed their development over time. Most presidents in Kempner's study moved from being hierarchical to inspirational leaders; his research findings illustrate the learning that needs to take place for leaders to transition their cognitive maps. Another approach to studying the cognitive frameworks of leaders is examining their development through a four-stage model (Amey, 1991). In the first or *imperial stage,* the individual's frame of reference is focused on personal goals and agenda. In the second stage, the *interpersonal stage,* leaders reflect on the interests of others and experience trust, commitment, and mutuality. In the third stage, the *institutional stage,* leaders develop a subjective frame of reference allowing for self-definition in terms of internal allies and standards, not merely connecting to others. And in the fourth, the *inter-individual stage,* values are a focus, and a global worldview becomes the organizing process. With this approach, the cognitive development of leaders can be tested; the culture of the organization can also be assessed on these dimensions and the leader and organization compared for developmental compatibility. A leader, for example, may be more cognitively developed and have reached the fourth stage, while the organizational culture may still be at the interpersonal stage. Unless the leader can bring the organization along in its development, this discrepancy may present barriers to creating effective leadership.

Two researchers are currently working on important scholarship related to leadership and learning (Komives and others, 2005; McDade, 2004). Komives has been conducting a study of how student leaders learn and develop over their lifetime. Her life narrative study involves interviewing student leaders in depth and at multiple points in times, revealing key findings about how leaders develop. Drawing on this data, Komives has constructed a college student leadership development model with six stages. The first stage, *awareness,* entails recognizing that leadership is happening around you and being an inactive follower. The second stage, *exploration/engagement,* focuses on intentional involvement, seeking change, and taking on responsibilities as a follower or member. For the third stage, *leader identified,* leadership is seen as a positional role held by self and others. The students begin to see groups as comprising leaders and followers and believe that leaders are responsible for group outcomes. In the fourth stage, *leadership differentiated,* the individual moves away from positional views of leadership and begins to see that leadership can come from anywhere in the group and is a process. In the fifth stage, *generativity,* individuals make an active commitment to their personal passion and accept responsibility for the development of others and team learning. And the sixth stage, *internalization/synthesis,* occurs when the individual continues self-development and lifelong learning, striving for congruence, internal confidence, and organizational complexity across contexts in relation to leadership. The model is heavily influenced by role models and mentors who help students to move through the stages, peer group influences, meaningful involvements that serve as a training ground for leadership identity, structured opportunities for reflection, and changes in the student's views of self and others. A key transition is between stages three and four when individuals' use of leadership transitions from positional (leader centric) to collective and collaborative. In addition, McDade (2004) has been interviewing college presidents for almost a decade, attempting to identify what has affected their learning and development as leaders (results of the study are forthcoming).

Although not designated as research on leadership, two projects have been examining the role of learning for creating change in higher education: the equity scorecard project and the campus diversity initiative (Bensimon, 2005; Smith and Parker, 2005). Given the close connection between leadership and change, this research might be the first to emerge examining the relationship between organizational learning and leadership in higher education. In the equity scorecard project, change agents throughout the organization are engaged in a team process of examining disaggregated data by race and ethnicity, reviewing students' performance, and looking for gaps in achievement and areas where they can create improvement (Bensimon, 2005). The change agents are studied to identify the extent to which they undergo alterations in their cognitive frameworks, the assumption being that individuals who undergo dramatic changes to their cognitive framework will be able to become leaders in the area of equity. Another assumption is that leadership is an individual, not an institutional, construct and that people emerge as leaders when they are faced with cognitive dissonance and feel the need to act to make changes. The research emerging in this study demonstrates that individuals engaged in a team directed toward a collective vision that challenges their mental models are likely to undergo personal change that often results in taking on a leadership role in the institution (Bensimon, 2005). Similarly, Smith and Parker (2005) engage leaders in a collective, shared process of examining data and developing plans to challenge existing mental models about how to diversify college campuses. Her research also demonstrates a relationship between organizational learning and the work of leadership.

At this point, almost all the literature on leadership through the framework of organizational learning is advocacy for leaders to use this approach to organizational functioning; very little empirical research exists (Dever, 1997; Lakomski, 2001; Phipps, 1993). Even though the overall concept of organizational learning is not prevalent in higher education, several component parts have been examined, including mental models, building shared vision, and teams. The notion of mental models prevalent in organizational learning is studied in the research on leaders' cognitive frameworks. Building on the research on cognitive frames, it will be helpful for researchers to examine leaders' and followers' cognitive frameworks in relationship to issues of organizational learning. Amey's study (1991) began to examine this issue, but virtually no studies have been undertaken since the early 1990s. Last, the notion of teams as important to organizational learning has received some attention in higher education (Bensimon and Neumann, 1993). We hope that researchers will begin to think about the implications of organizational learning for higher education leadership. The research on cognitive frames pursued by a variety of different leadership researchers in higher education remains a vital line of research in the future. New areas of research are ripe for study such as how leaders develop over time and the role of learning and the leadership process.

Key Insights

Few leaders use multiple cognitive frameworks to analyze decisions and develop solutions; multiple frameworks may be related to better decision making.

Internal reflection about how leaders frame issues is necessary because it affects organizational outcomes.

Various units on campus have particular cultures that attract people with certain frameworks, which can limit cognitive complexity.

Alignment between followers' and the leader's cognitive frames affects the perception of effectiveness. Leaders are better served if they understand the perspective and history of those they work with.

Leaders can shape people's frameworks by the way they shape meaning on issues.

Leaders who identify and learn from their mistakes develop greater cognitive complexity.

Leaders develop over time and in stages; these stages may be related to different leadership outcomes.

Leaders can use data to challenge cognitive frameworks and create cognitive dissonance and to move individuals and institutions beyond the status quo.

Cultural and Symbolic Theories

Leadership research over the last fifteen years has reinforced the importance of leaders in shaping culture, developing community, providing meaning, and reinforcing an institution's values orientation. Research has also demonstrated that leadership itself is a cultural construct that is context bound and affected by the values and beliefs of the college or university where it takes place.[4] In higher education, culture has been used as a framework to examine the context-based and processual nature of leadership. In the general leadership research, this approach is often characterized under contingency theory.

Culture and Leadership

A variety of researchers in higher education have examined cultural and symbolic theories in more recent years; this research has added to our knowledge about leadership as a cultural construct. Perhaps the most significant contribution to a cultural view of leadership is Birnbaum's *How Academic Leadership Works* (1992), which illustrates how leadership processes need to be aligned with campus culture, demonstrates the way that campus context affects the leadership process, and reviews the importance of leaders' being inspirational, using cultural strategies, and helping to manage ambiguity. In this book, Birnbaum posits that viewing leadership in colleges and universities from a cultural (and social constructivist) perspective is perhaps the most important lens for understanding the nature of leadership. The key question that cultural studies address is under what conditions leaders can make a difference. The emphasis is on understanding the culture or climate of an institution and then aligning the leadership to the values and beliefs that undergird and make up the culture. Birnbaum questions the dominant beliefs of earlier leadership theories that a single best way to lead exists, whether it be certain traits, behaviors, or power and influence strategies. He notes that in most organizations "there is neither an agreed-upon definition of leadership nor a viable measure of it" (p. 51). Instead, good or effective leadership looks different based on the culture of a particular institution (see also Neumann, 1991). Further, if leaders want to impact or change the culture of institutions, they must become familiar with the institution, carefully studying and understanding it.

Another major work on the relationship between culture and leadership is *The Four Cultures of the Academy* (Bergquist, 1992). Using data collected over two decades from more than three hundred colleges and universities and eight hundred faculty and administrators, Bergquist introduces a theoretical framework of four cultures that exist in institutions of higher education that affect leadership: collegial, managerial, developmental, and negotiating. This study serves leaders by demonstrating the influence of organizational culture on daily practices and change initiatives. The collegial culture is described as being consistently informal in nature, autonomous, and supportive of diversity. Power in this culture is shared, and decisions tend to be made democratically. The managerial culture is considered rigid and bureaucratic. As a result of this culture's origins in community colleges and Catholic colleges, strict standards are observed and specific roles of authority are designated. The developmental culture emphasizes teaching and learning and personal and organizational development. This culture is reflective and open to alternative approaches to learning and promotes collaborative decision making. The negotiating culture is one founded on individuality and values equity and egalitarianism above all. As a result this culture often fosters a highly political climate in which conflict is resolved through negotiation and compromise. Each organization may have more than one culture operating at a time and various subcultures throughout the organization. Understanding these models as well as the interplay between them is one approach Bergquist suggests leaders can use to be more effective.

In the institutional leadership project, Birnbaum (1992) examined the interactions of faculty and presidents, focusing on faculty views of presidential leadership to understand how faculty support affects views of effectiveness around certain areas such as presidential communication and actions early in their term. He noted that culture and history have a significant effect on whether leaders can have an influence on campus. A history of distrust, deep conflict, extreme decentralization, and other historical factors can limit a leader's ability to have an influence. Presidents need to develop the skills of inspiration and motivation, characteristic of interpretive leadership, to be successful in the long term. Several studies have emerged over the last decade that embrace the notion that we cannot understand leadership outside the cultural context of an institution.

The Effect of Leadership and Culture on Each Other

Some studies see culture and leadership as more fluid and dynamic, shaping each other and changing over time. One such study is by Anna Neumann (1995), who conducted a case study of how members of a college experienced a change in leadership. Over a period of two years, Neumann studied the entry of a new college president at one institution and examined the cultural and contextual interactions among faculty, administrators, and the new president. She paid special attention to understanding how the culture and organizational members were changed by the new leader as well as how they changed the new president. Because of the reciprocal emphasis of this study, leadership is considered a two-way relationship emphasizing cognition, experience, and the construction of social reality. A primary contribution of this study is its rejection of a singular institutional perspective, which is replaced by a number of different but simultaneous cultural experiences related to the introduction of the new president. In this analysis Neumann looked not only at the way a leader is perceived through the initial phases of the presidency but also at the socially constructed nature of leadership culture that in this case consisted of multiple realities that were complex and difficult to unravel.

Leaders as Cultural Workers

Another major work from a cultural perspective is Rhoads and Tierney's *Cultural Leadership in Higher Education* (1992). This work puts forth eight cultural principles for leaders in higher education based on several different research studies: (1) every college or university exists as a distinct organizational culture; (2) leadership in an academic culture requires putting people first; (3) leadership in an academic culture requires connecting people;

(4) introducing innovation and change involves changing values and beliefs; (5) building strong academic cultures requires enhancing diversity; (6) effective socialization involves linking new members to institutional change and commitment; (7) understanding organizations as cultures means viewing them beyond their physical boundaries; and (8) leadership and academic culture involve practicing effective cultural practices.

Rhoads and Tierney note that the first principle is the linchpin or the foundation on which all the other principles build, because once leaders realize organizations are cultures they will begin to focus on areas that are important in a cultural approach such as values, people, and socialization. Rhoads and Tierney (1992) posit that effective leadership of academic institutions demands that administrators understand their organizations as distinct cultures and recognize the importance of institutional history, traditions, and symbolic meaning and come to terms with institutional values and beliefs. Each principle reviewed focuses on the process of meaning making and relationship building. For example, in putting people first, the leader must understand the experiences of others, invest in people, be careful to make sure to send the right message, and encourage diverse backgrounds and opinions. Moreover, many of the principles relate to connecting people and developing relationships between various subcultures on campus such as academic and student affairs or in helping new members to understand the organization through socialization processes.

Empirical evidence suggests that higher education leaders have embraced the mantle of cultural leadership. Kempner's study of community college presidents (2003) found that they see themselves as cultural leaders whose work is to empower, energize, heal, inspire, reveal, and cultivate the organization and its participants. Presidents now tend to see their role as empowering rather than trying to control the organization; these retired leaders described their transition from hierarchical to inspirational leaders. The leaders' stories themselves show how, over time, people change their socially constructed views of leadership. One may wonder what views of leadership we may encounter next.

In addition, leaders play a role as cultural workers, helping faculty and staff manage the ambiguity of organizational life and providing meaning and a sense of purpose in the organization. Birnbaum (1992) notes, "A cultural view of leadership emphasizes the importance of leaders in developing and sustaining systems of belief that regenerate participants' commitment. Leaders accomplish this through the use of language, symbolism, and ritual that cause others to interpret organizational actions in ways consistent with the values of the leader" (p. 10).

Vision, Loyalty, and Values: Detailing Cultural Constructs

Building off Chaffee's work (1984) on interpretive strategy that acknowledges a more collective approach to direction setting such as including stakeholders' views, studies have examined the importance of a collective vision that emerges from a relational dynamic between the grassroots and hierarchical structures of the institution (Chermak, 1990). Yet some studies still focus on vision from a more conventional view—top down from the leader—examining the resistance these leaders experience (Kempner, 2003; Pearce, 1993). As described in "Transformational Leadership," visionary leadership from the top down may be necessary to create change when changes are counter to an institution's culture or when the institution is at great risk (Pearce, 1993, 1995; Zhang and Strange, 1992).

New lines of research have also emerged as a result of a cultural orientation to leadership such as the role of loyalty in leadership (Guido-DiBrito, 1995). A study of four campuses (Guido-DiBrito, 1995) found that loyalty was important to perceptions of effective leadership and that leaders and followers can improve their relationship by discussing and documenting expectations of loyalty. Although implicit to organizational expectations, loyalty increases when discussed openly. The author also discovered that organizational structures shape the ways in which loyalty is fostered. Less bureaucratic organizations that are horizontal in structure support the types of interactions that produce loyalty in organizations and their cultures. Open communication, including listening by leaders, also encourages loyalty and establishes a reciprocal sense of trust. Other elements that inspired loyalty were leaders' levels of power and the impact of the organizational mission and goals. Although not a major area of research, the role of values in the leadership process has been examined by a few scholars. Curry (1992) explained the role of leaders and their beliefs in facilitating or obstructing organizational transformation.

Because individuals enter change processes with their own agendas that reflect their values, efforts to change are inevitably affected by leaders' core visions and beliefs. Leaders who are aware of their values can ensure they are not too dogmatic on the one hand but clear enough on the other to help shape and frame values systems in the organization.

Gender and Race

Similar to the general literature on leadership, one of the main areas of inquiry in cultural theories of leadership during the last fifteen years has been examining the influence of gender and race on leadership. Some of the main findings include that women tend to be rated more highly on measures of transformational leadership (Daughtery and Finch, 1997), have less hierarchical and more collective views of leadership (Kezar, 2002c), are oriented toward care (Gillett-Karam, 2001), and are oriented toward empowerment (Duncan and Skarstad, 1995; Howard-Hamilton and Ferguson, 1998; Komives, 1994). Studies examining gender differences with respect to followers' preferences and perceptions demonstrate that both male and female followers tend to prefer to be supervised by men (Irby and Brown, 1995). Yet research findings differ from other studies, suggesting that the gender of the leader made no difference in satisfaction or effectiveness (Johnson, 1993; Komives, 1991b).

Few studies have examined the overlap of race, gender, and other aspects of identity. An exception is Kezar's ethnographic study of faculty and administrators (2000, 2002c), which examined leadership beliefs and contextual conditions that affect diverse perspectives. Results suggest that individuals' positionality (by gender, race, ethnicity, role in the institution, discipline, or field of study, among other characteristics) appears to be related to variations in the leaders' beliefs. For example, a woman in a vocational discipline might be interested in leading collaboratively based on her experience as a woman but, based on her vocational background, may approach the process in a more hierarchical way. People's experiences overlap and create distinctive approaches to leadership. This study also used an important new theory for examining leadership: positionality. Researchers using positionality theory assume that people have multiple overlapping identities; thus, people make meaning from various aspects of their identity (Longino, 1993). Therefore, in studying leadership it is important to conceptualize women and people of color (and faculty, staff, or students) as possessing multiple and fluid identities (multiple standpoints or positionalities) rather than possessing essentialist or singular identities (such as gender). The strong relationship between positionality and leadership beliefs suggests that educational institutions should acknowledge and accept multiple forms of leadership.

Kezar's research (2000, 2002c) also suggests the need for leaders to embrace a new approach to leadership called "pluralistic leadership," which entails three primary principles: (1) awareness of identity, positionality, and power conditions; (2) acknowledgement of multiple views of leadership; and (3) negotiation among the multiple views of leadership. Because some individuals lacked awareness of their biases and their own identity, they did not see that others might have valid perspectives based on having different experiences. Hierarchy and power conditions often isolate people and make these biases more extreme. In addition, awareness that each individual holds a particular leadership belief should lead to an acknowledgment and exploration of multiple perspectives of leadership, fostering communication and moving beyond groupthink. Faculty and staff can begin to compare, mediate, and perhaps even appreciate the different perspectives.

In addition to examining differences in style and approach to leadership, other studies have looked at the experiences of women leaders and leaders of color, focusing on issues that affect advancement (see Chliwniak, 1997, and Glazer-Raymo, 1999). Glazer-Raymo reviewed data collected by the American Council on Education that demonstrate that although the number of women executives in colleges and universities is increasing, they still remain significantly underrepresented—accounting for approximately 15 percent of chief academic officers and college presidents and approximately 25 percent of deans nationally. Bensimon and Neumann (1993) posit that women remain underrepresented because leaders form socially homogeneous management teams with people like themselves and are reluctant to appoint women. Women currently make up approximately 25 percent of private and 27 percent of public boards. They also receive unequal pay and a lower salary than male senior administrators. Glazer-Raymo's interviews with women presidents, vice presidents, and deans demonstrate the problems they encounter as they move into senior leadership positions such as having to act in feminine ways to make male counterparts comfortable, being held to different standards than men, enjoying limited support systems and networks, lacking mentors, encountering difficulty balancing personal and professional positions, and being discriminated against.

More recent studies have also examined the experience of leaders of color (Arminio and others, 2000). A phenomenological study demonstrates that students of color disdain the label "leader"; experience personal costs while holding leadership positions; have very different experiences being a leader in a group that is predominantly white, multiracial, or the same race; experience conflict between loyalty to their race and their individual needs; and need more staff and faculty role models to be successful as a leader.

Many important findings have emerged from research adopting the cultural perspective. The findings tend to be overly generic, and specific topics have not been pursued; the study on loyalty, for example, shows promise for providing more detailed data on specific cultural constructs. Continued use of this perspective is necessary, however, to fine-tune key areas of study. We may know what a leader who is a cultural worker needs to do, but we have few detailed studies that explain the challenges of putting people first in an environment of academic capitalism that rewards entrepreneurship. What happens if you understand the organizational culture and need to challenge certain areas that prevent effective leadership? What is the role of leaders at different levels of an organization to create effective socialization? These and many other cultural leadership questions need to be addressed in future research.

Key Insights

Leadership processes need to be aligned with campus culture, which affects the leadership process; archetypes of campus cultures (collegial, political, negotiating, managerial) help leaders negotiate and align the process.

Good or effective leadership differs based on the culture of a particular institution.

Leaders help to manage ambiguity and complexity by shaping meaning for others.

Inspirational leaders are more effective and enhance the morale of followers.

Although culture and history of the campus affect whether a leader can have influence, leaders' actions simultaneously affect how they are perceived and whether they can have influence.

Leaders can improve their chances of effectiveness by understanding the history, traditions, symbolic meaning, and values of the campus.

Leaders will be more successful if they are cultural workers: attentive to people, morale building, and working to socialize new members.

Vision is best fostered at the nexus between grassroots and top-down approaches.

Loyalty increases the chance of effective leadership and is fostered through less bureaucratic organizational structures and more openness among leaders.

Leaders in higher education from various racial, gender, and disciplinary backgrounds may have different approaches to leadership that should be acknowledged and encouraged.

Women and people of color in higher education continue to be hampered in their advancement to leadership.

Teams and Relational Leadership

Given the tradition of collegial governance and leadership in higher education, it is not surprising that the notion of teams has been used widely in recent years to understand the phenomenon of leadership. In addition, many writers point out that having a professional and well-trained faculty and staff makes the notion of leadership and followership seem unnecessary when each has valuable expertise to provide any leadership process. Recent books on leadership have given team building and collaboration a central role, for example, *Strengthening Departmental Leadership: A Team-Building Guide for Chairs in Colleges and Universities* (Lucas, 1994). Books such as Lucas's help leaders understand ways to develop a shared vision and community among faculty and provide supportive communication that helps manage conflict. Kouzes and Posner's *The Jossey-Bass Academic Administrator's Guide to Exemplary Leadership* (2003) is based on their research of collaborative forms of leadership over the last decade. They provide detailed examples of the key skills for team or collaborative leaders such as creating a shared vision, empowering others to act, and encouraging everyone in the organization to take a role in leadership. The majority of research in this area focuses on techniques and strategies for being an effective collaborative or team leader.

Another comprehensive book on team forms of leadership in higher education is Bensimon and Neumann's *Redesigning Collegiate Leadership* (1993). A key finding related to teams and their role in leadership is that teams lead to more cognitively complex decision making than individual leaders. But Bensimon and Neumann make the key distinction that decision making is improved only among teams that are "real" and not among teams that are "illusory." Real teams are characterized by open communication, trust, a willingness to challenge each other, a lack of hierarchy or power among people in the group, and limited politics. Teams also serve more than a cognitive decision-making function, serving an expressive function as well, making people feel better about their work environment and providing a sense of purpose in the institution. Although the research is focused on presidential cabinets, it is probable that teams throughout colleges and universities make better decisions than individual decision makers.

The research identifies key roles that help make up a real team such as a person who helps synthesize ideas, a person who operates as the emotional monitor checking in on how people on the team feel, or the critic who challenges the thinking of the team, helping them refrain from groupthink. In total, eight roles emerge as important for real teams: the definer, the analyst, the interpreter, the critic, the synthesizer, the disparity monitor, the task monitor, and the emotional monitor. The composition of a team also shapes its ability to become a real team as well as the cognitive complexity developed (Knudson, 1997). For example, a team that is missing a key area of expertise (such as finance or legal issues), that is missing racial diversity, or that has individuals from very similar cognitive frames of reference (all human relations, for example) will not be able to create the same depth of decision making. Therefore, presidents and other leaders who choose individuals for the team must be careful to think about functional expertise, cognitive frames of reference, and diversity. This research is critical in helping campuses to understand the characteristics of healthy and functional teams characterized by the metaphor of the real team as well as roles that individuals in the team need to play to make it more effective.

Some researchers have focused on team and collaborative forms of leadership and envision this practice as part of a democratic form of organizing. In *Building Communities of Difference: Higher Education in the Twenty-First Century,* Tierney (1993a) articulates the need for leaders to foster inclusiveness and ensure equal opportunity on higher education campuses through the initiation of shared decision-making mechanisms such as collaborative teams or reduced hierarchy. In sharp contrast to traditional forms of academic governance characterized by hierarchal and centralized decision making, Tierney draws on critical theory, postmodernism, and observations from five ethnographic case studies to frame a portrait of critical leadership that is primarily concerned with establishing decentralized organizational structures, teams, and decision-making processes that foster dialogue across different perspectives and functional roles. "From a postmodern perspective, decentralization enables distinctly different voices to arise, and from a critical perspective, decentralization enables oppositional voices to speak" (p. 99). Thus, for Tierney, the role of leaders and teams in higher education is to cultivate communities of difference characterized by multivocal dialogue and shared decision making.

Other research examines elements of the organization that help support collaborative and team forms of leadership. For example, team-oriented forms of leadership are enhanced by structural changes such as breaking down disciplinary and bureaucratic "silos," creating rewards for leading collaboratively, and developing new cross-unit structures (Kezar, 2001a, 2001b, 2002a, 2002b, 2002c, 2002d, 2003a, 2003b, 2005a, 2005b, forthcoming; Kezar and Eckel, 2002a, 2002b; Telford, 1995). In addition, the values and mission of the campus can be reoriented to support collaborative and team forms of work and leading (Kezar, 2005a, 2005b; Telford, 1995). Training and development can also help reorient people from leading in individualistic ways to thinking about leadership as a collective process (Schoenberg, 1992). Clear and open communication systems are particularly important to develop in team and collaborative forms of leadership. Many colleges and universities have hierarchical systems of governance and communication. These systems need to be reworked to foster team forms of leadership throughout the campus (Schoenberg, 1992; Telford, 1995).

Team leadership has been shown to have great potential to improve decision making and operations in colleges and universities if properly developed and sustained (Bensimon and Neumann, 1993). Colleges and universities have climates and cultures, however, that are often not conducive to a team approach. Research by Kezar (1998) demonstrates that creating a team environment may be extremely challenging. In a ten-year case study of a campus that was moving to a team-oriented form of leadership, the researcher demonstrated that many barriers emerged from politics and divisive subcultures and that the history of the campus can affect trust for years. Even as parts of the campus start to move toward a team-oriented form of leadership, groupthink is often likely to emerge. Because it is so difficult to move to a team-oriented form of leadership, criticism is often squelched to try to create the right atmosphere for collaboration. But in working to create a more harmonious environment, many campuses end up moving from real teams to illusory teams founded on groupthink. Neumann (1991) found that the various roles on leadership teams could lead to tension and conflict. For example, the task monitor and the emotional monitor may end up feeling conflict; the synthesizer and the critic might also be at odds with each other. The person who is in the definer role, who generally sets the direction for the group, can become a domineering person if the position is held by only one person in the group. It helps to have more than one definer on a team. Strong teams can isolate themselves from the overall organization and become what Neumann labeled a "cognitive clique." If team members spend extended amounts of time together and grow to appreciate each other, they may start attending to the needs of the administrative team over the needs of the particular administrative division they represent.

Key Insights

Several resources can help leaders to develop skills as team leaders such as creating shared visions or empowering others to act.

Leadership teams help make more cognitively complex decisions.

Real teams, characterized by open communication, trust, a willingness to challenge each other, lack of hierarchy or power among people in the group, and limited politics, need to be carefully developed and fostered.

Decentralization is a key aspect of redesigning organizations to collaborate, particularly to bring out marginalized voices and create communities of difference.

Organizations need to be redesigned to foster teams and collaborative forms of leadership by, for example, breaking down hierarchical and bureaucratic structures.

Breaking down traditional structures and moving to ones that enable collaboration is proving difficult.

Summary

Higher education research and practice have indeed experienced a revolution in the way that leadership is conceptualized. No longer is the college president considered the sole leader on campus or the campus hierarchy the place to look for change agents. Instead, both practitioners and researchers realize that leadership is a collective process that is found among many different individuals and groups on campus and usually involves the work of teams and collaboration. Leaders themselves are conceptualized quite differently. Task orientation is no longer seen as more important than developing relationships and being a strong communicator. Effective leadership is a combination of relational and task skills and involves both transformational and transactional qualities. Successful leaders need to develop cognitive complexity and become skilled in acting as a symbolic leader, become politically savvy, maintain attention to goals and objectives, and also build strong relationships on campus. In addition, they recognize that leadership takes place in a particular context that has a culture they need to learn and with which they must align their leadership practices. Leaders who foster learning can create change.

Although our understanding of leadership now embraces an understanding of the way culture affects leadership, the importance of leaders' developing cognitive complexity, the impact of leaders' and followers' mental models on the leadership process, and the effect of leaders' backgrounds and experience on their views and behavior as leaders, many areas in higher education leadership remain unstudied. For example, we need more empirical studies about how leaders can help campus constituents in learning and developing. And although we have research on best practices for team leadership and research on the barriers in creating a team leadership environment, we need more research on how campuses have moved to a team leadership environment and the way they overcame those barriers. (These areas are elaborated on in the final chapter on future directions for research.)

Three case studies are provided in the appendix to make the concepts in this chapter more understandable. These case studies describe a leadership situation and an analysis of the key concepts from organizational learning, chaos theory, and cultural theories of leadership. In addition, an extended scenario related to the case study has a set of questions for the reader to help with his or her own analysis.

Revolutionary Leadership Concepts in Higher Education

MOST OF THE THEORIES that have emerged in the general leadership literature have been applied to the context of higher education with the exception of chaos theory. Few of the new concepts have been examined, however, and they reflect important areas for future research. This chapter reviews the higher education literature that has examined ethics, collaboration, empowerment, social change, globalization, entrepreneurialism, and accountability. Collaboration and empowerment have received the most attention. The following sections describe the character of these concepts in higher education, main themes when they exist, empirical research, and potential areas of future research.

Ethics and Spirituality

Although ethics and spirituality have been subject to great attention in the general leadership literature, they have received less attention in higher education, particularly in empirical research. The majority of the existing literature has been written by college presidents and examines the moral role of higher education institutions; this literature tends to be prescriptive and not empirically based (Hesburgh, 1994; Olscamp, 2003; Vaughan, 1992; see also a journaling project for college presidents from the Institute of College Values, http://www.collegevalues.org/institute.cfm). Many writers suggest that academic work life is laden with values and has a moral dimension that is often ignored in the higher education literature. Current leadership challenges around diversity, community engagement, globalization, and others reflect issues that have ethical dimensions and require leaders to have experience with ethical decision making. These writers also emphasize the importance of ethics and moral leadership because of the role higher education plays in society, its responsibility to the public good, and its status as tax exempt and with a lay board of governors responsible to a host of stakeholders (Olscamp, 2003; Weingartner, 1999). They make the case that historically leadership was invested with a particular moral responsibility that has waned over the years. These books emphasize higher education institutions' obligations to society and inherent ethical responsibility to ensure quality teaching and to act in ways that reflect integrity to their mission, public charter, and stakeholders' concerns.

In addition to the calls for moral leadership among college presidents, other literature suggests particular approaches to establishing an ethical environment. For example, Wilcox and Ebbs (1992) suggest a model of ethical decision making to help inform the practices of successful leadership in higher education institutions and to provide a strong ethical base. They recommend that college and university leaders develop an ethos of ethics on their campuses. Typically, an ethical tone is not set by top leadership; the authors believe this missing tone affects leadership throughout the campus, which is missing an ethical dimension. Ethics are so important that they cannot be left up to individuals but must be integrated into the fabric of the institution—its structures, culture, and value system.

In terms of empirical research, studies of trait theories of leadership conducted in the 1960s and 1970s found that integrity was perceived to be one of the most important characteristics of leaders among followers and among the perceptions of leaders themselves. More recently, Birnbaum (1992) found that presidents who emphasize strong values are considered more effective. As Birnbaum notes, "Effective presidents act with a moral foundation that permits them to retain their equilibrium even as they are being buffeted by events" (p. 183). Principled and consistent action is important in the midst of uncertainty and ambiguity. If leaders compromise values, it often causes faculty and staff to question their decision-making ability and reduces their capacity to influence. Campus support for presidents was highest when they appeared to make decisions out of a commitment to transcendent values such as furthering the growth and development of individual learners or creating knowledge. Research has also examined specific strategies leaders can use to enhance the ethical environment. Establishing a code of ethics, conducting an ethics audit to attempt to determine what students, faculty, and staff members value, including ethical questions as part of the hiring process, including ethics as part of the curriculum, and starting a service-learning program have all been identified as ways to move toward a culture of ethical leadership (Vaughan, 1992). Almost no research has examined ethical decision making among college leaders, and research is limited on ethical development among student leaders (Vaughan, 1992).

Other leadership research on ethics and spirituality tends to be descriptive. As noted earlier, research on leaders of color and woman such as Garner's *Contesting the Terrain of the Ivory Tower* (2004) explore the spiritual dimensions of leadership among women presidents, demonstrating how their spiritual background helped them develop a form of leadership strongly based on care, service, and humility. A few historical pieces examine moral leadership among college presidents such as Nelson's *Leaders in the Crucible* (2000), which examines college presidents such as James Angell, Theodore Hesburgh, Nicolas Butler, and Edward Mobley and describes the key aspects of their presidencies from a moral or ethical perspective. These presidents faced challenges to academic freedom and institutional autonomy, cared about shaping students' character, maintained and sustained the institutional mission, and worked to expand the public service mission of their institutions. The descriptive research provides models for leaders seeking ways to understand how to be an ethical or moral leader.

But in general, ethics and spirituality have not been pursued in empirical research in more recent years (although it was emphasized in earlier trait theories of research). One recent study, *Spirituality in Higher Education* (Higher Education Research Institute, 2005), shows promise of expanding our understanding of spirituality in higher education. Although not focused specifically on leadership, the results of this study may help us to better understand how spirituality is understood in this setting and may have insight into student leadership. It may be that the culture of universities has affected its openness to issues of spirituality and ethics. Much of the research in higher education focuses on research universities, where the scientific ethic or value system is extremely strong. Studies of leadership in liberal arts colleges, for example, might help to develop an understanding of the ethical components of leadership that might be more prevalent in these institutional contexts. In summary, models of ethical leadership can help guide practitioners, but they remain mostly untested in empirical research.

Empowerment

Empowerment has been a major focus in studies of higher education. The new orientation toward empowerment is most strongly represented in the literature on women leaders and leaders of color. For example, studies of women presidents, provosts, department chairs, and deans have found that they are less likely to rely on bureaucratic and hierarchical forms of leading and that they work in more collegial ways and distribute power to others they work with (Duncan and Skarstad, 1995; Howard-Hamilton and Ferguson, 1998; Kezar, 2000, 2002b; Komives, 1994).

Empowerment has been studied across a host of academic leadership studies. For example, Birnbaum (1992) found that presidents who are not responsive to the agenda of others and who do not encourage leadership by others are seen as less effective and have less influence on their own campuses. He also found that sharing leadership and power entails more than increasing presidential influence: "When leadership is shared, a college has multiple ways of sensing environmental change, checking for problems, and monitoring campus performance. Shared leadership is likely to provide a college with a more complex way of thinking" (p. 187). Leaders create empowerment by encouraging and rewarding participation, collecting and disseminating data of interest to constituents, providing forums for constituents to talk together, and promoting a campus climate of openness. Through these processes, presidents are able to identify informal leaders whom they can empower to be part of the shared leadership. The growth of research on shared approaches to leadership provides evidence for the importance of empowerment in successful leadership processes.

Another way that empowerment is reflected in the higher education literature is in the growth of research on deans, directors, and chairs as campus leaders (Gmelch and Burns, 1993; Martin, 1993; Montgomery, 1990; Stark, Briggs, and Rowland-Poplawski, 2002). Almost all research in the 1970s and 1980s on leadership in colleges and universities focused exclusively on college presidents and occasionally on provosts or boards of trustees. In addition, the studies focused almost exclusively on transformational change or strategic planning processes that affected the overall institution. Recent studies of leadership are much more likely to include leadership of the curriculum or the creation of an innovative program in a particular division (Aspland, Macpherson, Brooker, and Elliott, 1998; Outcalt and others, 2001; Stark, Briggs, and Rowland-Poplawski, 2002). Our views of who is empowered to be leaders and the role of leaders in empowering others to be a part of the leadership process have been extended in recent years. In addition, decentralized forms of decision making, budgeting, and authority such as revenue-centered management are being used on many different campuses. Some studies have examined the growth of these new approaches to leadership and governance, finding that faculty and staff prefer these participative and empowering forms of leadership (Brown-Wright, 1996).

As assumptions and beliefs about leadership change, research also needs to focus on what might be barriers to empowerment and shared forms of leadership. One area of concern related to empowerment is research on power conditions and how they affect the leadership process. Kezar (2002b) found that individuals' beliefs about leadership are affected by oppression they have experienced and that many individuals will not feel empowered or will have difficulty embracing an empowering environment if they have experienced environments that limit their power and influence in the past. In addition to barriers to empowerment, details about successful models of empowerment still need to be developed.

Social Change

Research and dialogue on leadership in higher education from the perspective of social movement and social change have primarily centered on undergraduate leadership education. An ensemble of leadership educators from across the country developed the social change model of leadership development (Higher

Education Research Institute, 1996), which is organized around seven core values beginning with the letter C (the model is often referred to as "the seven C's"). The values are organized into a three-level model that includes individual values (consciousness of self, congruence, commitment), group process values (collaboration, common purpose, controversy with civility), and community/societal values (citizenship and change). According to the authors, "Change is the value 'hub' [that] gives meaning and purpose to the 7 C's. Change, in other words, is the ultimate goal of the creative process of leadership—to make a better world and a better society for self and others" (p. 21). The model is visually represented as three circles with interacting arrows as a means of underscoring that the pursuit of positive social change requires working interactively at the individual, group, and community or society level. The social change model of leadership development and the seven C's of social change have played a prominent role in shaping the curricula and formats of undergraduate leadership education initiatives in colleges and universities throughout the country. For example, Outcalt, Faris, and McMahon's *Developing Non-Hierarchical Leadership on Campus* (2001) spotlights a number of model programs and best practices grounded in the social change theory of leadership.

Work is limited outside student leadership educators; one notable exception is the W. K. Kellogg Foundation monograph *Leadership Reconsidered: Engaging Higher Education in Social Change* (Astin and Astin, 2000). This book surveys the higher education leadership environment with a specific focus on more fully engaging colleges and universities in service to society and the processes of social change. To advance their vision of higher education leadership for social change, the authors articulate definitions of both leader and leadership that are explicitly grounded in the work of social change and encompass the roles and responsibilities of all campus constituencies. With respect to the social justice objectives of leadership, the authors are equally unequivocal, asserting "the value ends of leadership should be to enhance equity, social justice, and the quality of life; to expand access and opportunity; to encourage respect for difference and diversity; to strengthen democracy, civic life, and civic responsibility; to promote cultural enrichment, creative expression, intellectual honesty, the advancement of knowledge, and personal freedom coupled with social responsibility" (p. 11).

Leadership is a process, not a position, requiring individual commitment, empowerment, and collective action. Accordingly, Astin and Astin (2000) identify five individual and five group leadership characteristics essential for the process of social change. The individual qualities are self-knowledge, authenticity/integrity, commitment, empathy/understanding of others, and competence. The five group characteristics are collaboration, shared purpose, disagreement with respect, division of labor, and a learning environment. After offering a brief introduction to each of the leadership qualities and underscoring the interactive nature of individual and group attributes—"each of the ten qualities reinforces every other quality" (p. 13)—the remainder of the book outlines strategies for integrating social change leadership campuswide. Despite the best efforts of the authors to establish a foundation on which to build continued dialogue, administrative practice, and research focused on advancing a social change agenda for higher education, few higher education scholars and administrators outside the ranks of undergraduate leadership educators have systematically pursued the development and assessment of higher education leadership practices grounded in social change. Three notable exceptions are described below.

The work by Astin and Leland (1991) is among the few empirical studies in higher education to focus on leadership through the perspective of social change. Their study examined the women's movement (a social movement) and the way leaders conceptualize their role. The model of leadership that developed was quite different from traditional models of leadership in that it emphasized creating change as the primary objective of the leader. A similar focus on leadership for social justice is described in Garner (2004), as social change is fundamental to the African American leaders interviewed. Birnbaum (1992) examined the issue of campus renewal, defined as ways the college enriches individual lives, promotes the search for knowledge, and assists the human quest to achieve a civil and just social community. Campus renewal becomes a way that leadership serves society and moves beyond individual agendas and influence. Renewing a college requires reaffirming values, replenishing energy and commitment, and helping people find satisfaction in their collective enterprise. The concept of campus renewal has some parallels with the concept of social change. Campuses that move toward renewal have presidents who are not overly conscious of status, actively listen to and seek the opinion of others, and allow themselves to be influenced by many campus constituents, creating more of a social movement than a top-down approach to leadership. Campuses oriented toward renewal have strong shared governance processes with expectations of mutual influence between faculty and administration. Hart (2003) has an emerging research agenda that examines the role of faculty in grassroots organizations, especially focusing on feminist organizations in two universities.

An informative and growing body of literature focuses on student leaders as agents of social change; however, limited empirical research has been conducted in this area. Noticeably absent are research and dialogue on leadership for social change in the other four campus constituencies identified in *Leadership Reconsidered* (Astin and Astin, 2000): faculty, student affairs professionals, students, and presidents. Future research initiatives informed by social change and social movement theories of leadership will need to examine the individual practices and organizational structures that facilitate as well as hinder higher education engagement in leadership for social change.

Collaboration and Partnering

The notion of collaboration and partnering has also received a great deal of attention in higher education; three major themes have emerged—new players, new models, and facilitators or barriers. In terms of new players, one of the important directions for research related to collaboration and partnering has been improving faculty leadership. For many years, studies of leadership focused exclusively on administrators, particularly college presidents. A key partner that has been identified as part of shared leadership is the faculty; creating mechanisms to collaborate with faculty in leadership is another important part. Birnbaum (1992) suggests that providing appropriate recognition for faculty who are involved in the campus senate is a key strategy in building collaboration. In addition, presidents can consult more regularly with the senate, making it an integral part of institutional policy development. Doing so often improves the composition of the faculty senate, bringing in individuals who now see that the president values collaboration with faculty on leadership and decision making. In addition, better communication networks need to be developed to facilitate a collaborative approach to leadership. Providing opportunities for senate leaders to attend presidential cabinet meetings or to meet formally or informally with influential people on campus helps open up communication channels.

Another major trend in the literature of new players has been research on the efficacy of various units or individuals in units working together to lead institutions. Most research has been conducted in the area of student and academic affairs collaboration, demonstrating that these partnerships help meet important institutional goals, improve morale, and create greater institutional effectiveness (Kezar, Hirsch, and Burack, 2002; also see *Powerful Partnerships* by the American Association of Higher Education, American College Personnel Association, and National Association of Student Personnel Administrators, 1998). Ferren and Stanton's *Leadership Through Collaboration* (2004) reviews research that examines how chief academic officers can be more successful in leading colleges and universities if they work with others—institutional researchers, business officers, student affairs staff, technology staff, and faculty—to meet academic goals.

Models of collaboration are also debated in the literature. Some authors have examined the dilemma of creating a functional type of collaboration on campus and charting a middle ground between authoritarianism, the old paradigm of leadership, and collectivism or managing by committee, the model of collegiality known to most campuses (Palmer, 1998a). Palmer notes that "academic leaders need to be direct and honest about the extent to which shared governance has actually institutionalized collaborative values and intentions" (p. 13). Most campuses simply assume that if leadership is shared, then they have collaboration, which is not accurate. Parker presents principles for developing a collaborative process: developing a shared knowledge base, fostering concern with external constituencies, recognizing the ways in which roles and structures inhibit true collaboration, modeling collaborative behavior, providing rewards for collaboration, and showcasing successful efforts. Like Birnbaum (1992), she identifies that many structural and cultural changes need to be made to support a collaborative form of leadership. In addition, administrators need to decide consciously how collaboration is defined. For example, disagreement exists about whether collaboration means allowing people voice or power over decision making. Some administrators believe true collaboration entails a broader group's having decision-making authority rather than being merely advisory.

A third area of research is focused on enablers and barriers to collaborative leadership processes. For example, research on enablers of collaboration demonstrates that understanding the culture of various units is important for success in a collaborative leadership approach (Ferren and Stanton, 2004; Kezar, Hirsch, and Burack, 2002). Research demonstrates that leaders who are not conscious of differences in various subunits are less likely to be successful in a shared leadership approach. Ferren and Stanton (2004) also caution that collaborative leadership needs to be built over time and that individuals first need to concentrate on sharing information, expertise, and ideas that build trust and empower people to ask; enhanced responsibility comes later. Campuses often do not have formal ways to share leadership; for example, they do not have regular meetings across units, exchange ideas, or have a shared operational vision. Campuses that create such mechanism facilitate shared leadership.

In an effort to comprehensively understand enablers, Kezar (forthcoming) studied how campuses could move from contexts that support individual leadership to campuses that support collaborative leadership and identified several aspects that need to be changed to overcome barriers. The mission of the institution needs to be altered to include collaboration, structures need to be developed to encourage collaborative work such as interdisciplinary research centers, networks need to be developed and fostered, rewards need to be provided and the tenure and promotion process adjusted to support collaborative work, external pressures need to be invoked to create a narrative about why collaboration is important, campus values and beliefs need to incorporate notions of collaboration, and professional development needs to include discussions of the benefits of and approaches to collaboration.

Researchers also describe barriers to collaboration: a culture of mistrust between divisions, resource allocation strategies that create competition, a history of fragmentation and working alone, different departmental cultures, and miscommunication about authority (Ferren and Stanton, 2004; Gayle, Tewarie, and White, 2003; Kekale, 2001; Kezar, Hirsch, and Burack, 2002).

Two examples of such studies provide more detail. Gayle, Tewarie, and White's study of leadership and governance (2003) discovered barriers to collaboration such as disagreement about who should be part of the decision-making processes, conflicting agendas, misunderstandings about who ultimately decides, and different views about the extent of inclusiveness and the optimal depth of consultation, mirroring Parker's observations (2001). Kekale (2001) used his research on the relationship between disciplinary background and leadership to examine departmental cultures of leadership on various campuses. Because of different departmental leadership cultures, collaboration and team leadership can be difficult on many campuses. Departments of sociology and political science, for example, showed strong democratic leadership cultures, physics and biology departments leadership cultures based more on oligarchy, and history and some physics departments strong individual leadership cultures.

Future research needs to examine other new players such as students, alumni, and external groups that still remain misunderstood in the literature, which has little guidance about how to best integrate these groups. In terms of models, a typology of different models of collaborative leadership and an examination of what types work in what situations will be needed. A greater understanding of barriers to collaborative leadership and the effects of interaction among these many barriers is needed to help practitioners negotiate these challenges. More research on facilitators of collaborative leadership is needed to complement the larger body of literature on barriers.

Emotions

Several authors make the link between emotional intelligence among leaders and the ability to successfully collaborate, empower, and provide ethical leadership. Because collaboration and empowerment have been explored extensively in higher education, it is likely that we will begin to see studies of emotions in relationship to leadership as well, but at present few exist. A few studies have begun to examine the importance of emotional intelligence for leaders to be effective. Neumann's study (1991) of college presidents from a social constructivist perspective demonstrates that presidents who are attentive to the emotional needs of campus constituents are able to improve morale even in difficult financial times. Similarly, in her studies of campus teams a key role that emerged in "real" teams was that of emotional monitor (Neumann, 1995). Healthy and functional leadership teams require members who check in with the feelings and emotions of various members on the team; emphasizing the cognitive function of the team only leads to less effective teams and less complex decision making. Teams serve a functional and cognitive purpose, but they also have an expressive function that relates to emotions. Campuses that are successful in team and collaborative forms of leadership do not overlook the expressive or emotional aspect of teams. Teams helped to identify, communicate, and translate campus value systems and emotions that are important in informing decision making and leadership. Birnbaum (1992) noted that leaders who are open to influence and talk regularly to stakeholders become less isolated and remain more in tune with the emotional pulse of the campus.

Other studies have focused specifically on techniques for leaders to hone their emotional intelligence by examining significant events in their lives and using this knowledge to more fully appreciate others in the organization (Beatty, 2000; Kezar, 2002c). In "Capturing the Promise of Collaborative Leadership and Becoming a Pluralistic Leader," Kezar (2002a) illustrates how leaders who reflect on their experiences with leadership (such as mentors, formative aspects of their identity and leadership development, earlier work experiences, and experiences with individuals who tried to suppress their ideas) become aware that they possess different views of leadership based on their own experiences. This practice, especially if it is conducted in leadership teams, helps leaders remain connected to other people and to not become isolated in their beliefs. In addition, leaders often become shielded from and forget about ways they have been disempowered. By remembering their own experiences, they can emotionally tap into the experience of others and be more effective leaders.

Like spirituality, emotions are likely to be met with resistance in academic research on leadership and may be one reason it is currently understudied. Many important areas need to be researched related to emotions and leadership. How will embracing an emotional workplace affect leadership? What barriers will leaders face in trying to create an academic organization that embraces emotions as critical to decision making, change, and other aspects of leadership? How can we best train leaders in higher education to be emotionally intelligent? It is hoped such questions will be addressed in the future.

Globalization

Although scholarship on the globalization of higher education continues to expand (Burbules and Torres, 2000; Levin, 2001; Rhoads and Torres, 2005), few researchers have examined the specific impact of globalization on the theories and practices of academic leadership. One related strand of inquiry, however, that holds tremendous potential for advancing our understanding of higher education leadership from a global perspective is research on the rise of the new managerialism (Currie and Newson, 1998; Deem, 1998, 2001) and academic capitalism (Slaughter and Leslie, 1997; Slaughter and Rhoades, 2004) as guiding ideologies in academic administration. Grounded in the neoliberal framework of economic and political globalization that emphasizes "the primacy of the market, privatization, and a reduced role for the public sphere" (Currie, 1998, p. 17), theories of new managerialism and academic capitalism inform the development of administrative practices and policies centered on the pursuit of efficiency, accountability, and excellence (Deem, 2001). Although conceptually distinct (that is, the scholarship of academic capitalism focuses on the integration of higher education into the new knowledge economy of the twenty-first century, while studies of new managerialism emphasize the increasingly prominent role of for-profit business practices and values in the administration of public institutions), both bodies of scholarship are inextricably linked to the processes of globalization and offer valuable insights on the global dimensions of higher education leadership.

Paramount to full understanding of the leadership implications embedded in new managerialism and academic capitalism is recognition of the prominent role the market plays in determining organizational policy and individual behavior such as leadership. For example, both Slaughter and Rhoades (2004) and Currie and Newson (1998) articulate the central role of department chairs, presidents, and trustees in advancing the market-driven agenda of higher education in the era of globalization. In their discussion of corporate managerialism in the public sphere of education, Currie and Vidovich (1998) call particular attention to the expanding leadership responsibilities of university presidents, observing that "CEOs are busy developing corporate images for their universities that will help develop their niche markets. The images created are more of efficient businesses selling university places both overseas and at home, cooperating with industries, and selling research products and professional services" (p. 157). Research on new managerialism also demonstrates that campuses are being pressured to centralize power, develop top-down authority structures, cut costs, move away from shared forms of leadership, and adopt corporate management practices, pressures that all run counter to the forms of leadership that are part of the leadership revolution.

Although much more research is needed to understand how the conceptualization of university leaders as entrepreneurs and marketing experts is translated to the day-to-day practice of academic leadership, one possible manifestation is the recent increase in the number of university presidents who are hired from outside the academy. A 2001 survey conducted by the American Council on Education found "that while presidents hired from outside higher education remain a minority, their ranks have doubled in recent years" (Basinger, 2002, p. A32). The largest increases were found at public institutions, with public doctoral universities showing a growth from 2.2 percent in 1998 to 10.6 percent in 2001. One possible explanation for the pursuit of academic leaders outside the academy is the shifting nature of postsecondary management priorities such as entrepreneurialism, corporate leadership and values, political lobbying, and marketing in the context of globalization. Moreover, the rise in outsourcing and other efficiency-oriented practices has been associated with new managerialism.

In the frameworks of globalization, academic capitalism, and new managerialism, the scope of academic leadership is no longer limited by the boundaries of the institution, the state, or the nation. Instead, higher education leadership is marked by participation in a global market without boundaries. What new leadership skills, behaviors, and cognitive frameworks are required to successfully navigate higher education leadership on a global scale? What are the ethical implications embedded in leadership practices and processes informed by a neoliberal framework of globalized higher education? How do academic leaders pursue a balance between the institutional mission of democratic education and the administrative practices of globalization and new managerialism? These questions highlight a void in the existing literature on globalization and leadership that must be addressed from diverse leadership theories and perspectives to generate insights that speak to the economic, political, and cultural dimensions of globalization.

Entrepreneurialism

Many recent books and articles have emphasized the importance of college presidents and leaders in institutional fundraising and advancement (Fisher and Koch, 2004; Martin and Samels, 2003; Murphy, 1997; Slinker, 1988). The emphasis on leaders' being entrepreneurial and playing a role in fundraising emerges from the tight budget times in the 1990s and the new managerialism described in the previous section. In addition to leaders at all levels playing a role in fundraising for the institution, leaders are called on to build local, national, and international networks that enhance campus capacity, from additional facilities to human resources in the community to support from community groups (Murphy, 1997). Leaders are spending more time off campus and are increasingly considered external leaders. The emphasis on developing external links with business and community groups also brings up the issue of ethical policies and practices that leaders need to consider (see Bowyer, 1992). Entrepreneurialism is studied through a more narrow definition in most research focused on academic capitalism and the marketplace. The emphasis on grassroots leadership, creativity, and learning in the general leadership literature is not reflected in higher education. One exception to this statement, however, is Love and Estanek's description of "intrapreneurship" (2004). Building on their definition of pervasive leadership (described earlier), Love and Estanek call on higher education leaders in general and student affairs administrators in particular to bring about positive change and innovation in their organizations by demonstrating the values, attitudes, and skills of entrepreneurship. In contrast to traditional entrepreneurialism frameworks that encourage leaders to focus their efforts on structures and opportunities external to the organization, however, intrapreneurs focus their attention on internal organizational structures, challenging organizational norms and assumptions that serve to stifle innovation and change. Another feature of the Love and Estanek model is the simultaneous focus on individual action and the common good. Love and Estanek assert, "To be a successful intrapreneur, an individual needs a firm grasp of the organization's mission, which acts like a field directing ideas and activities within an overall framework. Intrapreneurs think and act as individuals but are connected to others in the organization through the mutual understanding of the mission" (pp. 70–71). Similar to their model of pervasive leadership, Love and Estanek assert that all members of the organization can and should demonstrate a commitment to innovation and the principles of intrapreneurship. To achieve this goal, student affairs administrators must pay attention to ideas and pursue them despite the presence of obstacles, solicit feedback from diverse sources as a means of sharpening ideas and identifying potential roadblocks, use organizational slack (excess resources in an organization such as underused or extra personnel, spare time, unused capital, and extra supplies) to support innovation efforts, and recruit a core of trusted collaborators who can help bring ideas to life. Although the primary audience for *Rethinking Student Affairs Practice* is obviously student affairs administrators, the concepts and processes in Love and Estanek's description of intrapreneurship transcend organizational boundaries and illustrate the relevance and potential of new leadership paradigms for reshaping administrative practices across campus. To truly understand the implications of "intrapreneurship" for student affairs organizations and higher education institutions, however, scholars must begin to systematically examine the processes, strategies, and contextual conditions associated with grassroots leadership and innovation.

As described earlier and illustrated above, some forms of entrepreneurialism are consistent with new, empowering forms of leadership, while others reinforce efficiency and maximization of profits. Only the type that focuses on efficiency and maximization of profits has received much attention in higher education research. The major study conducted in this area is by Fisher and Koch (2004), *The Entrepreneurial College President*. Fisher and Koch note that in most earlier studies of leaders and leadership, entrepreneurialism is not thought of as a trait or process of academic leadership. They reviewed research that found that liberal arts college presidents need to be entrepreneurial to help these campuses survive extremely difficult times: had the leaders not operated in this fashion, it is unlikely these campuses would exist today. Fisher and Koch describe entrepreneurialism as part of transformational leadership and risk taking and attempt to illustrate entrepreneurialism as central to academic leadership. Their survey study of 371 presidents examined whether effective presidents exhibit entrepreneurial characteristics and found a statistically significant relationship between effectiveness and being entrepreneurial. Women presidents were found to be more entrepreneurial than men; minority presidents were the least likely to exhibit entrepreneurial traits, even at historically black colleges and universities. The authors rightly suggest that presidents of color might be averse to taking risks, given that they are new to the college presidency and face legitimacy issues that white presidents may not. Effective leaders were also individuals who partnered with business and government frequently, took risks, and did not believe heavily in organizational structure or let it limit their actions. The book also highlights cases studies of entrepreneurial presidents, describing how they worked to transition their institutions. Although the book focuses on college presidents, the authors note that entrepreneurialism is important to leaders across the campus and to the leadership process in general, and they describe how institutions can become entrepreneurial leadership environments.

Other authors provide evidence that leaders today face market dynamics that early leaders did not have to address and that they are no longer shielded as they had been in the past (Deem, 2001; Nixon, 2003; Ruch, 2001; Smith, 2000). Leaders in most types of academic institutions are required to seek external grants and funds, launch spin-off companies, build endowments (even community colleges), raise tuitions, recruit international students, develop licensing agreements, engage in contract industry training, eliminate less marketable programs, increase section sizes, and cultivate business-education partnerships (Nixon, 2003; Slaughter and Leslie, 1997). These trends extend to all sectors of higher education, with different institutions focusing on different strategies that fit their niche. The role of leaders is to carefully analyze the strategies available in relation to the external market and develop the appropriate strategy. Leaders who do not diversify their funding sources and negotiate the marketplace dynamics run the risk of compromising the survival of their institutions.

Various studies identify successful entrepreneurial practices as well as some of their potential risks and dangers (Deem, 2001; Nixon, 2003; Ruch, 2001; Slaughter and Leslie, 1997; Smith, 2000). For example, leaders who focus externally may compromise daily operations. External stakeholders may gain such prominence that internal stakeholders such as faculty and staff feel compromised, lowering morale. In addition, entrepreneurial activities that are not closely tied to the mission can lead an institution astray, pursuing funding while leaving their mission unfulfilled. In summary, research is emerging about the relationship of entrepreneurialism to leadership as well as ways to be successful in undertaking these activities. Entrepreneurialism is certainly not new to leadership, even in higher education. In tough financial times, leaders have often been asked to examine approaches for enhancing the capacity of the institution and setting a new direction. Research has not focused on this area until recently, however. This burgeoning area of research is likely to continue to grow in coming years.

Accountability

A limited amount of research in higher education has examined the link between leadership and accountability. Although much has been written in the past two decades about the increased accountability demanded by federal legislators and state officials, boards of trustees, alumni groups, and foundations, interest is not apparent in understanding how leaders can foster accountability or success in meeting accountability mandates (Steelman, Lew, and Snell, 2004). Campuses are being required more than ever to meet accountability mandates, so the lack of research about the role of leaders in this area is surprising.

A plethora of anecdotal research describes suggested techniques or practices of accountability, including assessment, testing, and audits (Steelman, Lew, and Snell, 2004). The limited empirical research that has been conducted on accountability systems, however, tends to focus on their inadequacy in the ways that leaders meet bureaucratic mandates for accountability, not on ways that accountability could be used to improve campus operations or a better learning environment (Peterson and Dill, 1997).

Accountability practices such as data-based decision making, assessment, and benchmarking have been related to organizational learning in a variety of studies (Zangwill and Roberts, 1995). In particular, researchers have found that organizational change, a core aspect of the leadership process, is linked to getting people to think differently, which can be achieved through organizational learning. Advocates for diversity, technology, interdisciplinarity, and other important innovations in higher education may rely on accountability techniques to have these innovations institutionalized. The link between accountability mechanisms and organizational learning may result in more studies in the future of the potential to improve leadership processes through learning. One study that examines the use of Total Quality Management–based benchmarking practices at colleges and universities found that institutions that employ these techniques enhance creativity and innovation and survive by attracting funding during times of budgetary cutbacks (Zangwill and Roberts, 1995). These institutions tended to engage more in organizational learning and brainstorming than other institutions that tended to be more isolated by not examining practices of other institutions. Research suggests that revising reward systems to be aligned with the institutional mission can help leaders create environments that are more accountable (Diamond, 2002), that performance funding can lead to improved programs (Banta and Moffett, 1987), that faculty evaluation can lead to stronger teaching and research (Theall, 2002), and that academic program review enhances departmental leadership and performance (Wergin, 2002).

These studies suggest that more research should focus on the link between accountability systems and effective leadership. The limited research on accountability may be related to the fact that many researchers perceive accountability to be associated with assessment, benchmarking, and other scientific management tools that have been found to have limited potential in higher education (Birnbaum, 2000). Others have described accountability as part of the new managerialism and neoliberal philosophy that is critiqued in various circles for emphasizing efficiency over effectiveness and institutional interests over stakeholders (Currie and Newson, 1998).

Summary

Some aspects of the leadership revolution appear to be moving more slowly into the higher education setting than others. Perhaps it is not surprising that collaboration and empowerment were easily embraced in colleges and universities because of their tradition of shared governance and decentralized authority among departments. Although collaboration and empowerment are different from the collectivism that has been a part of higher education's past, these new concepts fit in with higher education's history. Concepts that challenge the rigid scientific ethos, however, are being met with much greater resistance, in particular ethics, spirituality, and emotions. Higher education is tradition bound, and the concept of social change is likely not welcome. Entrepreneurialism, globalization, and accountability, which have been received easily in corporate settings, are also met with resistance in higher education, as they conflict with higher education's tradition of autonomy, focus on mission over money, and anticorporate orientation. Yet these concepts will likely continue to knock at higher education's door in the coming years and will be important for practitioners to consider and researchers to continue to examine. These three trends are increasing in importance; we need leaders to engage these issues and researchers to help us understand how to best link entrepreneurialism, accountability, and globalization to higher education leadership.

Practical Implications for the Leadership Revolution

MANY BOOKS ON LEADERSHIP TEND to provide a particular perspective on how individuals should lead—as transformational leaders or through a political approach. Our task in this book is quite different, however. It is to summarize the many lessons we have learned from leadership research. We hope that we have provided a broad set of tools to guide leaders as they tackle challenges and situations. In one situation, organizational learning will be particularly important, while in another collaboration will take precedence. We hope this volume can be a source for leaders in developing their skills. The environment for leadership and the tools needed to successfully engage it have become increasingly complex.

Bensimon, Neumann, and Birnbaum (1989) were concerned that practitioners were not embracing new approaches to leadership and were clinging to an authoritative and traditional view. They noted in particular resistance to social constructivist views of leadership, especially the more radical strands that suggest leadership itself is an illusion used by the powerful to control others or that leadership itself can have minimal effect on organizational outcomes and effectiveness. In our experience teaching leadership, the traditional, functionalist behavior, or power and influence strategies are easier for practitioners to understand initially as they are part of our popular culture and take less analytic work to tackle. These earlier theories also provide specific advice in terms of behaviors that can be used immediately to revise performance. As Bensimon, Neumann, and Birnbaum (1989) caution, "As long as leaders look to researchers to identify specific activities that will enable them to be more effective, they are doomed to disappointment. Research can provide only trivial and superficial responses to those who seek specific answers" (p. 69). This sentiment remains an important reminder for readers today. As work by Kuhn (1996) demonstrated, researchers who maintain strict paradigms and are not willing to examine primary assumptions are often blind to data that do not fit their underlying assumptions. Being open to questioning our assumptions is important. Leadership research, particularly chaos theory, demonstrates leadership to be a complex, dynamic phenomenon with few quick answers or easy solutions.

Yet we have seen many leaders in higher education embrace a view of leadership from the perspectives of critical theory, postmodernism, and social constructivism with some time and thought. These approaches suggest that leadership is about developing certain habits of mind, developing emotional intelligence, and connecting to spiritual insights, which takes time. It is a longer-term investment. We encourage leaders to consider the value of these new approaches for developing a sophisticated view of leadership that can have a lifetime effect. This suggestion does come in direct contradiction to others such as Burns (1978) and Rost (1991), who believe that the many different schools of thought and leadership beliefs are problematic and confusing for practitioners. They conducted exhaustive reviews of the leadership literature trying to develop a single definition of leadership and to discard the majority of the leadership literature as dealing with peripheral issues or not addressing leadership but some other social phenomenon such as management. Rost believes that reducing the complexity is the best approach and that we need one clear picture of what leadership is. He notes that people find "only contradictory and confusing understanding of the nature of leadership and almost no explanation of how leaders and followers really do leadership" (p. 221). Even though Rost believes leadership is socially constructed and we must change our assumptions to match the postindustrial age, we argue that he does not seem to realize that these assumptions will then change again as time evolves. His single paradigm will become outdated and will prevent movement toward helpful new ideas for leaders.

Reductionism, we believe, has never served the leadership literature well. Instead, we find social constructivist and critical scholars returning to important ideas that were discarded fifty or sixty years ago when scientific management theories rose into prominence and suggested easy answers to leadership challenges by developing formulaic approaches to problems. These formulaic behavioral and contingency theories are limited in helping leaders address complex challenges. Through the case studies in the appendix, we hope to demonstrate the way leaders can embrace leadership as a complex process, grounding the various lessons from this synthesis of the research.

What are some of the implications of the research synthesized in this volume? In terms of the paradigms presented, research from a social constructivist perspective has provided evidence that leadership is socially constructed and that the frameworks and assumptions of individuals affect what they perceive to be effective leadership, the way leaders enact their role, and the relationship between leaders and followers. What it means for leaders is that they must spend time understanding their own frameworks and assumptions as well as others in the leadership process. Communication and relational skills posited by many researchers as important for leadership have been demonstrated to be critical competencies that leaders need to spend time developing. Leaders need to challenge their own essentialist views that certain traits or behaviors will serve them in all situations. Individual leaders need to carefully understand the various individuals they are working with and how these individuals' backgrounds and experiences might affect their views of leadership. Additionally, leaders need to spend more time understanding the institutional contexts in which they are involved, particularly institutional culture. An important lesson that emerges from this research is that perception is reality and that leaders need to focus on people's perceptions. (See Birnbaum, 1992, for a detailed description of the implications of the social constructivist framework, with many specific examples of how leaders need to operate differently because leadership is a social construction.)

Unfortunately, limited research exists from a critical or postmodern paradigm, and the implications for higher education leaders are therefore not clearly understood. The one major strand of research from a critical paradigm has demonstrated that gender, race, and ethnicity affect views and approaches to leadership. In addition, earlier representations of leadership were overly narrow and represented mostly a white male perspective. Further, hierarchical, individualistic, and directive models of leadership have been thoroughly challenged as the most effective approach to leading. The research on gender, race, and ethnicity provides opportunities for leaders to expand the range of activities they consider successful to leading organizations—as we have seen, empowerment, collaboration, and a collective process of leadership are now seen as effective approaches.

A few studies from a critical theory perspective (Kezar, 2000, 2002c) have demonstrated that people tend to have biases that make them blind to the various ways that individuals from different backgrounds perceive and enact leadership. Individuals in positions of authority in particular tend to become removed from power conditions and dynamics that disempower many groups in the leadership process; moreover, they are oblivious to the ways people may feel disempowered. In addition, research has demonstrated that many people seek positions of authority to mandate and control an organization (Kempner, 1989). This research suggests that individuals in positions of authority need to spend more time in self-reflection, understanding their own biases and reaching out to others to expand their views of appropriate leadership. Research also suggests the importance of leaders' not surrounding themselves with a small group of individuals such as a cabinet, which can isolate them from varied perspectives and power dynamics throughout the campus. Various authors found that successful leaders and leadership processes remain open to influence from many different stakeholders and campus constituents (Bensimon and Neumann, 1993; Birnbaum, 1992; Kezar, 2000).

Although the postmodern paradigm has not been researched in any detail in higher education, the implications of the general leadership literature suggest that leaders will be best served if they use as many frameworks as they can to address complex problems. For example, leaders will be more effective if they can see organizations as cultures, can use symbols and stories effectively, can relate to people from different cultural backgrounds, are politically savvy, can carefully identify power dynamics, can understand techniques to create empowerment, are careful listeners, and are able to use a variety of accountability mechanisms. Birnbaum's notion of cognitive complexity (1992) fits in well with assumptions of the postmodern paradigm in which successful leaders develop skills in gathering input, listening, and learning so that they are better able to adapt to the rapidly changing external environment. In addition, Heifetz's work (1994) supports the notions that adaptive leadership requires mobilizing expertise from a variety of individuals from the institution and the importance of people's learning collectively so that they can create novel solutions. The message seems clear: seek feedback broadly, avoid routine responses, attempt to see situations as complexly as possible, and focus on learning and innovation.

The leadership literature has changed vastly in the past two decades. Many models are no longer leader centric. Practitioners need to grapple with what it means to be part of a phenomenon that is a process, not a person as is often described in popular culture and in the history of leadership. As a process, leadership is context bound and organizationally determined. Practitioners would be wise to shift their view from traits, behaviors, and cognitive mindsets alone to place them in a context. This step is often hard cognitively, as our popular culture has trained us to see and understand leadership as embodied in single, heroic leaders. It is also important not to see the context as an objective reality. As demonstrated in a variety of studies, different people interpret the same context in very different ways. Therefore, leaders need to gather information about the way various people experience and understand the organizational context. In practical terms, it can also mean that it is very difficult to understand all the individual ways that people perceive a situation (Bolman and Deal, 2003). We need research that helps us to understand the strategies leaders adopt to make sense of what is going on in the environment without being overwhelmed by complexity.

In addition to acknowledging that leadership is context bound and organizationally determined, it is important to realize that leadership is a cultural process. Practitioners need to consider that good leadership varies by institutional environment and that an approach on one campus may not work on the next. A key strategy for leaders is to carefully analyze the institutional culture as they begin engaging in a leadership process. Understanding that leadership is a cultural process intrinsically ties leadership to values, history, traditions, and other key components of culture. See Bergquist (1992); Birnbaum (1992); Bolman and Deal (2003); and Rhoads and Tierney (1992) for a detailed account of the implications for practitioners seeing leadership as a cultural process.

The endurance and popularity of transformational leadership, even in studies in higher education settings, suggest that a leadership process may have some essential elements such as creating a shared vision, fostering collaboration and self-development, motivating and encouraging others, and showing integrity and morality. These skills or areas are key for leaders to develop and will likely be important across various institutional contexts and in varying leadership initiatives. In addition, Birnbaum's study (1992) of academic leadership demonstrates a set of core skills that leaders should foster such as seeking input, listening to others, embracing integrity, fostering a shared process, and the like. Montez's review (2003) of the leadership literature identifies five key skills for leaders—integral, relational, credibility, competence, and direction or guidance. This work provides a set of skills and competencies to which higher education administrators must pay careful attention. Even though we have learned from studies on culture and contingency that leadership processes vary based on institutional context and conditions, certain characteristics appear to be essential to leadership. Therefore, leaders are urged to learn a set of basic skills and competencies but to be sensitive to varying their approach based on institutional culture and context or the situation at hand.

The emphasis on process and the importance of gathering multiple inputs relate to the importance of operating in a team and or a collaborative structure. Most practitioners see the value of a team approach, but successfully achieving that approach can be a great challenge. Much of the research synthesized in this volume provides ideas for leaders to structure and select a leadership team as well as barriers that they might encounter and ways to overcome them (see Bensimon and Neumann, 1993; Bolman and Deal, 2003; Kezar, forthcoming).

Because leadership is a relational process, practitioners need to consider their own relationship skills and focus more on people than strategies and data, often a mistake among leaders (see Bolman and Deal, 2003, Kezar, 2000, and Rhoads and Tierney, 1992, for specific guidance). Doing so will improve one's work in teams or networks, the form most leadership takes in a "power-sharing world." The research on spirituality and emotions demonstrates that leaders are whole people and that the leadership processes involve parts of people outside their professional spheres. People bring a history and a life outside involving families, community, and activities to the leadership process that need to be taken into account. Leaders need to reflect on their own background and experience and see how they affect their potential as a leader (Kezar, 2002c). In addition, individuals involved in the leadership process need to try to understand the frameworks and assumptions of all individuals they are working with. Various pieces of literature synthesized in this volume suggest likely differences that will shape people's frameworks—race, gender, disciplinary backgrounds, departmental culture—and serve as guides to help people interact with one another. It is another important context component that must be considered. As a result of these findings, personal reflection and journaling are key leadership practices that should be emphasized in leadership training and development.

For many leaders, personal reflection, self-development, journaling, and examining one's emotions are uncomfortable and difficult. A variety of techniques for self-development are described in the social change model of leadership development (Higher Education Research Institute, 1996; see also Goleman, 1998). Throughout one's career, most leaders will have been rewarded for their cognitive abilities, and the suggestion to focus on emotional capacities seems counter to one's experience. The leadership research does suggest, however, that successful leadership processes and leaders are in touch with their emotions, are authentic and behave with consistency, can read the emotions of others, and attend to the emotional aspects of the organization. In recent years, the evidence from leadership research is that an internal journey is necessary to be a successful leader. The research on culture also supports these findings.

The rebirth of spirituality and ethics in the leadership literature has important implications for practitioners. It is clear that leaders need to consider ethical frameworks and decision-making models rather than continuing to ignore the values inherent in the leadership process (Wilcox and Ebbs, 1992). Several authors described in this volume provide specific ethical decision-making frameworks. Other authors offer historical examples of moral leaders as case studies that can help leaders to shape their own approach (Nelson, 2000). Campuses should help develop an ethos of ethics throughout the campus environment to support leaders (Weingartner, 1999; Wilcox and Ebbs, 1992).

Another implication of the leadership research is that we need to clearly define what collaboration and empowerment mean. In a world of increasing accountability, it is becoming difficult to delegate authority and to provide individuals throughout the organization with real decision-making power. The clash of accountability and empowerment needs to be considered by practitioners as well as future research. As noted in many of the studies, higher education and leadership are characterized more by collectivism then by real models of collaboration and empowerment. Leaders need to examine their own campuses and honestly ask whether true collaboration and empowerment exist and what a desirable mix would be. In some contexts if accountability is a concern, collaboration and empowerment may not be real options.

Last, the relationship between entrepreneurialism and effectiveness and the increasing influence of the marketplace suggest that leaders should hone their entrepreneurial skills, although it may be difficult for many individuals who in the past have been rewarded for being politically savvy or for not rocking the boat. Research needs to examine what happens when leaders of color are entrepreneurial and whether it negatively affects views of their effectiveness. Evidence at present suggests that leaders of color are less likely to be entrepreneurial. Perhaps research in this area would empower leaders of color to take on a more entrepreneurial role (Fisher and Koch, 2004). At present, accountability and globalization have few implications for practice, and research on the relationship between leadership and accountability and globalization is needed.

Many of the implications described will be challenging for higher education leaders, moving them in directions where they might not have spent much time such as developing their emotional intelligence, risk taking, and carefully assessing the cultural implications of one's actions. Research has revealed, however, that the benefits of undergoing this personal revolution in one's beliefs have been demonstrated to lead to more effective leaders. We encourage readers to continue to grapple with the implications of this new research as they read the case studies in the appendix.

As we have emphasized throughout this book and this chapter, we believe the true benefit of the lessons presented is best obtained by combining the insights from various theories and concepts. The accompanying vignette about diversifying a college campus provides a lens for successfully engaging leadership and demonstrates the ways the information in this book can inform leadership.

Diversifying the Faculty and Students of Rio Rancho College

Located in a traditionally rural and homogenous region of the West, Rio Rancho College is one of the largest educational institutions in the state. Because of its emphasis on agronomy and its strong hotel industry program, many top students compete to attend Rio Rancho and become part of the "Mustang Tradition." After a recent visit by the regional board of accreditation, a major institutional dilemma surfaces. Although they commend Rio Rancho for its pioneering spirit, tradition, and success as an academic institution, members of the accrediting body point out a serious lack of gender and ethnic diversity, which is out of sync with shifting demographic populations and the institution's purported mission: to prepare students to lead into new frontiers.

In response to this new revelation, a town hall meeting is convened and the results of the accrediting body shared, after which the chancellor, provost, president of the faculty senate, student senate representatives, core faculty members, and a number of staff union representatives meet to develop a plan of action. They unanimously decide to fill all remaining administrative and faculty vacancies with female candidates or minorities. They also create benchmarks that will measure and assess hiring practices, rewarding campus departments with the most diversity with increased funding possibilities and additional campus resources such as larger classrooms. A second part of the benchmarking includes quarterly public reports by each department on its hiring practices and progress. Because of a strong emphasis on and belief in meritocracy, identified as one reason faculty of color often are not hired, the group decides to start "growing its own" underrepresented faculty, meaning it wants to hire advanced doctoral candidates from selective institutions, introduce them to the Mustang culture, and groom them at Rio Rancho to meet their expectations. Doing so will allow them to increase the size of the applicant pool, which is usually quite small because of the college's location. If they pay doctoral candidates to finish their dissertations while teaching, however, Rio Rancho might develop more diversity and talent among candidates.

(Continued)

Diversifying the Faculty and Students of Rio Rancho College (*Continued*)

To bolster support for this new multifaceted plan of action, the group decides it is important to explain the significance and fiscal implications of being accredited to the campus and local community. Part of having to explain why they must make progress in diversifying their campus requires increasing their understanding about why they have not had more success in the past. Through dialogues and some honest reflection, the group arrives at some new realizations—including the fact that although the college is competitive, it is not a nationally recognized institution. Moreover, aside from being located far from any major cities or diverse communities, it offers low pay and has experienced a number of hate crimes in the past that have gone relatively unattended. A final means of addressing the lack of diversity is to change the makeup of the search committees. The new plan calls for representatives from many departments, students and women, and the two minority faculty members on the staff.

The Rio Rancho strategy to diversify students and faculty represents the integration of multiple theories and concepts from the leadership literature. It illustrates that rather than selecting one theoretical approach, it is possible and often more beneficial to combine concepts. This brief analysis serves to identify specific theories employed in this plan of action.

The first step taken by the group, to reserve all vacant positions for women and minority faculty, reflects trait, style, and behavioral theories. By filling central positions with traditionally underrepresented candidates, Rio Rancho hopes to model desired hiring practices and communicate openness to diversity and non-traditional populations. By providing incentives to increase diversity in hiring through rewards and public assessments, Rio Rancho also uses power and influence theories. The group asked themselves what would make department heads be more inclusive in their hiring practices. Aside from having new minority leaders in key positions, the next best thing is incentives. A major step for Rio Rancho that signified true progress is the recognition of the perceived meritocracy.

Through the use of cultural theory, the group realizes their culture has been deeply entrenched in the school's rugged pioneering history, which did not consider important social realities that stratified and excluded certain populations. Acknowledging these cultural tendencies and applying cognitive theories, the group identifies certain mental models related to diversifying, which encourages them to reconsider current practices. In doing so they realize that aside from significant mental barriers and preconceived notions about diversity, Rio Rancho in all of its pioneering glory does not appeal to many populations. From the perspective of complexity theory, they realize that their contextual circumstances contribute to why so few minorities and women are drawn to their remote and homogenous campus. Combined with contingency theory, it becomes apparent that past racial incidents and current attitudes and cultural values present a structure that is not inviting to faculty or students of color. The few women and minorities who have attended Rio Rancho appear not to have benefited from their decisions to attend. In response to the overwhelming complexity of this call for change, the final part of the Rio Rancho diversity strategy is built on team leadership theory. Because the traditional hiring committee is not capable of recruiting and hiring minority candidates for administrative and faculty positions, a new team has been compiled. Consisting of individuals with a number of differing perspectives, this new team is designed to complement and support each other in achieving the desired objective of increased diversity.

Framing Leadership Research
in a New Era

BENSIMON, NEUMANN, AND BIRNBAUM (1989) hoped that research in the future would allow leadership to be considered in new ways. For example, they called for the consideration of nonpositional leaders, leadership teams, and multiple sources of leadership throughout the organization. They also suggested that research needed to focus on understanding how a leader's behavior is part of the larger organizational phenomenon and that the role of interpretation between and among leaders and followers needed examination. And the authors implored that more multivariate and complex approaches to leadership be considered. In the last fifteen years, researchers have made major progress on this ambitious agenda. Teams, nonpositional leaders, organizational context, interpretation, and complexity are now commonly studied in leadership. But what are the leadership challenges for the future? This chapter draws on both unanswered questions and the remaining gaps in the literature to map out a research agenda that will serve to expand our understanding of the current revolution in leadership research and to foster the methodological flexibility essential for navigating the uncharted waters of future revolutions.

In terms of paradigms, the expansion in viewpoints has been exceedingly helpful in providing the complexity and richness Bensimon, Neumann, and Birnbaum hoped for in 1989. Social constructivism has been the framework used by the majority of researchers in higher education who have moved beyond functionalist assumptions to frame research. Following up on the work of Birnbaum (1992) and Neumann (1991, 1995) on the interaction of higher education presidents with individuals across campus, we need more studies that examine the interaction of individuals in the leadership process. New research needs to focus on campus teams and groups involved in shared leadership.

Critical theory has been applied in modest ways, mostly focused on strategies for opening up the manner in which leadership is defined and described (for example, including the perspectives and experiences of women or people of color). Study of the power dynamics surrounding leadership has been minimal (exceptions being the challenge to traditional hierarchy and transactional or exchange models of leadership and the emerging focus on empowerment). Little examination has occurred of the way leadership may contribute to or prevent oppression in workplaces. Exploration into the subtle power dynamics related to the leadership process has been minimal, especially in the newer models and definitions. How does power operate in team leadership or in the social change model? How might leaders use values and spirituality to manipulate rather than create leadership (a concern in the transformational leadership literature)? Conflict is also an understudied issue that critical theorists often investigate. Many scholars have pointed out that team and collaborative forms of leadership are likely to lead to more conflict, yet minimal research has focused on identifying strategies for negotiating and managing conflict in the leadership process or explicitly addressed the ways conflict enriches leadership (with the exception of Tierney, 1993a). A rich body of literature on conflict could be used to shape and frame particular studies in higher education (see Bolman and Deal, 2003).

Few studies have examined leadership from a postmodern perspective (Bergquist, 1993). Although research has been done about how leadership is context based, this finding has not been translated into a way to rethink leadership to challenge (or alter) the many universal models that exist. The postmodern emphasis on context needs further elaboration, cultivating a better understanding of the effect local contexts have on leadership environments as well as the nexus between universal and culturally contingent models of leadership. For example, studies of urban community colleges might develop a set of leadership characteristics that can inform leaders in these particular contexts. Sector and regional differences are rarely studied.

Two other areas of study in postmodernism show promise. First, leadership research has often focused on best practices and leaders' effectiveness. We may learn more if we study the ambiguities and problems encountered in the leadership process, studying failed attempts at change and examining why leadership does not emerge around various initiatives. Many untold stories on many different campuses might, with careful analysis, shed more light on leadership than continued studies of best practices. Second, given the very limited research on the implications of globalization for leadership, we have almost no understanding of how leadership may need to be enacted differently, given the current changes and challenges in the environment. Adaptive approaches including entrepreneurialism and accountability remain understudied and need additional attention. Last, few research studies have combined assumptions from more than one paradigm. Future studies should try to examine leadership from both a social constructivist and critical or postmodern perspective (see Kezar 2000 and 2002b for examples of studies using both social constructivism and critical theory).

The new theories and models of leadership that have emerged in the last fifteen years also present numerous opportunities for further investigation. Although these theories are grounded in long-standing bodies of research—organizational learning, complexity and chaos theory, team research, feminist theory—each needs careful study as it is applied to leadership in higher education. Because each approach is newly applied to leadership, empirical studies in support of these "revolutionary" theories are slowly emerging, but large research gaps remain. For example, we need more research on when transformational leadership is necessary. Only one or two studies have examined the role of transformational leadership in addressing complex issues that challenge the status quo of campuses.

Very limited research exists related to complexity and chaos theory in higher education. The research detailed in Birnbaum's *How Academic Leadership Works* (1992) provides some empirical research to build from with respect to cognitive complexity. In addition, he examines higher education institutions as complex organizations. Work by Wheatley (1999) or Heifetz (1994) could be used to frame studies of complexity and chaos in higher education institutions that examine critical campus leadership challenges: (1) mobilizing expertise, (2) developing novel solutions, (3) using outside environments to create innovation, (4) creating networks, (5) using a decentralized environment to develop solutions to problems, and (6) establishing a balance between autonomy and accountability in the leadership process. Several key research questions need to be addressed: What are the best ways to approach adaptive leadership in higher education? What skills and understandings do leaders need to be boundary spanners? How do leaders most effectively develop the skills of systems thinking and interdependence?

The relationship between learning and leadership is an important area for future research as well. We need research that demonstrates effective strategies for leaders to use in developing learning among change agents on college and university campuses. Research that helps us understand how individual leaders themselves grow and develop is very limited, although some research in this area is forthcoming. In examining learning theories, we might consider how one develops the communication skills of the constructivist leader, when different strategies of communication are best used, how leaders build a creative tension between the vision of where the organization is going and the current reality, and whether certain personality types are more comfortable with this approach. In addition, we have little appreciation of how leaders develop cognitive mind-sets and the ways in which they change. We have research that demonstrates that leaders' cognitive mind-sets affect the way they enact leadership and their effectiveness, yet we have little understanding of how they develop these frameworks. We also know little about the training and development mechanisms that might help to expand the mind-sets individuals bring to leadership.

In terms of social and cultural theories of leadership, it will become important to examine and apply cross-cultural studies of leadership as more institutions start building satellite campuses in other countries. Approaches to leadership that have been effective on U.S. campuses may not be effective in other countries. Research studies examining the impact of globalization for leadership of U.S. institutions are also needed. Research on culture and globalization helps us understand the skills needed for new leadership processes embedded in global contexts. This research tends to be developed from a U.S.

perspective, but reviewing research from other countries or teaming with researchers from other countries to conduct research might help provide a more comprehensive picture of the global leadership needed to meet future challenges. We still have mixed results related to the degree to which social and cultural differences affect leadership models; some say the impact is significant, while others believe the impact is negligible, with the evidence leaning toward its being a fairly significant factor. This area needs a meta-analysis of the various studies conducted. Research that examines the overlap of race, gender, ethnicity, and other factors such as class or sexual orientation is also limited. We need to understand the dynamic ways that identity affects leadership (see Kezar, 2000, 2002a, and 2002c for examples).

Most studies of culture have been macro in nature, studying the impact of the overall environment or context (Birnbaum, 1992; Rhoads and Tierney, 1992). Fewer studies have pursued specific cultural constructs such as the use of symbols, vision, story telling, or values. Although they are advocated as important in the prescriptive literature, research is limited on how practitioners can best use these specific cultural strategies. The vague generalizations offered in most texts ("recognize your organization is a culture," "use symbols to motivate followers") are wholly inadequate to guide practice. Having taught practitioners for years, we know they want to understand how to use symbols and stories effectively yet need more guidance in the translation of cultural theory to administrative practice.

Research is needed to understand how the increasingly political and top-down nature of higher education environments will affect or transform current leadership trends. How will collaboration and empowerment be compromised in the increasingly capitalist and globalized marketplace? What role will external agents play in campus leadership in coming years? How can entrepreneurialism temper or fuel these trends from the outside?

Research from a social movement perspective could greatly enhance higher education leadership. For example, we need research that examines how commitment can be formed and used to drive collective leadership efforts. We understand very little about the passion and intensity that people bring or could bring to leadership. Only a few studies have examined leaders' work to develop a common purpose or shared vision for an institution. More work needs to be done in this area, examining the impact of institutional structure and culture as well as different types of leadership initiatives.

A significant need exists for research related to the processual approach to leadership. Understanding how context affects leadership is perhaps one of the most important areas of future research in this new era of non-leader-centric models. Researchers in the processual tradition might ask several questions: Which context factors are the most significant at each level—micro, meso, or macro? What is the relationship between these levels? Some research in higher education has focused on the impact of the organizational context, but we have less of an understanding of some of the microdynamics that occur in specific units or divisions as well as the macroconditions that affect leadership processes. In future years, studies that examine leadership from a multilevel perspective, looking at all these contextual conditions, will enhance our understanding.

With greater emphasis on a collaborative and team approach to leadership, we need more research to support practitioners operating in new ways. How can personal relationships be developed that transform the workplace and enhance the leadership process? How can we better work through personality clashes that may unfold as we bring more of the personal into the workplace? Bureaucratic structures and hierarchy were used to remove emotions and relationships from the workplace; however, little work has been done on how we manage these new dynamics that occur as we redefine the leadership process in a collaborative and shared way. We need more research on how campuses have moved to team leadership and the way they overcame barriers. A key area for study will be ways that leaders negotiate conflict as they try to include people from varying backgrounds in the leadership process. The work of Bensimon and Neumann (1993), Tierney (1993a), and H. S. Astin (1996) has begun to examine this issue, but more research is needed.

In terms of the concepts described in recent leadership literature, many of the topics need study but may prove difficult to study with traditional methodologies and approaches. The way ethics and spirituality are connected to leadership needs greater study. Although we understand it is important to various groups and individual leaders, we know less about the specific dynamics of how ethics affect learning, complexity, teams, change, and other aspects important to the leadership process. Although collaboration and empowerment have been analyzed more since they have been seen as tools for effectiveness in the new paradigms of leadership, we need more study of how to be sure collaboration and empowerment are authentic and not merely collectivism (Terry, 1993). Many critics of Total Quality Management noted that empowerment and collaboration were used as management tools to encourage greater commitment by employees but that empowerment and collaboration in the end were really illusory.

In terms of social change, we need to understand whether and when it is desirable and how change agents might most effectively build the case for social change. We need empirical research on the social change model of leadership, highlighting the challenges encountered as well as strategies for institutionalizing such a leadership process. We also need to know how entrepreneurialism might be a helpful approach for individuals with a less social or risk-taking orientation but who want to work toward change at the grassroots level. We need more research that examines the interaction of grassroots efforts and leadership with top-down approaches, as many leadership processes operate interactively at both levels. Entrepreneurialism, empowerment, and social change models or social movement theory can provide lenses for studies of some of these grassroots efforts at leadership and their interaction with top-down approaches. Very little research has been conducted on the relationship between accountability and leadership, an important area for future research that will enhance the potential of assessment, program review, and data practices.

The following research agenda is indeed ambitious, but leadership scholars and practitioners must begin to address these important issues and tough questions if we are to develop a deep and textured understanding of leadership that reflects the complex, diverse, and dynamic nature of contemporary society.

Use critical and postmodern paradigms to uncover new ways to conceptualize leadership.

Start developing studies using several paradigms.

Conduct explicit examinations of power dynamics embedded in leadership processes.

Focus on failed examples of leadership.

Study the implications of globalization for leadership.

Increase research on entrepreneurialism and accountability.

Use complexity and chaos to understand higher education leadership.

Study the relationship between learning and leadership.

Focus on cross-cultural leadership.

Conduct empirical studies of specific cultural phenomena that affect leadership in higher education such as symbols or story telling.

Develop empirical research from a social movement perspective.

Study the interaction of various levels (micro, meso, macro) and aspects (different units) of the higher education context.

Conduct research on negotiating the conflicts that are inevitable with collective forms of leadership.

Initiate interdisciplinary research to understand ethics, global leadership, and empowerment.

Study leadership over time.

If there is one thing we have learned in the last twenty years, it is that no single way exists to be a "good" leader or that a universally "appropriate" leadership process exists. Thus, we need to consider leadership as a multidimensional phenomenon. If leadership, as social constructivist theory suggests, is an evolving concept that has changed over time as social mores and beliefs have changed, then researchers will continuously reconstruct new visions that fit the emerging social understandings and needs. In the coming years, with more information on how context, interpretation, power dynamics, ethics and spirituality, empowerment, and the host of new paradigms, theories, and concepts influence leadership processes, we are confident that both leadership scholars and practitioners will create an understanding of leadership that fits the needs of an evolving society. We hope (and believe) that the leadership research will continue to revolutionize itself on an ongoing basis to meet the dynamic needs of organizations and societies.

Notes

1. The word *constructivist* is used in this model to refer to constructivist learning theories rather than the social constructivism paradigm. Constructivist learning, related to social constructivism as described earlier, posits that learning is the process of reforming what we know, believe, and value based on the connections between new and already held knowledge, values, and beliefs. People are in a constant state of learning to enhance their existence.

2. In 1989, few researchers had examined leadership in higher education from a contingency perspective (examining how traits and behaviors are affected by situational dynamics and the organizational context), which is still true today.

3. As a reminder, transactional leadership focuses on the exchange between leaders and followers based on needs, the ability to allocate resources, and motivations.

4. Several valuable cultural lessons were summarized in the last ASHE-ERIC monograph on leadership (1989), including (1) the importance of leaders' being sensitive to the interpretation and views of followers as a means of eliciting faculty and staff support; (2) the significance of leaders' taking an interpretive approach to strategy, which incorporates how individuals on campus see, understood, and feel about their lives and using this approach to maintain the identity and integrity of the institution; and (3) the need for leaders to pose cultural questions to help them identify characteristics of the organizational environment critical to effective leadership (Chaffee, 1984; Chaffee and Tierney, 1988; Neumann 1989; Tierney 1988).

Appendix: Three Case Studies

Case Study One
University of Portsmouth at Doonsbury: Chaos, Complexity, and Change

Institutional Background

The University of Portsmouth at Doonsbury (UPD) is a large public selective institution located in a major city. Founded at the turn of the twentieth century, UPD has a rich legacy of educating some of the nation's most preeminent researchers, particularly in science, math, and engineering. Aside from academic rigor, this university of thirty thousand students has one of the nation's best basketball programs. The continued success of UPD has caused it to move up in the national rankings from among the top twenty universities to among the top ten. This shift in the rankings has also caused an increase in an already high volume of admissions applications each fall.

A recent addition to the UPD family is Byron Applegate, the new dean of admissions hired from a prestigious private research university known for its success and efficiency in the admissions process. Much of the success enjoyed by Dean Applegate in his previous work resulted from his implementation of new and creative admissions policies as well as his willingness to use new technology. One of the reasons Dean Applegate was recruited for UPD is the university's need to overhaul its current admissions practices, which are expensive and overburdened by the current number of applications. After his first six months at UPD and as a result of many conversations with a wide range of staff members, the new dean proposed to move from traditional paper-based admissions file reading to all-electronic files. This suggestion also coincided with a statewide budget shortfall that eliminated UPD's budget for hiring additional admissions file readers.

To implement the suggested changes, Dean Applegate held a retreat where the admissions staff could share their ideas and feedback. As a result of this retreat, small committees were formed in the admissions division to brainstorm and lead whatever change efforts were needed to maximize their collective efficiency. The groups suggested a reorganization of admissions practices. Rather than have one set task such as reading or processing files, the entire admissions division (from high-level administrators to phone operators) would temporarily share the duties. To assist in the process of converting the incoming files to e-files, the admissions cycle was divided into three phases. The first phase lasted for three months and entailed the electronic entry of the incoming files by all staff members (including the dean). The second phase also included all staff members and involved setting up interviews, answering inquiries and phone calls, and processing and sorting applications. The final phase was the actual admissions decision process and was limited to experienced readers and admissions officers. As a result of this new structure, within one year the admissions division at UPD was entirely paperless and much more efficient.

Theoretical Analysis

On a theoretical level this case depicts many of the central elements of chaos and complexity theories. Beginning with his rejection of a hierarchical approach and his recognition of a need to decentralize decision making, Dean Applegate emphasized organizational interdependence. The dean recognized his limitations as a leader and supported an innovative, less traditional approach to change where roles and boundaries were blurred. He behaved as a shepherd and committed himself to new ways of influencing change—in this case through small groups, committee decisions, and open communication. A direct result of the collectivism that was emphasized was learning, which is also characteristic of chaos and complexity theories. Because the admissions personnel had to learn the different aspects of the various jobs in their division, skills and knowledge were exchanged among staff members.

Phone operators, who had always been taken for granted, experienced newfound respect from their colleagues for their tact and communication skills with angry, frustrated, and often disgruntled callers. Support staff, who coordinated events and travel schedules, were also appreciated more fully as administrators and counselors realized the intricacies and complex time-management challenges involved in running the division. Admissions officers, often considered the high-maintenance darlings of the division, also experienced newfound appreciation from their colleagues, who discovered their stamina and ability to perform many tasks under pressure. Before sharing their tasks, none of the personnel interacted with each other, and consequently there was no sense of collegiality in the admissions division. Since the new initiatives were implemented, the entire division works in a collectivist fashion, with individuals supporting each other in many innovative cross-collaborations. Overall the admissions staff realized the importance of their interdependence, which greatly increased their productivity. Although staff members do not need to interact with each other as much as they used to as a result of the convenience of electronic files, the admissions division now operates as one whole unit with many linked parts.

Institutional Dilemma

A major challenge facing UPD lies in the School of Engineering. Because of its reputation as one of the top engineering programs in the nation, UPD has one of the most prestigious faculties in the world, including a former astronaut and two Nobel Laureates. A strong international presence is apparent in both faculty and students; however, representation of minorities and women remains low. In the campus community the UPD School of Engineering is considered among the most rigid, traditional, and closed to outside influences. Because of its success, however, the chancellor and board of regents have allowed the school a tremendous amount of autonomy and respect. In recent years it has become evident that gender inequity exists among both students and faculty in the School of Engineering. Of the school's eighty faculty members, for example, only four are women and only one of them has received tenure. Among students, less than 5 percent of engineering students are women, even though 54 percent of undergraduates are women. Aside from their low representation, female students and faculty also do not share in the same level of research grants and lab space as their male counterparts. Recent comments by students and administrators have called attention to this equity gap.

Analytical Questions

1. In what ways could complexity or chaos theories be applied to address issues of gender inequity at the UPD School of Engineering?
2. Specifically, how can the traits of these theories such as collectivism, flexibility, decentralization, and adaptability be applied?
3. Because chaos theory suggests that replicated patterns underlie organizations, would it be necessary for UPD to assess its overall treatment of gender equity in other departments and the entire campus? Or is this an instance of extreme gender inequity in the School of Engineering?
4. How would complexity theory be used to answer this question?
5. Identify how the concept of fractals from chaos theory relates to the institutionalization of gender equity.

Case Study Two
Quaker College: Collegiality, Culture, and Tradition

Institutional Background

Quaker College (QC) is a small private liberal arts college situated in a tiny bucolic college town known for its pleasant environment and Quaker legacy. Because of its proximity to the center of town, most administrators, faculty, and students live within walking distance of campus. The pace of the town and the college is slow and mellow. Although very productive and efficient, the campus community keeps the hustle and bustle of everyday life at a minimum. Above all, this community prides itself on its friendly atmosphere and on the fact that everyone knows everybody else on a first-name basis.

After more than a century of male presidents, Quaker College has just elected its first female president, Martha Riley. As a respected academic and the former president of a prominent liberal arts college in the East, President Williams brings with her a legacy of prestige. In fact, one reason she was selected was the community's desire to promote its image and recognition nationally. One way President Williams would like to do it is through new public relations strategies intended to promote the hidden virtues of the college. An important source of support for President Williams is the faculty at the college led by Bob Montgomery, president of the faculty senate. Aside from heading the search for the new president, Professor Montgomery also serves as dean of student services and plays a central role in the university administration.

A primary agenda item for President Williams is fundraising. In recent years admissions numbers have been low, which is problematic because this college relies to a great deal on tuition revenue. In an effort to recruit full-paying students who do not require financial aid from the college and at the suggestion of a committee spearheaded by Dean Montgomery, the admissions office has started to recruit students internationally. As a result, in recent years the campus has seen an increase in affluent international students from Asia, Africa, and Europe who are seeking an American college education. Another significant trend at QC is a shift in local demographics. Although this college has traditionally served a predominantly white student population, in recent years it has admitted many Latino students who are the children of local farm workers. Both these trends have transformed the landscape and population of QC into a majority minority campus where diversity is palpable.

In preparation for the arrival of President Williams, Dean Montgomery and the faculty senate held a retreat where they developed their campus vision and mission statements. By creating these documents, the faculty hoped to assist the new president in her transition and in understanding their community and culture. Two themes that emerged during the retreat were the need to capitalize on and promote their newfound diversity and the need to embrace the academic middle (the level at which QC students perform). Often the students were not admitted to more competitive institutions or have generally struggled in their academic endeavors. At QC these students thrive because of the individualized attention they receive, which is a hallmark of the institution.

During the first official meeting with a small group of high-level campus administrators, President Williams expressed her excitement to be at Quaker College and at the potential for change. She also took the opportunity to introduce some important ideas she had developed with the board of trustees. First, she explained they had decided it would be good for the school's image to update recruitment publications and use a high-end New York–based company known for its skill in institutional image transformation. The president and trustees also expressed a desire to rise in the national rankings and increase student selectivity. One way of doing so would be to attract a higher caliber of faculty and students to breathe life into what they suggested might be considered an unexciting college atmosphere. After this meeting, Dean Montgomery was confronted with a number of comments from fellow administrators about the new president's "cutting edge" and "innovative" ideas. Roughly translated in the context of QC, faculty and administrators were expressing their concerns about the changes discussed.

Theoretical Analysis

This case exemplifies the significance of cultural and symbolic theories. One of the central tenets of cultural leadership is the alignment and sensitivity of leadership with the campus culture. In this case President Williams did not behave in ways that acknowledged the deeply rooted culture of QC. Instead of considering the collegial context of the college, she proceeded in ways that were countercultural and unnatural to this community. Because a big part of cultural leadership is the fact that different leadership styles work for different types of institutions, President Williams needed to understand the new college better before unveiling her agenda. By not interpreting the symbolism and meaning embedded in the QC campus culture and not considering its rich historical context, President Williams alienated many key constituents such as Dean Montgomery. A more effective approach from the perspective of cultural and symbolic theories would have been less hierarchical and more inspirational ideas. By taking the time to work with the community and engage people in this process, President Williams had the potential to inspire the campus and build morale and loyalty.

Another problem that directly related to not using a cultural or symbolic approach was her inability to understand the campus culture's needs and desires. What President Williams mistook to be a desire for a new campus image and identity was actually QC's desire to embrace and celebrate its community legacy and whom they have become. By publicly touting diversity and individualized student attention, QC was setting itself apart from its competitors. Rather than change its image, President Williams would have been better off borrowing from the most recent mission statement, which described QC as "a campus family committed to accepting and supporting all individuals in their pursuit of their hopes and dreams."

Institutional Dilemma

Another significant challenge facing President Williams and administrators is a movement led by a group of students frustrated by QC's current and limited curriculum. Because most students pay full tuition, they feel entitled as consumers to a broader variety of general education courses. The current curriculum focuses on many traditional literature and philosophy courses that have been the mainstay of QC courses for decades. The new diversified student body is more interested in courses they can relate to with more global and practical scopes. Specific classes that have been requested include information technology, international business, Chicano literature, and a course on postmodernism. Although these subjects are mentioned in a few of the current courses, they do not receive the attention these students feel is necessary. The QC student senate supports adding to the curriculum and has passed a senate bill requesting curricular reform at QC.

Analytical Questions

1. How can administrators at QC address curricular reform in a collegial but transformative process?
2. Based on cultural and symbolic theories, what roles do the backgrounds and histories of the current student population (international, working class, and multiethnic) play in their requests for additional courses?

3. What strategy or approach would be useful for administrators invited to speak about curricular reform in front of the student senate?
4. Because of QC's strong community emphasis, if the president and Dean Montgomery were to form a committee to address this issue, who should be invited to serve on the committee, or how should it be structured?
5. In what ways should this issue be presented to faculty, particularly those who have had courses cut as a result of budgetary constraints?

Another Institutional Dilemma

Before the arrival of the new president, a team of administrators representing different parts of campus were invited to form an assessment committee to support the professor who serves the campus as an institutional researcher. The goal of this committee was to evaluate the performance of students to identify weaknesses and areas for improvement as well as strengths to build on. Using the data, this committee is also to propose benchmarks for improvement and identify areas that can be used to better market QC. The committee is to present its work in a formal report to the president at a public meeting traditionally attended by the whole campus community. Professor Shah, a math professor and head of institutional research, has recently participated in a number of workshops related to data-based organizational change where new and innovative measurements and techniques have been employed. Using these techniques to guide her committee, she had administrators collect, analyze, and discuss data for over a year. The findings were surprising and presented the committee with a challenge. Although committee members were aware of the success of international students across the board, the new data indicated that affluent domestic students who did not receive any financial aid, particularly white males, were performing the worst of any students. Also surprising was the fact that many first-generation working class students, particularly Latina women, outperformed all other students in grades and time to degree completion. The reason it is a problem is that QC focuses on increasing the population that performs the worst (white males who pay full tuition) and has limited resources to provide financial aid for the population that performs the best (working class students who need financial aid). The shocking and indisputable data are also problematic because the information is not appropriate for the public presentation the committee is scheduled to make in one month.

Analytical Questions

1. From the standpoint of cultural and symbolic theory, rituals such as the public reading of the report are important. How should administrators handle this situation? Should they make a public presentation? If so, how much of the information should they report, knowing the QC culture and the context of the data?
2. If the report is presented, who should present it—the committee or higher-ranking administrators?
3. For a tightly knit and traditional community like QC, what are the implications of these findings?
4. In light of the new president's initial misunderstanding of the QC culture, how should these data be presented to her and the board of trustees?
5. In what ways can these data be used effectively in QC's cultural context to produce change and improve student outcomes?

Case Study Three
Green River Community College: A Different Kind of Leadership

Institutional Background

Green River Community College (GRCC) is a modest campus located in a suburban setting. Established as a land-grant institution, GRCC is one of a handful of two-year colleges that feeds into the state university system. This medium-sized college serves approximately eleven thousand students, many of whom are nontraditional students, and as a result has a strong technical component. One of the finer attributes of GRCC is its culinary certificate program, which is known for its annual food fair. GRCC is known as a good place to work because of its highly paid administrative and teaching positions. In fact, many faculty members have remained there longer than anticipated because of their high salaries, making job openings at GRCC scarce and highly coveted. It is also well known that the students are not academically well prepared. Because many instructors are jaded, they often blame the students for their mediocre academic achievement and constantly question their work ethic and intellectual aptitude. The more successful faculty at GRCC are those who feel sorry for the students and acknowledge their efforts to get ahead.

One anomaly of an education at GRCC is Vince Lopez, a GRCC alumnus and current adjunct music and math instructor. When not playing classical guitar at restaurants and clubs in the evenings, Vince teaches music history, precalculus, and statistics. After two years at GRCC, this single father, who put himself through school by working nights, transferred to the local four-year college, where he graduated with dual degrees in classical guitar and music education. Inspired by his educational experiences, Vince worked for a master's degree in math and is pursuing an Ed.D. with an emphasis in math education.

In his first two years of teaching at GRCC, Vince was surprised by the potential and intellectual curiosity of some of his students. Contrary to everything he had been told by other instructors, many of the students were similar to him when he was at GRCC—committed to learning but lacking guidance and social capital. Another phenomenon Vince realized were the persistent gatekeeping practices, which had also existed when he was a student. It was particularly true in the math department, where most of the faculty considered it their duty to weed out students who do not excel in math. Because of such attitudes, very few students ever make it to higher-level math courses—especially calculus, which is required of all students who want to transfer to premed or engineering departments at four-year universities. In response to the frustration expressed by some of his students, Vince designated Tuesday nights as a study hall where he tutors any student interested in statistics, precalculus, and calculus. After four months of Tuesday night study halls filled with students, Vince tried to convince other instructors to donate their time to tutor more students. None would do it unless they were paid. As a result, Vince went to the administration with some of the newest research on math remediation, which emphasized the importance of tutoring, and requested additional resources and funding. He explained his interest in tutoring students as something to build his résumé and as a first step in obtaining grant money for GRCC. By devoting time and resources to teaching underserved populations in math, Vince explained, he had a better chance of getting state grant money earmarked for math remediation. Because of his research for his doctoral degree and experience in the field of math education, the administrators were convinced of Vince's credibility and decided to fund an additional adjunct position to help him. Two years after the addition of this position, GRCC math students tripled their transfer rates into four-year colleges, especially into premed and engineering departments.

Theoretical Analysis

In this case Vince illustrates cognitive theory and organizational learning. He presents his ideas using visionary framing, which indicated his ability to see the potential in his students and their futures. He was strategic about his approach with administrators because he had the advantage of assuming multiple cognitive frames. Aside from being a current instructor, he was a former GRCC student, a former transfer student, a researcher, and, like many students at GRCC, a working-class person of color. He understood the complexity behind why many students are not more successful in math and could reframe the issues in such a way that appealed to administrators incapable of appreciating students' positions. Another use of cognitive frames was his ability to understand what mattered most to the administrators and key decision makers at GRCC—the fiscal bottom line. He realized that by appearing to be self-interested in his intentions and explaining the advantage of possible grant money, administrators would more likely buy into his plan than if he went to them asking for money because students were allegedly underserved. In this case he aligned his endeavor with the broader institutional culture, which was not student centered. Because his previous attempts using the sympathetic approach failed to garner resources, Vince learned that a new approach and fundraising strategy were necessary. A characteristic of organizational learning is individuals' learning from their mistakes. Thus, Vince knew better than to go directly to the math department, and he knew better than to appeal sentimentally to the administration. Moreover, he used data in his strategy. Equipped with quantitative research studies and fresh institutional data, Vince was able to achieve his objectives. After some quantitative data analysis, Vince was finally able to dispel many institutional myths about the inability of GRCC students to succeed in math.

Institutional Dilemma

Other gatekeeping practices many of his students experienced were poor transfer counseling and institutional discouragement. The counseling staff, which consists of only two people for eight thousand students, does not actively encourage students to transfer to other schools. Many students who ask about transferring to a four-year college after fulfilling their general education requirements are told they should stay and take their electives. As a result, students often complete more units than the four-year colleges are willing to accept. Thus, students waste their limited resources and precious time in taking courses they will have to repeat when they are able to transfer elsewhere. Another mythology perpetuated by the GRCC counselors is that students of GRCC who have a chance of being admitted to a four-year school will not be able to afford tuition. Because they do not want to set up students for disappointment, both counselors and many faculty have learned to tell students to limit their choices to the least expensive public colleges. These myths pose additional problems for Vince's math students, who are already preoccupied with overcoming other institutional hurdles.

Analytical Questions

1. Using a cognitive theory approach, in what ways can student advocates like Vince address institutional gatekeeping practices and mythologies?
2. Is it possible for students at GRCC to produce organizational learning? If so, how? If not, why not?
3. Name some of the cognitive frames that might be used to deconstruct these campus myths. What specific cognitive processes or thoughts must be examined?
4. What institutional resources could be employed to assist in organizational learning in this case?
5. What is it about the context and leadership of GRCC that allows gatekeeping practices and false assumptions to be perpetuated?

References

Adler, N. J. (2001a). Conclusion: Future issues in global leadership development. In M. E. Mendenhall, T. M. Kuhlmann, and G. K. Stahl (Eds.), *Developing global business leaders: Policies, processes, and innovations* (pp. 255–271). Westport, CT: Quorum Books.

Adler, N. J. (2001b). Global leadership: Women leaders. In M. E. Mendenhall, T. M. Kuhlmann, and G. K. Stahl (Eds.), *Developing global business leaders: Policies, processes, and innovations* (pp. 73–97). Westport, CT: Quorum Books.

Aguirre, A., Jr., and Martinez, R. O. (2002). Leadership practices and diversity in higher education: Transitional and transformational frameworks. *Journal of Leadership Studies, 8*(3), 53–62.

Ah Chong, L. M., and Thomas, D. C. (1997). Leadership perceptions in cross-cultural context: Pakeha and Pacific Islanders in New Zealand. *The Leadership Quarterly, 8*(3), 275–293.

Allen, K. E., and Cherrey, C. (2000). *Systemic leadership: Enriching the meaning of our work.* Lanham, MD: University Press of America.

Alston, J. A. (2002). *Multi-leadership in urban schools: Shifting paradigms for administration and supervision in the new millennium.* Lanham, MD: University Press of America.

American Association of Higher Education, American College Personnel Association, and National Association of Student Personnel Administrators. (1998). *Powerful partnerships: A shared responsibility for learning. A joint report.* Washington, DC: American College Personnel Association. (ED 441 195)

Amey, M. J. (1991, April). *Constructive/development theory and leadership: A question of perceived leadership.* Paper presented at an annual meeting of the American Educational Research Association, Chicago, IL. (ED 333 539)

Amey, M. J., and Twombley, S. B. (1992). Re-visioning leadership in community colleges. *Review of Higher Education, 15*(2), 125–150.

Anderson, P. (1999). Complexity theory and organization science. *Organization Science, 10*(3), 216–232.

Antonakis, J., Avolio, B. J., and Sivasubramaniam, N. (2003). Context and leadership: An examination of the nine-factor full-range leadership theory using the multifactor leadership questionnaire. *The Leadership Quarterly, 14*(3), 261–295.

Arminio, J. L., and others. (2000). Leadership experiences of students of color. *NASPA Journal, 37*(3), 496–510.

Aronson, E. (2001). Integrating leadership styles and ethical perspectives. *Canadian Journal of Administrative Sciences, 18*(4), 244–256.

Ashcroft, B., Griffiths, G., and Tiffin, H. (Eds.). (1995). *The post-colonial studies reader.* New York: Routledge.

Aspland, T., Macpherson, I., Brooker, R., and Elliott, B. (1998, April). *Establishing and sustaining a critical and reconstructive network of engagement in and about curriculum leadership through the use of narrative and conversation.* Paper presented at an annual meeting of the American Educational Research Association, San Diego, CA. (ED 420 643)

Astin, A. W. (1996). The role of service in higher education. *About Campus, 1*(1), 14–19.

Astin, A. W., and Astin, H. S. (Eds.). (2000). *Leadership reconsidered: Engaging higher education in social change.* Battle Creek, MI: W. K. Kellogg Foundation.

Astin, H. S. (1996). Leadership for social change. *About Campus,* 4–10.

Astin, H. S., and Leland, C. (1991). *Women of influence, women of vision.* San Francisco: Jossey-Bass.

Avolio, B. J., and Bass, B. M. (1991). The full range of leadership development. Binghamton, NY: Center for Leadership Studies, Binghamton University, State University of New York.

Avolio, B. J., and Gardner, W. L. (2005). Authentic leadership development: Getting to the root of positive forms of leadership. *The Leadership Quarterly, 16*(3), 315–338.

Axelrod, R., and Cohen, M. D. (1999). *Harnessing complexity: Organizational implications of a scientific frontier.* New York: Free Press.

Ayman, R. (1993). Leadership perception: The role of gender and culture. In M. M. Chemers and R. Ayman (Eds.), *Leadership theory and research: Perspectives and directions* (pp. 137–166). San Diego: Academic Press.

Banks, C.A.M. (1995). Gender and race as factors in educational leadership and administration. In J. A. Banks and C.A.M. Banks (Eds.), *Handbook of research on multicultural education* (2nd ed., pp. 65–80). New York: Macmillan.

Banta, T. W., and Moffett, M. S. (1987). Performance funding in Tennessee: Stimulus for program improvement. In D. F. Halpern (Ed.), *Student outcomes assessment: What institutions stand to gain.* New Directions for Higher Education, no. 59. San Francisco: Jossey-Bass.

Barker, R. A. (2001). The nature of leadership. *Human Relations, 54*(4), 469–494.

Barker, R. A. (2002). *On the nature of leadership.* New York: University Press of America.

Basinger, J. (2002). Casting a wider net. Colleges are more likely to find presidents outside academe; Most chiefs are still white men. *Chronicle of Higher Education, 49*(16), A32.

Bass, B. M. (1985). *Leadership and performance beyond expectations.* New York: Free Press.

Bass, B. M. (1997). The ethics of transformational leadership. In Kellogg Leadership Studies Project (Ed.), *KLSP: Transformational leadership working papers* (pp. 89–119). College Park, MD: Academy of Leadership Press.

Bass, B. M., and Steidlmeier, P. (1999). Ethics, character, and authentic transformational leadership behavior. *The Leadership Quarterly, 10*(2), 181–217.

Beatty, B. R. (2000). The emotions of educational leadership: Breaking the silence. *International Journal of Leadership in Education, 3*(4), 331–357.

Bell, B. S., and Kozlowski, S.W.J. (2002). A typology of virtual teams: Implications for effective leadership. *Group and Organization Management, 27,* 14–49.

Bell, C. S. (1988). Organizational influences on women's experience in the superintendency. *Peabody Journal of Education, 65*(4), 31–59.

Bennis, W. G., and Goldsmith, J. (1997). *Learning to lead: A workbook on becoming a leader.* Reading, MA: Perseus Books.

Bensimon, E. M. (1989a). A feminist reinterpretation of presidents' definitions of leadership. *Peabody Journal of Education, 66*(3), 143–156.

Bensimon, E. M. (1989b). The meaning of "good presidential leadership": A frame analysis. *Review of Higher Education, 12*(2), 107–123.

Bensimon, E. M. (1990). Viewing the presidency: Perceptual congruence between presidents and leaders on their campuses. *The Leadership Quarterly, 1*(2), 71–90.

Bensimon, E. M. (1993). New presidents' initial actions: Transactional and transformational leadership. *Journal for Higher Education Management, 8*(2), 5–17.

Bensimon, E. M. (2005). *Equality as a fact, equality as a result: A matter of institutional accountability.* Washington, DC: American Council on Education.

Bensimon, E. M., and Neumann, A. (1993). *Redesigning collegiate leadership: Teams and teamwork in higher education.* Baltimore: Johns Hopkins University Press.

Bensimon, E. M., Neumann, A., and Birnbaum, R. (1989). *Making sense of administrative leadership: The "L" word in higher education.* ASHE-ERIC Higher Education Report. Washington, DC: School of Education, George Washington University.

Bergquist, W. H. (1992). *The four cultures of the academy: Insights and strategies for improving leadership in collegiate organizations.* San Francisco: Jossey-Bass.

Bergquist, W. H. (1993). *The postmodern organization: Mastering the art of irreversible change.* San Francisco: Jossey-Bass.

Birnbaum, R. (1986). Leadership and learning: The college president as intuitive scientist. *Review of Higher Education, 9*(4), 381–395.

Birnbaum, R. (1988). *How colleges work: The cybernetics of academic organization and leadership.* San Francisco: Jossey-Bass.

Birnbaum, R. (1989). The implicit leadership theories of college and university presidents. *Review of Higher Education, 12*(2), 125–36.

Birnbaum, R. (1992). *How academic leadership works: Understanding success and failure in the college presidency.* San Francisco: Jossey-Bass.

Birnbaum, R. (2000). Management fads in higher education: Where they come from, what they do, why they fail. San Francisco: Jossey-Bass.

Blackmore, J. (1999). *Troubling women: Feminism, leadership, and educational change.* Buckingham, UK: Open University Press.

Bolman, L. G., and Deal, T. E. (1995). *Leading with soul: An uncommon journey of spirit.* San Francisco: Jossey-Bass.

Bolman, L. G., and Deal, T. E. (2003). *Reframing organizations: Artistry, choice, and leadership* (3rd ed.). San Francisco: Jossey-Bass.

Bowyer, K. A. (1992). Business and community linkages. In G. B. Vaughan (Ed.), *Dilemmas of leadership: Decision making and ethics in the community college.* San Francisco: Jossey-Bass.

Bradford, D. L., and Cohen, A. R. (1998). *Power up: Transforming organizations through shared leadership.* San Francisco: John Wiley & Sons, Inc.

Brown, C. R., and Mazza, G. J. (1997). *Healing into action: A leadership guide for creating diverse communities.* Washington, DC: National Coalition Building Institute.

Brown-Wright, D. (1996, May). *A qualitative/quantitative analysis of the Administrative Management Institute at Cornell University.* Paper presented at an annual meeting of the Ohio Academy of Science, Canton, OH. (ED 400 740)

Burbules, N. C., and Torres, C. A. (Eds.). (2000). *Globalization and education: Critical perspectives.* New York: Routledge.

Burns, J. M. (1978). *Leadership.* New York: Harper & Row.

Calas, M. B., and Smircich, L. (1992). Re-writing gender into organizational theorizing: Directions from feminist perspectives. In M. Reed and M. D. Hughes (Eds.), *Rethinking organization: New directions in organizational theory and analysis* (pp. 97–117). Beverly Hills, CA: Sage.

Cantor, D. W., and Bernay, T. (1992). *Women in power: The secrets of leadership.* New York: Houghton Mifflin.

Carroll, J. B., and Gmelch, W. H. (1992). *The relationship of department chair roles to importance of chair duties.* Paper presented at an annual meeting of the Association for the Study of Higher Education, Minneapolis, MN. (ED 352 910)

Caruso, D. R., and Salovey, P. (2004). *The emotionally intelligent manager: How to develop and use the four key emotional skills of leadership.* San Francisco: Jossey-Bass.

Chaffee, E. E. (1984). Successful strategic management in small private colleges. *Journal of Higher Education, 55*(2), 212–241.

Chaffee, E. E., and Tierney, W. G. (1988). *Collegiate culture and leadership strategies.* Washington, DC: American Council on Education.

Chemers, M. M. (1997). *An integrative theory of leadership.* Mahwah, NJ: Lawrence Erlbaum Associates.

Chemers, M. M., and Ayman, R. (1993). *Leadership theory and research: Perspectives and directions.* San Diego: Academic Press.

Chermak, G. D. (1990). Cultural dynamics: Principles to guide change in higher education. *CUPA Journal, 41*(3), 25–27.

Chliwniak, L. (1997). *Higher education leadership: Analyzing the gender gap.* ASHE-ERIC Higher Education Report, Vol. 25, No. 4. Washington, DC: Graduate School of Education and Human Development, George Washington University.

Ciulla, J. B. (Ed.). (1998). *Ethics, the heart of leadership.* Westport, CT: Quorum Books.

Cohen, M. D., and March, J. G. (1974). *Leadership and ambiguity: The American college president.* New York: McGraw-Hill.

Conger, J., and others. (1994). *Spirit at work: Discovering the spirituality in leadership.* San Francisco: Jossey-Bass.

Conger, J. A., and Kanungo, R. N. (1988). The empowerment process: Integrating theory and practice. *The Academy of Management Review, 13*(3), 471–482.

Connors, R., Smith, T., and Hickman, C. (1994). *The Oz principle: Getting results through individual and organizational accountability.* Englewood Cliffs, NJ: Prentice Hall.

Cooper, J. E., and Ideta, L. M. (1994). *Dealing with difference: Maps and metaphors of leadership in higher education.* Paper presented at an annual meeting of the Association for the Study of Higher Education, Tucson, AZ.

Cornwall, J. R. (2003). *From the ground up: Entrepreneurial school leadership.* Lanham, MD: Scarecrow Press.

Cox, T., Jr. (1993). *Cultural diversity in organizations: Theory, research, and practice.* San Francisco: Berrett-Koehler.

Crosby, B. C. (1999). *Leadership for global citizenship: Building transnational community.* Thousand Oaks, CA: Sage.

Crotty, M. (1998). *The foundations of social research: Meaning and perspective in the research process.* Thousand Oaks, CA: Sage.

Currie, J. (1998). Globalization practices and the professoriate in Anglo-Pacific and North American universities [electronic version]. *Comparative Education Review, 42*(1), 15–29. Retrieved December 3, 2003.

Currie, J., and Newson, J. (Eds.). (1998). *Universities and globalization: Critical perspectives.* Thousand Oaks, CA: Sage.

Currie, J., and Vidovich, L. (1998). Micro-economic reform through managerialism in American and Australian universities. In J. Currie and J. Newson (Eds.), *Universities and globalization: Critical perspectives* (pp. 153–172). Thousand Oaks, CA: Sage.

Curry, B. K. (1992). *Instituting enduring innovations: Achieving continuity of change in higher education.* ASHE-ERIC Higher Education Report, No. 7. Washington, DC: School of Education and Human Development, George Washington University.

Cutright, M. (Ed.). (2001). *Chaos theory and higher education: Leadership, planning, and policy.* New York: Peter Lang Publishing.

Daughtery, L. H., and Finch, C. R. (1997). Effective leadership of vocational administrators as a function of gender and leadership style. *Journal of Vocational Education Research, 22*(3), 173–186.

Dawson, P. (1994). *Organizational change: A processual approach.* London: Paul Chapman Publishing.

Day, D. V., Gronn, P., and Salas, E. (2004). Leadership capacity in teams. *The Leadership Quarterly, 15*(6), 857–880.

Deal, T. E., and Peterson, K. D. (1999). *Shaping school culture: The heart of leadership.* San Francisco: Jossey-Bass.

Deem, R. (1998). New managerialism and higher education: The management of performances and cultures in universities in the United Kingdom. *International Studies in Sociology of Education, 8*(1), 47–70.

Deem, R. (2001). Globalization, new managerialism, academic capitalism, and entrepreneurialism in universities: Is the local dimension still important? *Corporate Education, 37*(1), 7–20.

Den Hartog, D. N., and others. (1999). Culture specific and cross-culturally generalizable implicit leadership theories: Are attributes of charismatic/transformational leadership universally endorsed? *The Leadership Quarterly, 10*(2), 219–256.

Depree, M. (1989). *Leadership is an art.* New York: Doubleday.

Depree, M. (1992). *Leadership jazz.* New York: Doubleday.

Dess, G. G., and others. (2003). Emerging issues in corporate entrepreneurship. *Journal of Management, 29*(3), 351–378.

Dever, J. T. (1997). Reconciling educational leadership and the learning organization. *Community College Review, 25*(2), 57–63.

Diamond, R. M. (Ed.). (2002). *Field guide to academic leadership.* San Francisco: Jossey-Bass.

Dickson, M. W., Den Hartog, D. N., and Mitchelson, J. K. (2003). Research on leadership in a cross-cultural context: Making progress, and raising new questions. *The Leadership Quarterly, 14*(6), 729–768.

Dickson, M. W., Smith, D. B., Grojean, M. W., and Ehrhart, M. (2001). An organizational climate regarding ethics: The outcome of leader values and the practices that reflect them. *The Leadership Quarterly, 12*(2), 197–217.

Dorfman, P. W. (1996). International and cross-cultural leadership research. In B. J. Punnett and O. Shenkar (Ed.), *Handbook for international management research* (pp. 267–349). Cambridge, MA: Blackwell.

Druskat, V. U., and Wheeler, J. V. (2004). How to lead self-managing teams. *MIT Sloan Management Review, 45*(4), 65–71.

Duncan, P. K., and Skarstad, K. (1995, October). *How women administrators are perceived by others: A case study examining the relationship between leadership temperament, use of power, and success.* Paper presented at an annual meeting of the Mid-Western Educational Research Association, Chicago, IL. (ED 417 485)

Eddy, P. L. (2003, April). *The influence of presidential cognition and power on framing change at community colleges.* Paper presented at an annual meeting of the American Educational Research Association, Chicago, IL. (ED 480 123)

Edmondson, A., Bohmer, R., and Pisano, G. (2001). Speeding up team learning. *Harvard Business Review, 79*(9), 125–132.

Eggert, N. J. (1998). *Contemplative leadership for entrepreneurial organizations: Paradigms, metaphors, and wicked problems.* Westport, CT: Quorum Books.

Ensari, N., and Murphy, S. E. (2003). Cross-cultural variations in leadership perceptions and attribution of charisma to the leader. *Organizational Behavior and Human Decision Processes, 92*(1–2), 52–66.

Entrialgo, M., Fernandez, E., and Vazquez, C. J. (2000). Linking entrepreneurship and strategic management: Evidence from Spanish SMEs. *Technovation, 20*(8), 427–436.

Erb, M. J. (1991, May). Making-sense of "participation": An exploratory study of the relationship between leadership and the sense-making process of subordinates. Paper presented at an annual meeting of the International Communication Association, Chicago, IL. (ED 335 723)

Fagin, C. M. (1997). The leadership role of a dean. New Directions for Higher Education, no. 25. San Francisco: Jossey-Bass.

Fairholm, G. W. (2001). *Mastering inner leadership.* Westport, CT: Quorum Books.

Ferguson, K. E. (1984). *The feminist case against bureaucracy.* Philadelphia: Temple University Press.

Ferren, A. S., and Stanton, W. W. (2004). *Leadership through collaboration: The role of the chief academic officer.* Westport, CT: Praeger.

Fiedler, F. E. (1997). Situational control and a dynamic theory of leadership. In K. Grint (Ed.), *Leadership: Classical, contemporary, and critical approaches.* Oxford: Oxford University Press.

Fisher, J. L., and Koch, J. V. (1996). *Presidential leadership: Making a difference.* Phoenix, AZ: Oryx Press.

Fisher, J. L., and Koch, J. V. (2004). *The entrepreneurial college president.* Westport, CT: Praeger.

Fisher, J. L., Tack, M. W., and Wheeler, K. J. (1988). *The effective college president.* New York: American Council on Education/Macmillan.

French, J.R.P., and Raven, B. (1959). The bases of social power. In D. Cartwright (Ed.), *Studies in social power.* Ann Arbor: Institute for Social Research, University of Michigan.

Gardner, H. (1993). *Multiple intelligences: The theory in practice.* New York: Basic Books.

Garner, R. (2004). *Contesting the terrain of the ivory tower: Spiritual leadership of African American women in the academy.* New York: Routledge.

Gayle, D. J., Tewarie, B., and White, A. Q., Jr. (2003). *Governance in the twenty-first-century university: Approaches to effective leadership and strategic management.* Washington, DC: Office of Educational Research and Improvement. (ED 482 560)

Gerstner, C. R., and Day, D. V. (1994). Cross-cultural comparison of leadership prototypes. *The Leadership Quarterly, 5*(2), 121–134.

Gillett-Karam, R. (2001). Community college leadership: Perspectives of women as presidents. *Community College Journal of Research and Practice, 25*(3), 167–170.

Glazer-Raymo, J. (1999). *Shattering the myths: Women in academe.* Baltimore: Johns Hopkins University Press.

Gmelch, W. H., and Burns, J. S. (1993). The cost of academic leadership: Department chair stress. *Innovative Higher Education, 17*(4), 259–270.

Gmelch, W. H., and Wolverton, M. (2002, April). *An investigation of dean leadership.* Paper presented at an annual meeting of the American Educational Research Association, New Orleans, LA. (ED 465 343)

Goldsmith, M., Greenberg, C. L., Robertson, A., and Hu-Chan, M. (2003). *Global leadership: The next generation.* Upper Saddle River, NJ: Prentice Hall.

Goleman, D. (1995). *Emotional intelligence.* New York: Bantam Books.

Goleman, D. (1998). *Working with emotional intelligence.* New York: Bantam Books.

Gordon, J. U. (2000). *Black leadership for social change.* Westport, CT: Greenwood Press.

Greenleaf, R. K. (1977). *Servant leadership: A journey into the nature of legitimate power and greatness.* New York: Paulist Press.

Griffin, D. (2002). *The emergence of leadership: Linking self-organization and ethics.* London: Routledge.

Grint, K. (Ed.). (1997). *Leadership: Classical, contemporary, and critical approaches.* New York: Oxford University Press.

Guido-DiBrito, F. (1995). Student affairs leadership and loyalty: Organizational dynamics at play. *NASPA Journal, 32*(3), 223–231.

Hackman, J. R. (1990). Work teams in organizations: An orienting framework. In J. R. Hackman (Ed.), *Groups that work (and those that don't): Creating conditions for effective teamwork.* San Francisco: Jossey-Bass.

Handy, C. (1996). *Beyond certainty: The changing worlds of organizations.* Boston: Harvard Business School Press.

Hargrove, E. C., and Owens, J. E. (Eds.). (2003). *Leadership in context.* Lanham, MD: Rowman & Littlefield.

Harrison, R. T., and Leitch, C. M. (1994). Entrepreneurship and leadership: The implications for education and development. *Entrepreneurship and Regional Development, 6,* 111–125.

Hart, J. (2003, April). *Mobilization among women academics: The interplay between feminism and the profession.* Paper presented at an annual meeting of the American Educational Research Association, Chicago, IL. (ED 478 752)

Heifetz, R. A. (1994). *Leadership without easy answers.* Cambridge: Belknap Press.

Heifetz, R. A., and Linsky, M. (2002). *Leadership on the line: Staying alive through the dangers of leading.* Boston: Harvard Business School Press.

Helgesen, S. (1990). *The female advantage: Women's ways of leadership.* New York: Doubleday.

Hertel, G., Geister, S., and Konradt, U. (2005). Managing virtual teams: A review of current empirical research. *Human Resource Management Review, 15*(1), 69–95.

Hesburgh, T. M. (Ed.). (1994). *The challenge and promise of a Catholic University.* Notre Dame: University of Notre Dame Press.

Higher Education Research Institute. (1996). *A social change model of leadership development, guidebook version III.* Los Angeles: Higher Education Research Institute.

Higher Education Research Institute. (2005). *Spirituality in higher education: A national study of college students' search for meaning and purpose.* Los Angeles: Higher Education Research Institute.

Hodgkinson, C. (1991). *Educational leadership: The moral act.* Albany: State University of New York Press.

Hofstede, G. (1980). *Culture's consequences: International differences in work-related values.* Beverly Hills: Sage.

Hofstede, G. H. (1997). *Cultures and organizations: Software of the mind.* New York: McGraw-Hill.

House, R. J., and others. (Eds.). (2004). *Culture, leadership, and organizations: The GLOBE study of 62 societies.* Thousand Oaks, CA: Sage.

House, R. J., Wright, N., and Aditya, R. N. (1997). Cross-cultural research on organizational leadership: A critical analysis and a proposed theory. In P.C. Earley and M. Erez (Eds.), *New perspectives on international industrial and organizational psychology.* San Francisco: Jossey-Bass.

Howard-Hamilton, M. F., and Ferguson, A. D. (1998, November). *Women students' leadership styles and practices.* Paper presented at an annual meeting of the Association for the Study of Higher Education, Miami, FL. (ED 427 595)

Hunt, J. G. (1991). *Leadership: A new synthesis.* Thousand Oaks, CA: Sage.

Ilgen, D. R., Major, D. A., Hollenbeck, J. R., and Sego, D. J. (1993). Team research in the 1990s. In M. M. Chemers and R. Ayman, (Eds.), *Leadership theory and research: Perspectives and directions* (pp. 245–271). San Diego: Academic Press.

Irby, B. J., and Brown, G. (1995, April). *Constructing a feminist-inclusive theory of leadership.* Paper presented at an annual meeting of the American Educational Research Association, San Francisco, CA. (ED 384 103)

Johnson, R. S. (1993, April). *Female and male faculty: Expectations and interpretations of presidential leadership in a research university.* Paper presented at an annual meeting of the American Educational Research Association, Atlanta, GA. (ED 362 080)

Kayworth, T. R., and Leidner, D. E. (2001/2002). Leadership effectiveness in global virtual teams. *Journal of Management Information Systems, 18*(3), 7–40.

Kekale, J. (2001). *Academic leadership.* New York: Nova Science Publishers.

Kelly, G. (1998). *Team leadership: Five interactive management adventures*. Aldershot, UK: Gower Publishing.

Kempner, K. (1989). Getting into the castle of educational administration. *Peabody Journal of Education, 66*(3), 104–123.

Kempner, K. (2003). The search for cultural leaders. *The Review of Higher Education, 26*(3), 363–385.

Kerr, C., and Gade, M. L. (1986). *The many lives of academic presidents: Time, place, and character*. Washington, DC: Association of Governing Boards of Universities and Colleges.

Kezar, A. (1998). Trying transformations: Implementing team-oriented forms of leadership. In S. Frost (Ed.), *Using teams in higher education: Cultural foundations for productive change*. New Directions for Institutional Research, no. 100. San Francisco: Jossey-Bass.

Kezar, A. (2000). Pluralistic leadership: Incorporating diverse voices. *Journal of Higher Education, 71*(6), 722–743.

Kezar, A. (2001a). Investigating organizational fit in a participatory leadership environment. *Journal of Higher Education Policy and Management, 23*(1), 85–102.

Kezar, A. (2001b). Theory of multiple intelligences: Implications for higher education. *Innovative Higher Education, 26*(2), 141–154.

Kezar, A. (2002a). Capturing the promise of collaborative leadership and becoming a pluralistic leader: Using case stories to transform beliefs. *Metropolitan Universities: An International Forum, 13*(2), 68–79.

Kezar, A. (2002b). Expanding notions of leadership to capture pluralistic voices: Positionality theory in practice. *Journal of College Student Development, 43*(4), 558–578.

Kezar, A. (2002c). Overcoming obstacles to change within urban institutions: The mobile framework and engaging institutional culture. *Metropolitan Universities: An International Forum, 13*(2), 95–103.

Kezar, A. (2002d). Reconstructing static images of leadership: An application of positionality theory. *The Journal of Leadership Studies, 8*(3), 94–109.

Kezar, A. (2003a). Achieving student success: Strategies for creating partnerships between academic and student affairs. *NASPA Journal, 41*(1), 1–22.

Kezar, A. (2003b). Enhancing innovative partnerships: Creating a change model for academic and student affairs collaboration. *Innovative Higher Education, 28*(2), 137–156.

Kezar, A. (2004, Fall). Philosophy, leadership, and scholarship: Confucian contributions to a leadership debate. *Leadership Review, 4*, 110–131.

Kezar, A. (2005a). Moving from I to we: Reorganizing for collaboration in higher education. *Change: The Magazine of Higher Learning, 37*(6), 50–57.

Kezar, A. (2005b). Redesigning for collaboration with higher education institutions: An exploration into the developmental process. *Research in Higher Education, 46*(7), 831–860.

Kezar, A. (forthcoming). Redesigning for collaboration in learning initiatives: An examination of four highly collaborative campuses. *The Journal of Higher Education*.

Kezar, A., and Eckel, P. (2002a). The effects of institutional culture on change strategies in higher education: Universal principles or culturally responsive concepts? *The Journal of Higher Education, 73*(4), 435–460.

Kezar, A., and Eckel, P. (2002b). Examining the institutional transformation process: The importance of sensemaking, interrelated strategies, and balance. *Research in Higher Education, 43*(4), 295–328.

Kezar, A., Hirsch, D. J., and Burack, C. (Eds.). (2002). *Understanding the role of academic and student affairs collaboration in creating a successful learning environment.* New Directions for Higher Education, no. 116. San Francisco: Jossey-Bass.

Kezar, A., and Moriarty, D. (2000). Expanding our understanding of student leadership development: A study exploring gender and ethnicity identity. *The Journal of College Student Development, 41*(1), 55–69.

Kinlaw, D. C. (1998). *Superior teams: What they are and how to develop them.* London: Gower.

Klenke, K. (1996). *Women and leadership: A contextual perspective.* New York: Springer.

Knudson, L. S. (1997, November). *Team leadership in three Midwestern community colleges: The president's cognitive frame of reference and its relationship to real versus illusory teams.* Paper presented at an annual meeting of the Association for the Study of Higher Education, Albuquerque, NM. (ED 415 802)

Komives, S. R. (1991a). The relationship of hall directors' transformational and transactional leadership to select resident assistant outcomes. *Journal of College Student Development, 32*(6), 509–515.

Komives, S. R. (1991b). The relationship of same- and cross-gender work pairs to staff performance and supervisor leadership in residence hall units. *Sex Roles: A Journal of Research, 24*(5–6), 355–363.

Komives, S. R. (1994). Women student leaders: Self-perceptions of empowering leadership and achieving style. *NASPA Journal, 31*(2), 102–112.

Komives, S. R., Lucas, N., and McMahon, T. R. (1998). *Exploring leadership: For college students who want to make a difference.* San Francisco: Jossey-Bass.

Komives, S. R., and others. (2005). Developing a leadership identity: A grounded theory. *Journal of College Student Development, 46*(6), 593–611.

Kouzes, J. M., and Posner, B. Z. (2002). *The leadership challenge* (3rd ed.). San Francisco: Jossey-Bass.

Kouzes, J. M., and Posner, B. Z. (2003). *The Jossey-Bass academic administrator's guide to exemplary leadership.* San Francisco: Jossey-Bass.

Kuhn, T. (1996). *The structure of scientific revolutions* (3rd ed.). Chicago: University of Chicago Press.

Kurke, L. B. (2004). *The wisdom of Alexander the Great: Enduring leadership lessons from the man who created an empire.* New York: American Management Association.

Kyle, D. T. (1998). *The four powers of leadership: Presence, intention, wisdom, compassion.* Deerfield Beach, FL: Health Communications.

LaFasto, F.M.J., and Larson, C. E. (2001). *When teams work best: 6000 team members and leaders tell what it takes to succeed.* Thousand Oaks, CA: Sage.

Lakomski, G. (2001). Organizational change, leadership and learning: Culture as cognitive process. *International Journal of Educational Management, 15*(2), 68–77.

Lakomski, G. (2005). *Managing without leadership: Towards a theory of organizational functioning.* Amsterdam: Elsevier.

Lambert, L., and others. (2002). *The constructivist leader* (2nd ed.). New York: Teachers College Press.

Larana, E., Johnston, H., and Gusfield, J. R. (Eds.). (1994). *New social movements: From ideology to identity.* Philadelphia: Temple University Press.

LaRocque, L., and Coleman, P. (1993). The politics of excellence: Trustee leadership and school district ethos. *Alberta Journal of Educational Research, 39*(4), 449–475.

Lerner, J. S., and Tetlock, P. E. (1999). Accounting for the effects of accountability. *Psychological Bulletin, 125*(2), 255–275.

Levin, J. S. (1998). Presidential influence, leadership succession, and multiple interpretations of organizational change. *Review of Higher Education, 21*(4), 405–425.

Levin, J. S. (2001). *Globalizing the community college: Strategies for change in the twenty-first century.* New York: Palgrave.

Lipman-Blumen, J. (1996). *The connective edge: Leading in an interdependent world.* San Francisco: Jossey-Bass.

Lipman-Blumen, J. (2000). *Connective leadership: Managing in a changing world.* Oxford: Oxford University Press.

Lipman-Blumen, J. (2004). *The allure of toxic leaders: Why we follow destructive bosses and corrupt politicians—and how we can survive them.* Oxford: Oxford University Press.

Longino, H. E. (1993). Feminist standpoint theory and the problems of knowledge. *Signs, 19*(1), 201–212.

Love, P. G., and Estanek, S. M. (2004). *Rethinking student affairs practice.* San Francisco: Jossey-Bass.

Lucas, A. F. (1994). *Strengthening departmental leadership: A team-building guide for chairs in colleges and universities.* The Jossey-Bass Higher and Adult Education Series. San Francisco: Jossey-Bass.

Marion, R. (1999). *The edge of organization: Chaos and complexity theories of formal social systems.* Thousand Oaks, CA: Sage.

Marion, R., and Uhl-Bien, M. (2001). Leadership in complex organizations. *The Leadership Quarterly, 12*(4), 389–418.

Martin, J. L. (1993, April). *Academic deans: An analysis of effective academic leadership at research universities.* Paper presented at an annual meeting of the American Educational Research Association, Atlanta, GA. (ED 362 079)

Martin, J., and Samels, J. E. (2003). Eight skills of highly effective new presidents. *Trusteeship, 11*(5), 8–12.

McCauley, C. D., and Van Velsor, E. (2003). *The center for creative leadership handbook of leadership development* (2nd ed.). San Francisco: Jossey-Bass.

McDade, S. A. (2004, November). *Relationship of undergraduate school experiences of college presidents to their leadership development.* Paper presented at an annual meeting of the Association for the Study of Higher Education, Kansas City, MO.

McKee, J. G. (1991). Leadership styles of community college presidents and faculty job satisfaction. *Community/Junior College Quarterly of Research and Practice, 15*(1), 33–46.

Mendenhall, M. E. (2001). Introduction: New perspectives on expatriate adjustment and its relationship to global leadership development. In M. E. Mendenhall, T. M. Kuhlmann, and G. K. Stahl (Eds.), *Developing global business leaders: Policies, processes, and innovation* (pp. 1–18). Westport, CT: Quorum Books.

Meyerson, D. E. (2003). *Tempered radicals: How everyday leaders inspire change at work.* Boston: Harvard Business School Press.

Meyerson, D. E., and Scully, M. A. (1995). Tempered radicalism and the politics of ambivalence and change. *Organizational Science, 6*(5), 585–600.

Montez, J. (2003, April). *Developing an instrument to assess higher education leadership.* Paper presented at an annual meeting of the American Educational Research Association, Chicago, IL. (ED 477 446)

Montgomery, J. R. (1990, May). *Leadership in middle administration.* Paper presented at an annual forum of the Association for Institutional Research, Louisville, KY. (ED 321 680)

Morrison, A. M. (1991). *The new leaders: Guidelines on leadership diversity in America.* San Francisco: Jossey-Bass.

Morrison, A. M. (1996). *The new leaders: Leadership diversity in America.* San Francisco: Jossey-Bass.

Murphy, M. K. (Ed.). (1997). *The advancement president and the academy: Profiles in institutional leadership.* Washington, DC: American Council on Education.

Nelson, S. J. (2000). *Leaders in the crucible: The moral voice of college presidents.* Westport, CT: Bergin & Garvey.

Neumann, A. (1989, March). *Colleges under pressure: Budgeting, presidential competence, and faculty uncertainty.* Paper presented at an annual meeting of the American Educational Research Association, San Francisco. (ED 308 753)

Neumann, A. (1990). Making mistakes: Error and learning in the college presidency. *Journal of Higher Education, 61*(4), 386–407.

Neumann, A. (1991). Defining "good faculty leadership." *Thought and Action, 7*(1), 45–60.

Neumann, A. (1995). Context, cognition, and culture: A case analysis of collegiate leadership and cultural change. *American Educational Research Journal, 32*(2), 251–279.

Neumann, A., and Pallas, A. M. (2005). Windows of possibility: Perspectives on the construction of educational researchers. In C. Conrad and R. C. Serlin (Eds.), *The Sage handbook for research in education: Engaging ideas and enriching inquiry.* Thousand Oaks, CA: Sage.

Neumann, Y., and Neumann, E. F. (1999). The president and the college bottom line: The role of strategic leadership styles. *International Journal of Educational Management, 13*(2), 73–79.

Nixon, G. (2003). Academic capitalism forces and successful college leadership. *Dissertation Abstracts International 65*(01), 55.

Noddings, N. (1984). *Caring: A feminine approach to ethics and moral education.* Berkeley: University of California Press.

Northouse, P. G. (2004). *Leadership: Theory and practice* (3rd ed.). Thousand Oaks, CA: Sage.

O'Connor, P.M.G., and Quinn, L. (2004). Organizational capacity for leadership. In C. D. McCauley and E. Van Velsor (Eds.), *The Center for Creative Leadership handbook of leadership development* (2nd ed., pp. 417–437). San Francisco: Jossey-Bass.

O'Day, J. A. (2002). Complexity, accountability and school improvement. *Harvard Educational Review, 72*(3), 293–330.

Offermann, L. R., and Phan, L. U. (2002). Culturally intelligent leadership for a diverse world. In R. E. Riggio, S. E. Murphy, and F. J. Pirozzolo (Eds.), *Multiple intelligences and leadership* (pp. 187–210). Mahwah, NJ: Lawrence Erlbaum Associates.

Olscamp, P. J. (2003). *Moral leadership: Ethics and the college presidency.* Lanham, MD: Rowman & Littlefield.

Olson, H. A. (1991). *Power strategies of Jesus Christ: Principles of leadership from the greatest motivator of all time.* Chicago: Triumph Books.

Osborn, R. N., Hunt, J. G., and Jauch, L. R. (2002). Toward a contextual theory of leadership. *The Leadership Quarterly 13*(6), 797–837.

Outcalt, C. L., Faris, S. K., and McMahon, K. N. (2001). *Developing non-hierarchical leadership on campus: Case studies and best practices in higher education.* Westport, CT: Greenwood Press.

Outcalt, C. L., and others. (2001). A leadership approach for the new millennium: A case study of UCLA's Bruin Leaders Project. *NASPA Journal, 38*(2), 178–188.

Palestini, R. H. (1999). Leadership tendencies of continuing education administrators. *PAACE Journal of Lifelong Learning, 8,* 31–39.

Palestini, R. H. (2003). *The human touch in educational leadership: A postpositivist approach to understanding educational leadership.* Lanham, MD: Scarecrow Press.

Palmer, P. J. (1998a). *The courage to teach: Exploring the inner landscape of a teacher's life.* San Francisco: Jossey-Bass.

Palmer, P. J. (1998b). Leading from within. In L. C. Spears (Ed.), *Insights on leadership: Service, stewardship, spirit, and servant-leadership* (pp. 197–208). New York: Wiley.

Palmer, P. J. (2000). *Let your life speak: Listening for the voice of vocation.* San Francisco: Jossey-Bass.

Parker, P. S. (2001). African American women executives' leadership communication within dominant-culture organizations: (Re)conceptualizing notions of collaboration and instrumentality. *Management Communication Quarterly, 15*(1), 42–82.

Parry, K. W. (1998). Grounded theory and social process: A new direction for leadership research. *The Leadership Quarterly, 9*(1), 85–105.

Pearce, C. L., and Conger, J. A. (Eds.). (2003). *Shared leadership: Reframing the hows and whys of leadership.* Thousand Oaks, CA: Sage.

Pearce, S. D. (1993). Internal barriers to visionary leadership in university continuing education units. *Canadian Journal of University Continuing Education, 19*(2), 9–24.

Pearce, S. D. (1995). The nature of vision in organizational leadership: A study of deans of continuing higher education. *Continuing Higher Education Review, 59*(1–2), 25–44.

Pellicer, L. O. (2003). *Caring enough to lead: How reflective thought leads to moral leadership.* Thousand Oaks, CA: Corwin Press.

Peterson, M. W., and Dill, D. (1997). Understanding the competitive environment of the postsecondary knowledge industry. In M. Peterson, D. Dill, and L. Mets (Eds.), *Planning and management for a changing environment: A handbook on redesigning postsecondary institutions* (pp. 3–29). San Francisco: Jossey-Bass.

Petrick, J. A., and Quinn, J. F. (2001). The challenge of leadership accountability for integrity capacity as a strategic asset. *Journal of Business Ethics, 34*(3/4) 331–343.

Pettigrew, A. (1997). What is a processual analysis? *Scandinavian Journal of Management, 13*(4), 337–348.

Pettigrew, A. M., Woodman, R. W., and Cameron, K. (2001). Study of organizational change and development: Challenges for future research. *Academy of Management Journal, 44*(4), 697–713.

Phillips, R. L., and Hunt, J. G. (Eds.). (1992). *Strategic leadership: A multiorganizational-level perspective.* Westport, CT: Quorum Books.

Phipps, S. E. (1993). Transforming libraries into learning organizations: The challenge for leadership. *Journal of Library Administration, 18*(3–4), 19–37.

Popper, M. (2001). *Hypnotic leadership: Leaders, followers, and the loss of self.* Westport, CT: Praeger Publishers.

Rabbin, R. (1998). *Invisible leadership: Igniting the soul at work.* Atlanta: Acropolis Books.

Ramsden, P. (1998). *Learning to lead in higher education.* New York: Routledge.

Rantz, R. (2002). Leading urban institutions of higher education in the new millennium. *Leadership and Organization Development Journal, 23*(8), 456–466.

Regine, B., and Lewin, R. (2000). Leading at the edge: How leaders influence complex systems. *Emergence: A Journal of Complexity Issues in Organizations and Management, 2*(2), 5–23.

Rhoads, R. A., and Tierney, W. G. (1992). *Cultural leadership in higher education.* University Park, PA: National Center on Postsecondary Teaching, Learning, and Assessment.

Rhoads, R. A., and Torres, C. A. (Eds.). (2005). *The university, state, and market: The political economy of globalization in the Americas.* Stanford, CA: Stanford University Press.

Rhode, D. L. (Ed.). (2003). *The difference "difference" makes: Women and leadership.* Stanford, CA: Stanford Law and Politics.

Riggio, R. E., Murphy, S. E., and Pirozzolo, F. J. (Eds.). (2002). *Multiple intelligences and leadership.* Mahwah, NJ: Lawrence Erlbaum Associates.

Rosenbach, W. E., and Taylor, R. L. (Eds.). (2001). *Contemporary issues in leadership.* Cambridge, MA: Westview Press.

Rosener, J. B. (1990). Ways women lead. *Harvard Business Review, 68*(6), 119–125.

Rosenzweig, R. M. (1998). *The political university: Policy, politics, and presidential leadership in the American research university.* Baltimore: Johns Hopkins University Press.

Rosser, V. J., Johnsrud, L. K., and Heck, R. H. (2000, November). *Mapping the domains of effective leadership: The case of deans and directors.* Paper presented at an annual meeting of the Association for the Study of Higher Education, Sacramento, CA. (ED 449 703)

Rost, J. C. (1991). *Leadership for the twenty-first century.* New York: Praeger.

Rubin, H. (2002). *Collaborative leadership: Developing effective partnerships in communities and schools.* Thousand Oaks, CA: Corwin Press.

Ruch, R. S. (2001). *Higher Ed, Inc.: The rise of the for-profit university.* Baltimore: John Hopkins University Press.

Satish, U., and Streufert, S. (1997). The measurement of behavioral complexity. *Journal of Applied Social Psychology, 27*(23), 2117–2121.

Schein, E. H. (1985). *Organizational culture and leadership.* San Francisco: Jossey-Bass.

Schein, E. H. (1992). *Organizational culture and leadership* (2nd ed.). San Francisco: Jossey-Bass.

Schier, S. E. (Ed.). (2000). *The postmodern presidency: Bill Clinton's legacy in U.S. politics.* Pittsburgh: University of Pittsburgh Press.

Schoenberg, R. (1992). Community, culture, communication: The three C's of campus leadership. *Liberal Education, 78*(5), 2–15.

Scully, M., and Segal, A. (2002). Passion with an umbrella: Grassroots activism in the workplace. *Social Structure and Organizations Revisited, 19,* 125–168.

Seagren, A. T. (1993). *The department chair: New roles, responsibilities, and challenges.* ERIC Digest. Washington, DC: School of Education and Human Development, George Washington University. (ED 363 165)

Segil, L., Goldsmith, M., and Belasco, J. A. (Eds.). (2003). *Partnering: The new face of leadership.* New York: Amacom.

Senge, P. M. (1990a). *The fifth discipline: The art and practice of the learning organization.* New York: Doubleday.

Senge, P. M. (1990b). The leader's new work: Building learning organizations. *MIT Sloan Management Review, 32*(1), 7–23.

Shakeshaft, C. (1999). The struggle to create a more gender inclusive profession. In J. Murphy and K. S. Louis (Eds.), *Handbook of research on educational administration* (2nd ed.). San Francisco: Jossey-Bass.

Shamir, B., and Howell, J. M. (1999). Organizational and contextual influences on the emergence and effectiveness of charismatic leadership. *The Leadership Quarterly, 10*(2), 257–283.

Shapiro, A. (2003). *Case studies in constructivist leadership and teaching.* Lanham, MD: Rowman & Littlefield.

Shaver, H. (2004). *Organize, communicate, empower: How principals can make time for leadership.* Thousand Oaks, CA: Corwin Press.

Skrla, L. (2000). The social construction of gender in the superintendency. *Journal of Education Policy, 15*(3), 293–316.

Slaughter S., and Leslie, L. L. (1997). *Academic capitalism: Politics, policies, and the entrepreneurial university.* Baltimore: Johns Hopkins University Press.

Slaughter S., and Rhoades, G. (2004). *Academic capitalism and the new economy: Markets, state, and higher education.* Baltimore: Johns Hopkins University Press.

Slinker, J. M. (1988). *The role of the college or university president in institutional advancement.* Unpublished doctoral dissertation, Northern Arizona University. (ED 308 791)

Smith, C. W. (2000). *Market values in American higher education: The pitfalls and promises.* Lanham, MD: Rowman & Littlefield.

Smith, D., and Parker, S. (2005). Organizational learning: A tool for diversity and institutional effectiveness. In A. Kezar (Ed.). *Organizational learning in higher education.* New Directions for Higher Education, no. 131. San Francisco: Jossey-Bass.

Spears, L. C. (Ed.). (1998). *Insights on leadership: Service, stewardship, spirit, and servant-leadership.* New York: Wiley.

Stark, J. S., Briggs, C. L., and Rowland-Poplawski, J. (2002). Curriculum leadership roles of chairpersons in continuously planning departments. *Research in Higher Education, 43*(3), 329–356.

Starratt, R. J. (2004). *Ethical leadership.* San Francisco: Jossey-Bass.

Statham, A. (1987). The gender model revisited: Differences in the management styles of men and women. *Sex Roles, 16*(7/8), 409–430.

Steelman, L. A., Lew, P. E., and Snell, A. F. (2004). The feedback environment scale: Construct definition, measurement and validation. *Educational and Psychological Measurement, 64*(1), 165–184.

Streufert, S. (1997). Complexity: An integration of theories. *Journal of Applied Social Psychology, 27*(23), 2068–2095.

Streufert, S., and Nogami, G. Y. (1989). Cognitive style and complexity: Implications for I/O psychology. In C. L. Cooper and I. Robertson (Eds.), *International review of industrial and organizational psychology* (pp. 93–143). Chichester, UK: Wiley.

Telford, H. (1995, January). *Collaborative leadership in urban schools of Melbourne.* Paper presented at the International Congress of School Effectiveness and Improvement, Leeuwarden, Netherlands. (ED 382 692)

Terry, R. W. (1993). *Authentic leadership: Courage in action.* San Francisco: Jossey-Bass.

Theall, M. (2002). Leadership in faculty evaluation. In R. M. Diamond (Ed.), *Field guide to academic leadership.* San Francisco: Jossey-Bass.

Tierney, W. G. (1988). *The web of leadership: The presidency in higher education.* Greenwich, CT: JAI Press.

Tierney, W. G. (1991). Advancing democracy: A critical interpretation of leadership. *Peabody Journal of Education, 66*(3), 157–175.

Tierney, W. G. (1993a). *Building communities of difference: Higher education in the twenty-first century.* Westport, CT: Bergin & Garvey.

Tierney, W. G. (1993b). *Multiculturalism in higher education: An organizational framework for analysis.* University Park, PA: National Center on Postsecondary Teaching, Learning, and Assessment. (ED 371 675)

Tomlinson, H. (2004). *Educational leadership: Personal growth for professional development.* Thousand Oaks, CA: Sage.

Ulrich, D., Zenger, J., and Smallwood, N. (1999). *Results-based leadership.* Boston: Harvard Business School Press.

Vaill, P. B. (1991). *Managing as a performing art: New ideas for a world of chaotic change.* San Francisco: Jossey-Bass.

Vaill, P. B. (1996). *Learning as a way of being: Strategies for survival in a world of permanent white water.* San Francisco: Jossey-Bass.

Valverde, L. A. (2003). *Leaders of color in higher education: Unrecognized triumphs in harsh institutions.* Walnut Creek, CA: AltaMira Press.

Van Velsor, E., and Drath, W. H. (2003). A lifelong developmental perspective on leader development. In C. D. McCauley and E. Van Velsor (Eds.), *The Center for Creative Leadership handbook of leadership development* (2nd ed.). San Francisco: Jossey-Bass.

Vaughan, G. B. (Ed.). (1992). *Dilemmas of leadership: Decision making and ethics in the community college.* San Francisco: Jossey-Bass.

Wageman, R. (2001). How leaders foster self-managing team effectiveness: Design choices versus hands-on coaching. *Organization Science, 12*(5), 559–577.

Weick, K. E. (1976). Educational organizations as loosely coupled systems. *Administrative Science Quarterly, 21*(1), 1–19.

Weick, K. E. (1995). *Sensemaking in organizations.* Thousand Oaks, CA: Sage.

Weingartner, R. H. (1999). *The moral dimension of academic administration.* Lanham, MD: Rowman & Littlefield.

Wen, H. D. (1999). *A profile of community college presidents' leadership styles.* Unpublished doctoral dissertation, Mississippi State University. (ED 438 858)

Wenger, E. (1998). *Communities of practice: Learning, meaning, identity.* Cambridge: Cambridge University Press.

Wergin, J. F. (2002). Academic program review. In R. M Diamond (Ed.), *Field guide to academic leadership.* San Francisco: Jossey-Bass.

Wheatley, M. J. (1999). *Leadership and the new science: Discovering order in a chaotic world* (2nd ed.). San Francisco: Berrett-Koehler Press.

Wilcox, J. R., and Ebbs, S. L. (1992). *The leadership compass: Values and ethics in higher education.* ASHE-ERIC Higher Education Report, no. 1. Washington, DC: School of Education and Human Development, George Washington University. (ED 347 955)

Wolverton, M., Gmelch, W. H., Wolverton, M. L., and Sarros, J. C. (1999). Stress in academic leadership: U.S. and Australian department chairs/heads. *Review of Higher Education, 22*(2), 165–185.

Wood, J. A., Jr., and Winston, B. E. (2005). Toward a new understanding of leader accountability: Defining a critical construct. *Journal of Leadership and Organizational Studies, 11*(3), 84–95.

Woodard, D. B., Jr., Love, P. G., and Komives, S. R. (2000). *Leadership and management issues for a new century.* New Directions for Student Services, no. 92. San Francisco: Jossey-Bass.

Young, M. D., and Skrla, L. (Eds.). (2003). *Reconsidering feminist research in educational leadership.* Albany: State University of New York Press.

Yukl, G. (1998). *Leadership in organizations* (4th ed.). Upper Saddle River, NJ: Prentice Hall.

Zaccaro, S. J., Rittman, A. L., and Marks, M. A. (2001). Team leadership. *The Leadership Quarterly, 12*(4), 451–483.

Zacharatos, A., Barling, J., and Kelloway, E. K. (2000). Development and effects of transformational leadership in adolescents. *The Leadership Quarterly, 11*(2), 211–226.

Zangwill, W., and Roberts, H. V. (1995). Academic leadership from the top: Total quality for higher education. In H. V. Roberts (Ed.), *Academic initiatives in total quality for higher education* (pp. 563–590). Milwaukee, WI: ASQC Quality Press.

Zhang, C., and Strange, C. C. (1992, October). *Shaping institutional vision: The risk of presidential leadership in small colleges. A preliminary report.* Paper presented at an annual meeting of the Association for the Study of Higher Education, Minneapolis, MN. (ED 352 921)

Zigurs, I. (2003). Leadership in virtual teams: Oxymoron or opportunity? *Organizational Dynamics, 31*(4), 339–351.

Name Index

C

Calas, M. B., 21
Cameron, K., 59, 60
Cantor, D. W., 52, 53
Carroll, J. B., 104
Caruso, D. R., 84, 85
Chaffee, E. E., 59, 102, 127, 177
Chemers, M. M., 20, 45, 55, 56, 59
Chermak, G. D., 127
Cherrey, C., 77, 112
Chliwniak, L., 21, 129
Ciulla, J. B., 73
Cohen, A. R., 63, 76
Cohen, M. D., 39, 111, 114
Coleman, P., 107
Conger, J. A., 73, 77, 78
Conners, R., 94
Cooper, J. E., 113
Cornwall, J. R., 92
Cox, T., Jr., 54, 55
Crosby, B. C., 26, 27, 88, 89
Crotty, M., 18
Currie, J., 149, 150, 155
Curry, B. K., 127
Cutright, M., 111, 112

D

Daughtery, L. H., 128
Dawson, P., 59, 60
Day, D. V., 54, 55, 65, 66
Deal, T. E., 20, 47, 52, 74, 115, 161, 162, 170
Deem, R., 149, 153, 154
Den Hartog, D. N., 37, 54, 55, 87
Depree, M., 28, 39
Dess, G. G., 92
Dever, J. T., 122
Diamond, R. M., 155
Dickson, M. W., 54, 75
Dill, D., 155
Dorfman, P. W., 54
Drath, W. H., 48
Druskat, V. U., 67
Duncan, P. K., 128, 140

E

Ebbs, S. L., 138, 163
Eckel, P., 133
Eddy, P. L., 116
Edmondson, A., 66
Eggert, N. J., 92
Ehrhart, M., 75
Elliott, B., 141
Ensari, N., 54, 55
Entrialgo, M., 93
Erb, M. J., 119
Estanek, S. M., 4, 112, 113, 151, 152

F

Fagin, C. M., 104
Fairholm, G. W., 95
Faris, S. K., 142
Ferguson, A. D., 128, 140
Ferguson, K. E., 53
Fernandez, E., 93
Ferren, A. S., 76, 145, 146
Fiedler, F. E., 58
Finch, C. R., 128
Fisher, J. L., 92, 106, 107, 111, 151–153, 164
French, J.R.P., 106

G

Gade, M. L., 111
Gardner, H., 77
Gardner, W. L., 73
Garner, R., 75, 82, 139, 143
Gayle, D. J., 146, 147
Geister, S., 67
Gerstner, C. R., 54, 55
Gillett-Karam, R., 128
Glazer-Raymo, J., 129, 130
Gmelch, W. H., 104, 109, 110, 140, 141
Goldsmith, J., 48
Goldsmith, M., 76, 86
Goleman, D., 84, 85, 163
Gordon, J. U., 81, 82
Greenberg, C. L., 86

Greenleaf, R. K., 28, 73
Griffin, D., 73
Griffiths, G., 21
Grint, K., 15, 19–21, 23
Grojean, M. W., 75
Gronn, P., 65, 66
Guido-DiBrito, F., 127
Gusfield, J. R., 82

H

Hackman, J. R., 63
Handy, C., 39
Hargrove, E. C., 61
Harrison, R. T., 92, 93
Hart, J., 144
Heck, R. H., 107
Heifetz, R. A., 14, 39–41, 44, 47, 66, 72, 160, 161, 171, 172
Helgesen, S., 52, 53, 63
Hertel, G., 67
Hesburgh, T. M., 137, 139
Hickman, C., 94
Hirsch, D. J., 145, 146
Hodgkinson, C., 73
Hofstede, G. H., 54, 55
Hollenbeck, J. R., 62
House, R. J., 54, 55, 87
Howard-Hamilton, M. F., 128, 140
Howell, J. M., 37, 38, 59
Hu-Chan, M., 86
Hunt, J. G., 15, 39–42, 59, 60

I

Ideta, L. M., 113
Ilgen, D. R., 62
Irby, B. J., 128

J

Jauch, L. R., 41, 42, 59, 60
Johnson, R. S., 128
Johnsrud, L. K., 107
Johnston, H., 82

K

Kanungo, R. N., 78
Kayworth, T. R., 67, 68
Kekale, J., 117, 146, 147
Kelloway, E. K., 37
Kelly, G., 62
Kempner, K., 119, 126, 127, 160
Kerr, C., 111
Kezar, A., 15, 19, 21, 22, 24, 52–54, 117, 128, 129, 133, 134, 140, 141, 145, 146, 148, 160, 162, 163, 171, 173
Kinlaw, D. C., 62
Klenke, K., 59
Knudson, L. S., 132
Koch, J. V., 92, 106, 107, 111, 152, 153, 164
Komives, S. R., 11, 13, 27, 39, 48, 64, 68, 77, 78, 110, 120, 128, 140
Konradt, U., 67
Kouzes, J. M., 33, 35, 36, 131, 132
Kozlowski, S.W.J., 67
Kuhn, T., 158
Kurke, L. B., 33
Kyle, D. T., 33, 74, 84

L

LaFasto, F.M.J., 63, 76
Lakomski, G., 1, 2, 122
Lambert, L., 48
Larana, E., 82
LaRocque, L., 107
Larson, C. E., 63, 76
Leidner, D. E., 67, 68
Leitch, C. M., 92, 93
Leland, C., 51–53, 77, 78, 81, 104, 143
Lerner, J. S., 96
Leslie, L. L., 149, 153, 154
Levin, J. S., 107, 108, 149
Lew, P. E., 154
Lewin, R., 42
Linsky, M., 39–41
Lipman-Blumen, J., 3, 14, 22, 31
Longino, H. E., 128, 129
Love, P. G., 4, 13, 112, 113, 151, 152
Lucas, A. F., 131
Lucas, N., 11, 27, 48, 64, 68, 77

Subject Index

About the Authors

Adrianna J. Kezar is associate professor for higher education, University of Southern California. She holds a Ph.D. and M.A. in higher education administration from the University of Michigan and a B.A. from the University of California, Los Angeles. Her research focuses on change, leadership, organizational theory, governance, and diversity issues in higher education. She has participated actively in national service, including as an editorial board member for several journals.

Rozana Carducci is a doctoral student in the Division of Higher Education and Organizational Change, University of California, Los Angeles. She holds a M.S. in college student personnel from Miami University and a B.A. from the University of North Carolina–Chapel Hill. Carducci previously worked as the coordinator of leadership development programs at the University of Missouri–Columbia. Her research focuses on leadership in student affairs, organizational studies of higher education, and critical methodology.

Melissa Contreras-McGavin is a doctoral candidate in higher education policy at the Rossier School of Education, University of Southern California. She holds an M.A. in postsecondary administration and student affairs from USC. Her research interests include critical race theory and organizational change related to race in higher education. Contreras-McGavin previously worked as a college admission counselor.

About the ASHE Higher Education Reports Series

Since 1983, the ASHE (formerly ASHE-ERIC) Higher Education Report Series has been providing researchers, scholars, and practitioners with timely and substantive information on the critical issues facing higher education. Each monograph presents a definitive analysis of a higher education problem or issue, based on a thorough synthesis of significant literature and institutional experiences. Topics range from planning to diversity and multiculturalism, to performance indicators, to curricular innovations. The mission of the Series is to link the best of higher education research and practice to inform decision making and policy. The reports connect conventional wisdom with research and are designed to help busy individuals keep up with the higher education literature. Authors are scholars and practitioners in the academic community. Each report includes an executive summary, review of the pertinent literature, descriptions of effective educational practices, and a summary of key issues to keep in mind to improve educational policies and practice.

The Series is one of the most peer reviewed in higher education. A National Advisory Board made up of ASHE members reviews proposals. A National Review Board of ASHE scholars and practitioners reviews completed manuscripts. Six monographs are published each year and they are approximately 120 pages in length. The reports are widely disseminated through Jossey-Bass and John Wiley & Sons, and they are available online to subscribing institutions through Wiley InterScience (http://www.interscience.wiley.com).

Call for Proposals

The ASHE Higher Education Report Series is actively looking for proposals. We encourage you to contact one of the editors, Dr. Kelly Ward (kaward@wsu.edu) or Dr. Lisa Wolf-Wendel (lwolf@ku.edu), with your ideas.

Recent Titles

Back Issue/Subscription Order Form

Copy or detach and send to:

Jossey-Bass, A Wiley Imprint, 989 Market Street, San Francisco CA 94103-1741

Call or fax toll-free: Phone 888-378-2537 6:30AM – 3PM PST; Fax 888-481-2665

Back Issues: Please send me the following issues at $26 each
(Important: please include series abbreviation and issue number.
For example AEHE 28:1)

_____

_____

_____

$ _____   Total for single issues

$ _____   SHIPPING CHARGES: SURFACE   Domestic Canadian

	First Item	$5.00	$6.00
	Each Add'l Item	$3.00	$1.50

For next-day and second-day delivery rates, call the number listed above.

Subscriptions   Please ❏ start ❏ renew my subscription to *ASHE Higher Education Reports* for the year 2_____ at the following rate:

U.S.	❏ Individual $165	❏ Institutional $185
Canada	❏ Individual $165	❏ Institutional $245
All Others	❏ Individual $201	❏ Institutional $296

❏ Online subscriptions available too!

**For more information about online subscriptions, visit
www.interscience.wiley.com**

$ _____   Total single issues and subscriptions (Add appropriate sales tax for your state for single issue orders. No sales tax for U.S. subscriptions. Canadian residents, add GST for subscriptions and single issues.)

❏Payment enclosed (U.S. check or money order only)

❏VISA ❏ MC ❏ AmEx ❏ #_____ Exp. Date _____

Signature _____ Day Phone _____

❏ Bill Me (U.S. institutional orders only. Purchase order required.)

Purchase order # _____

Federal Tax ID13559302   GST 89102 8052

Name _____

Address _____

_____

Phone _____ E-mail _____

For more information about Jossey-Bass, visit our Web site at www.josseybass.com

ASHE-ERIC HIGHER EDUCATION REPORT IS NOW AVAILABLE ONLINE AT WILEY INTERSCIENCE

What is Wiley InterScience?

Wiley InterScience is the dynamic online content service from John Wiley & Sons delivering the full text of over 300 leading scientific, technical, medical, and professional journals, plus major reference works, the acclaimed Current Protocols laboratory manuals, and even the full text of select Wiley print books online.

What are some special features of Wiley InterScience?

Wiley Interscience Alerts is a service that delivers table of contents via e-mail for any journal available on Wiley InterScience as soon as a new issue is published online.

Early View is Wiley's exclusive service presenting individual articles online as soon as they are ready, even before the release of the compiled print issue. These articles are complete, peer-reviewed, and citable.

CrossRef is the innovative multi-publisher reference linking system enabling readers to move seamlessly from a reference in a journal article to the cited publication, typically located on a different server and published by a different publisher.

How can I access Wiley InterScience?

Visit http://www.interscience.wiley.com.

Guest Users can browse Wiley InterScience for unrestricted access to journal Tables of Contents and Article Abstracts, or use the powerful search engine. *Registered Users* are provided with a *Personal Home Page* to store and manage customized alerts, searches, and links to favorite journals and articles. Additionally, Registered Users can view free Online Sample Issues and preview selected material from major reference works.

Licensed Customers are entitled to access full-text journal articles in PDF, with select journals also offering full-text HTML.

How do I become an Authorized User?

Authorized Users are individuals authorized by a paying Customer to have access to the journals in Wiley InterScience. For example, a University that subscribes to Wiley journals is considered to be the Customer.

Faculty, staff and students authorized by the University to have access to those journals in Wiley InterScience are Authorized Users. Users should contact their Library for information on which Wiley journals they have access to in Wiley InterScience.

ASK YOUR INSTITUTION ABOUT WILEY INTERSCIENCE TODAY!

Printed in the United States
131888LV00005B/15/P